JOHANN MARTIN BOLZIVS
Erster Evangel: Prediger der Salzburg: Colonistengemeine
zu Ebenezer in Georgien.
geb. A. C. 1703. den 15ᵗᵉⁿ Decbr.   ordinirt 1733. den 11ᵗᵉⁿ Novbr.

From A Mezzotint in the De Renne Collection,
University of Georgia Library

Detailed Reports on the Salzburger Emigrants Who Settled in America ...

Edited by Samuel Urlsperger

VOLUME TWO, 1734-1735

Edited with an Introduction by
GEORGE FENWICK JONES

Translated by
Hermann J. Lacher

*WORMSLOE FOUNDATION PUBLICATIONS
NUMBER TEN*

UNIVERSITY OF GEORGIA PRESS
ATHENS

Contents

Erste
CONTINVATION
der ausführlichen Nachricht
von denen
Saltzburgischen
Emigranten,
die sich in America niedergelassen haben.
Worin die
Tage-Register
der beyden Saltzburgischen Prediger zu EbenEzer in Georgien vom
17 Iul. 1734 bis 1735 zu Ende, mit einigen hierzu gehörigen
Briefen enthalten sind:
Nebst einem gedoppelten Anhang
Bestehend
1) In einer im August 1735 zwischen Ihro Excellentz Herrn Jonathan Belcher,
Ritter, General-Capitain und Gouverneur en Chef in Neu-Engeland
und einigen Indianischen Nationen zu Deerfield gehaltenen Conferentz;
So denn
2) In M. Nathan. Appelletons, bey der Ordination des Herrn Johann Sar-
gent, unter den Indianern von Houssatonoe bestellten ersten Dieners des
Evangelii zu Deerfield in Neu-Engeland den 31 August 1735 gehaltenen
Predigt,
Und
einer Vorrede
herausgegeben von
Samuel Urlsperger,
Des Evangelischen Ministerii der Stadt Augsburg Seniore und Pastore
der Haupt-Kirchen zu St. Annen.

HALLE,
In Verlegung des Wäysenhauses, MDCCXXXVIII.

First
CONTINUATION
of the detailed report on the

SALZBURGER
EMIGRANTS

Who have settled in America.

Wherein are contained
The Daily Entries
of the two Salzburger Pastors at Ebenezer in Georgia from 17 July
1734 to the end of of 1735, together with some pertinent letters:

in addition a double appendix
consisting of

1) a report on a conference held in August, 1735, by His Excellency Mr. Jonathan Belcher, Knight, Commander-in-Chief, and supreme Governor of New England, with several Indian nations at Deerfield;

also

2) A sermon by Mr. Nathan Appleton, preached at the ordination of Mr. John Sargent, the first servant of the Gospel to be sent to the Indians of Houssatonic, who was ordained at Deerfield, New England on 31 August 1735,

and a Preface
published by

Samuel Urlsperger
Senior of the Protestant ministry in Augsburg
and Pastor of the Main Church of St. Anne.

Halle
Published by the Orphanage Press, MDCCXXXVIII

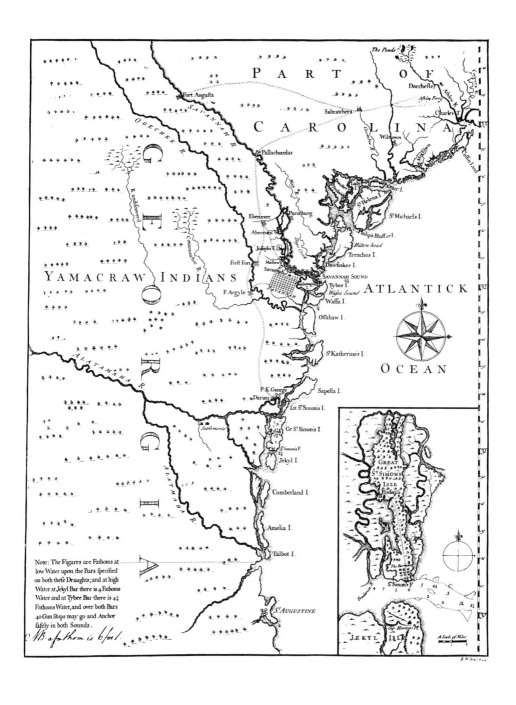

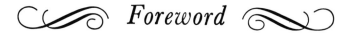 *Foreword*

THE Wormsloe Foundation is a non-profit organization chartered on December 18, 1951, by the Superior Court of Chatham County, Georgia. In the words of its charter, "The objects and purposes of this Foundation are the promotion of historical research and the publication of the results thereof; the restoration, preservation, and maintenance of historical sites and documents and the conduct of an educational program in the study of history in the State of Georgia, and in states adjoining thereto."

As its first important activity, the Foundation has begun the publication of a series of historical works and documents under the title of "Wormsloe Foundation Publications." They will consist of important manuscripts, reprints of rare publications, and historical narrative relative to Georgia and the South. The first volume appeared in 1955, written by E. Merton Coulter, the General Editor of the series, and entitled *Wormsloe: Two Centuries of a Georgia Family*. This volume gives the historical background of the Wormsloe Estate and a history of the family which has owned it for more than two and a quarter centuries. It is now out of print.

The second publication of the Foundation was *The Journal of William Stephens, 1741-1743*, and the third volume was *The Journal of William Stephens, 1743-1745*, which is a continuation of the journal as far as any known copy is extant. However, there is evidence that Stephens kept his journal for some years after 1745. These volumes were edited by the General Editor of the Wormsloe Foundation series and were published in 1958 and 1959, respectively. Both are now out of print.

The fourth volume of the series was the re-publication of the unique copy of Pat. Tailfer et al., *A True and Historical Narrative of the Colony of Georgia* . . . With Comments by the Earl of Egmont. This volume is in the John Carter Brown Library of Brown University. In this present publication there appears for the first time in print the comments of Egmont. With the permission of Brown University, this volume was edited by Clarence L. Ver Steeg of Northwestern University, Evanston, Illinois. The volume is now out of print.

The fifth volume in the series of Wormsloe Foundation Publications was the long-missing first part of Egmont's three manuscript volumes of his journal. It was edited by Robert G. McPherson of the University of Georgia. This volume contains the journal from 1732 to 1738, inclusive, and is owned by the Gilcrease Institute of American History and Art, Tulsa, Oklahoma, which gave permission for its publication.

In 1963 the Foundation published its sixth volume, *The Journal of Peter Gordon, 1732-1735,* which was edited by the General Editor of the Wormsloe Foundation Publication series. Gordon came to Georgia with Oglethorpe on the first voyage; he began his journal on leaving England. The original manuscript was acquired by the Wormsloe Foundation in 1957, which presented it to the General Library of the University of Georgia.

The seventh volume in the series is *Joseph Vallence Bevan, Georgia's First Official Historian.* It is a departure from the nature of the five volumes directly preceding, which are documentary. It was written by the General Editor, who brings to light a historiographer who was appointed Georgia's first official historian by the state legislature.

The eighth volume, *Henry Newman's Salzburger Letterbooks,* begins a series within the general series, for it is to be followed by several volumes of translations of the Urlsperger Reports (*Ausführliche Nachrichten . . .,* edited by Samuel Urlsperger, Halle, 1735ff, and dealing with the Georgia Salzburgers). This volume was transcribed and edited by George Fenwick Jones of the University of Maryland, who also will edit future volumes of the Salzburger translations.

The ninth volume of the Wormsloe Foundation Publications was the first of several volumes of the Urlsperger Reports in translation to be published in this series. It appeared in 1968. The second volume of the Urlsperger Reports is the present one, edited by George Fenwick Jones, as was the first. A third of the Urlsperger Reports is now in preparation by Professor Jones.

E. MERTON COULTER
General Editor

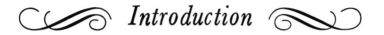 *Introduction*

IT is assumed that the reader of this volume is already familiar with Volume I of these reports. If not, suffice it to say that they were written by Pastor John Martin Boltzius and his assistant, Israel Christian Gronau, two young clergymen sent by the Francke Foundation in Halle, Germany, to administer to the Protestant exiles from Salzburg who emigrated to Georgia in 1733.

This volume, originally published as the *First Continuation,* covers the experiences of the Georgia Salzburgers from July 17, 1734, until the end of 1735, the period of their worst hardships, frustrations, and disappointments. It has the great advantage over Volume I of having been carefully collated with contemporary copies of the original documents, in as far as they still survive in the archives of the Francke Foundation.[1] Soon after reaching Europe, these reports were edited and published by Samuel Urlsperger,[2] chief pastor of St. Anne's in Augsburg and Senior of the Lutheran Ministry of that city, who remained the spiritual father of the Georgia Salzburgers to the end of his life. The worthy churchman's purpose in publishing these reports was to edify his readers and encourage them to continue their support of the Georgia colonists; and consequently he suppressed all information that might hinder this purpose or seem to contradict the promises made to the exiles before their emigration to America.

Since contemporary manuscripts survive for a part of this period, it has been possible to restore many passages deleted or changed by Urlsperger. This matter is indicated by brackets [ ], successive paragraphs of a single entry being indicated by only an introductory bracket [. A glance at these bracketed restitutions will quickly reveal Urlsperger's method, namely of suppressing all mention of misbehavior on the part of the Salzburgers, of squabbles between the pastors and the non-Salzburgers in the community, and of difficulties with the British authorities and their failure to fulfill their promises. Urlsperger also removed the names of several people about whom disparaging remarks were made, and he even omitted the names of towns in which they had so-journed in Germany lest these serve as a clue to their identity.

Despite these changes, we must admire Urlsperger's moral courage in admitting to so much disorder and hardship, which was in glaring contrast to the glowing reports published in his first volume. In this he was not alone to blame. The journey of the first transport, or group, of Salzburgers was so successful, and their arrival in Georgia so auspicious, that the young pastors themselves were thoroughly optimistic. Only when the first volume was ready to appear did conflicting reports come; and, since these seemed unconfirmed, Urlsperger ignored them in getting his copy ready for the printer.

A year and a half later, however, the awful truth could no longer be denied, if for no other reason than that the appalling death rate gave the lie to all accounts of Georgia's salubrious climate. Most of the settlers had arrived with scurvy; and all were immediately exposed to dysentery, malaria, and various fevers such as typhoid and typhus. It was not a question of avoiding contagion, but merely of surviving it; and only those with the proper antibodies did so. We cannot help but pity the druggist, Andreas Zwifler, who was blamed for failing to cure his miserable patients. Urlsperger also had to swallow his pride enough to confess that the land promised to the Salzburgers had not yet been allotted and that it was sterile as well as inaccessible, being usually either parched or innundated.

Within three months after the first transport reached Georgia, a wicked man named George Bartholomew Roth had the audacity to send a letter to Germany which was "written in such a manner as would give occasion for many Calumnies," as Urlsperger indignantly reported after the letter "happily" fell into his hands.[3] Despite all measures taken to maintain a tight censorship, unfavorable rumors had succeeded in trickling out; and even the schoolmaster, Ortmann, was accused of having smuggled a secret letter into Boltzius' packet, as we see from the entry of January 6, 1735.

To appreciate Urlsperger's righteous indignation at Roth's effrontery, we must remember that this was an age not only of righteousness, but also of self-righteousness, when it was still difficult for even the most introverted Christian to distinguish clearly between pride and conscience. But, besides the Old Adam found in every man, there was a real concern for salvation that is nearly lost today. It was not only hypocrisy that made men wish to appear sanctified, it was an inner need to feel sanctified and thus assured of salvation. Whereas the Puritans feared eternal damnation with fire and brimstone, the Pietists like Urlsperger and his spiritual children in Georgia rather feared to lose the inestimable love of Jesus. This anxiety about salvation helps explain the reluctance of Zwifler, Commissioner Vat, and Schoolmaster Ortmann to accept Boltzius' chastisements. It was less their fear of admitting their sinfulness to him or even to the congregation than their fear of admitting it to themselves, for this would have diminished their certainty of being washed in the blood of the Lamb.

We can therefore imagine Urlsperger's inner struggle in having to acknowledge in his preface to this *Continuation* that conditions in Ebenezer were not so good as first reported. Nevertheless, even though he relaxed his censorship somewhat, we see that he did still suppress facts that he felt better kept hidden. Boltzius himself had paved the way in this; for, as he mentioned in his entry for September 24, 1735, he preferred to report good things and hold back unpleasant circumstances as long as possible. We see, in his entry for January 15, 1735, that Boltzius at first indignantly rejected the attacks against Mr. Vat made by a certain Mr. Dietzius, yet he later drew the same conclusions himself. It will be noticed that he often failed to mention a sickness until it was necessary to do so for some specific reason. For example, on August 16, 1734, we learn that Rheinländer will go to Savannah as soon as he is stronger, but we have not yet heard that he was sick.

In addition to his deletions, Urlsperger made certain minor stylistic changes that do not show in translation. For example, he replaced Latinisms and Gallicisms with native German words: e.g. *vorbereiten* for *praeparieren, versorgen* for *accommodieren,* and *Unbequemlichkeit* for *Incommodität.* These lexical changes were not made to purify the language, but merely to make it more intelligible to a non-scholarly public. For the same reason he expanded many Biblical passages that Boltzius had given in abbreviated form: e.g. when Boltzius wrote "Set your affections on things above," Urlsperger added "not on things on the earth" (December 16, 1735). In this regard it might be mentioned that the Luther Bible which Boltzius cited sometimes differs slightly from the King James Bible in its verse-numbering. Urlsperger changed the subjunctives of indirect discourse from the past to the present tense, possibly to gain a more elegant tone. Incidentally, like all English translations from German, this one suffers from our inability to render the fine distinctions between direct and indirect discourse made possible by the German use of the subjunctive. As a substitute, and *inquit* such as "he said" or "she replied" has been added wherever the meaning requires.

The passages deleted by Urlsperger show, among other things, that Boltzius was not entirely devoid of humor. At least he had a flare for sarcasm, which he demonstrates, for example, when he declares that Zwifler is rapidly curing the congregation to death and when he quotes the medical jargon with which the semi-educated druggist tries to impress him (September 18, 1735).

In reading Boltzius' diary, we should remember that he usually uses the pronoun "we" to distinguish himself and his colleague Gronau from his Salzburger parishioners (e.g. August 27, 1935). Although both of them condescended to marry girls from their congregation, they, as scholars, felt superior to their flock (see appended letters of Sept. 1, 1735, Nos. V & X). It will be noted that all English benefactors, the commissioners, and even Zwifler and Ortmann are called *Herr* (Mr.), while the skilled artisans like Rheinländer and Tullius are called *Meister* (Master), but that the Salzburgers receive no titles. We should also remember that the term Salzburger was restricted to those who actually came from Salzburg, in contrast to other Germans such as the Bavarians Roth and Schweikert, the Swabian Rauner, the Swiss Zent, and the many Austrians of the third transport. Subsequently, through association and often through intermarriage, all the German speaking people of Effingham Country have become included in the term Salzburger.

This translation aims to render the original as faithfully as possible, without improving on Boltzius' style. Judged by eighteenth-century standards, Boltzius' syntax was exceptionally precise, even if it would be found wanting today. Like most of his contemporaries, he did not collect his thoughts into paragraphs, but rambled on as his ideas came to him. However, for typographical reasons this translation is arbitrarily forced into Procrustean paragraphs, even where the chain of thought does not entirely warrant it. Also for typographical economy, the names of the months have been removed from the margins of the pages, where Urlsperger placed them, and restored to the heading of each entry, where Boltzius had originally put them.

In Volume I, in cases where Christian names were not given in the text but could be ascertained from elsewhere, they were added to the text in brackets. Volume II, to the contrary, omits them because all names are given in full, if known, in the index. In the few cases of ambiguity, such as between August Hermann Francke

and his son Gotthilf August, the confusion is clarified in a foot-
note. This translation has expanded various abbreviations. Several
place names have been standardized or modernized. Purisburg has
given way to Purysburg, Haberkorn to Abercorn, Pellichokelis to
Pallachacolas, Charles Town to Charleston, and Ogizschy to Ogeechee. The word Salzburger appears without a *t*, since the older
spelling is no longer used, not even by the Georgia descendants.

Several of Boltzius' favorite words are difficult to render because
of their many meanings. He often refers to his congregation as
Zuhörer (hearers), even in contexts where there is no allusion to
their listening. He more often uses the word *Gemeinde* (community), since, with the exception of Commissioner Vat alone, who
was Swiss Reformed, all members of the community were members of the same congregation, as was usual in Europe. In this
translation the word *Gemeinde* is rendered by either "congregation" or "community," as the context seems to demand. Another
favorite word of Boltzius that lacks an exact English equivalent is
Vorstellung, which includes the meanings of representation, reprimand, remonstrance, admonition, intercession or good office, or
even fantasy. Here it is most often rendered as "representations."
Boltzius uses the word *Umstände* (circumstances) for many purposes, especially to denote one's spiritual, mental, physical, or even
educational condition. In interpreting Boltzius' Pietistic vocabulary, we should remember that spiritual values are always fore-
most. *Elend* (misery) retains some of its original meaning of
"exile," especially exile or separation from God. If we read that
someone is miserable, this could mean that he is naked, hungry,
or sick; but it more likely means that he is not happy in Jesus.
(See entry for April 21, 1735.) If Boltzius is referring to physical
misery, he usually states this clearly. Another word we often con-
front is *melden* (to announce), which usually means to announce
one's intention to take Holy Communion and to receive spiritual
preparation for this serious event, as is explained in the entry for
March 15, 1735. This concept is rendered here most often by "to
declare one's intention" or "to register for Communion."

This translation includes all of Urlsperger's *First Continuation*
except for the double appendix containing a report of a conference at Deerfield and a sermon by Nathan Appleton, which have
been omitted here because they have nothing to do with the
Georgia Salzburgers and because they are based on a printed
pamphlet that is still extant.[4] The larger part of this volume was
translated by Herman J. Lacher while he was a student at the

University of Georgia. The material added from the Halle manuscripts was translated by the present editor, and the appended letters from the two pastors were translated by Miss Marie Hahn of the University of Maryland, who was also kind enough to help correct the galleys.

I wish at this time to thank the authorities of the University and State Library of Sachsen-Anhalt in Halle, DDR, for their hospitality to me during my two visits to the Francke Foundation archives in 1966 and 1968 and also for their kindness in furnishing microfilms of the Ebenezer diaries. I also wish to thank the American Philosophical Society for subsidizing my two trips to Halle and the General Research Board of the University of Maryland for supporting the necessary filming and typing.

GEORGE FENWICK JONES
University of Maryland

To the

Well-Born, High-Nobly-Born, High-Noble,

Severe, Firm, Most Honorable, Provident,

High and Very Wise

Gentlemen

CITY COMMISSIONERS

Mayors

and

Council A. C.

of the very praiseworthy Free City of

Augsburg in the Holy Roman Empire,

MY GRACIOUS, BENEVOLENT,

High Ruling Lords

May the Allhighest give from His inexhaustible plenty

all the lasting good in time and in eternity.

Well-Born, High-Nobly-Born, High-Noble,

Severe, Firm, Most Honorable, Provident,

High and Very Wise

MY GRACIOUS, BENEVOLENT,

High-Ruling Lords

Just as I had sufficient reason to dedicate the complete report on the Salzburgers who settled in America, which was edited two years ago, to the Trustees or Commissioners who were charged by His Royal Majesty of Great Britain with the establishment of the new Colony of Georgia in America, and also to all of the very noble members of the very praiseworthy English Society for Promoting Christian Knowledge: so I have no less good reason for dedicating the first continuation of said complete report to Your Graces, the Very Noble, Firm, Strong, Wise, and Provident Lords.

For it is you who have not only looked with wonder, a few years ago, on this great Work of God, namely, the migration from the archbishopric of Salzburg of many thousands who confessed our Protestant religion, and particularly the guidance of one Protestant community of Salzburger Emigrants from Augsburg to England and from there across the great ocean to Georgia in America, but have also from time to time made laudable arrangements for the Christian reception of these strangers and for adequate care of their bodies and spirits (which, as we know, has awakened all of Germany and England and has inspired them to become followers with good works and giving). Thus you have joyfully followed the Word of God as written by John to the Regents: We must receive those who went forth for the sake of Christ's name so that we might be fellow helpers to the truth. 3 John 7-8.

These strangers whom we have harbored here have thankfully recognized this very unusual and fatherly care and have borne dignified witness for it before all congregations and before God. Along with them many thousands, near and far, recognize the same in the old and in the new world, and wish for our Protestant Augsburg and its inhabitants, but especially for you, most worthy Regents, in return for the good deeds done for these pilgrims and for the work done on their behalf, the Great Reward which God has promised to all those who let their faith be active with true love and who continue unto the end to follow His Son and obey His word.

Above all, I find myself obliged to concur with this wish and to give public thanks to you my gracious, very benevolent lords, for having lent a helping hand with the groups which left here on 31 Oct. 1733, on 23 Sept. 1734, and on 6 Sept. 1735, and for having given official and constitutional protection to the Colonists on all occasions, in accordance with requests from the Embassy of Great Britain and Brunswick in Regensburg, and for having spared no efforts towards making their brief stay here, and their voyage, easy and agreeable.

May the true God grant rich fulfillment of everything regarding you, your families, and households, the task entrusted to you in this city and, above all, the preservation and propagation of our most Holy Faith, for which He is being asked here by me, and in America by the congregation at Ebenezer.

And may the same true God continue to give me strength not only to pray for you, gracious, very benevolent and high lords, but also to encourage many others to do the same so that today and in the future Truth will become increasingly powerful in this city, pious conduct will be pursued more earnestly, justice and peace will embrace each other more beautifully, our commerce will prosper in a manner pleasing to the Lord, and that your enterprises will succeed so that we and our descendants may live a calm and peaceful life under a Christian regime, in true godliness and honor.

And with this I commend you, gracious, most benevolent and high lords, to the powerful, wise, and gracious government of the Lord of all lords and King of all kings and remain, myself and with mine, in obedient commendation to your grace, favor, and great graciousness, such as you have shown me and them for nearly fifteen years, Your Graces, Very Noble Lords, Strong, Firm, Provident and Wise, My Gracious, Benevolent, High Ruling Lords.

Your obedient servant and
faithful intercessor

Augsburg, 21 November 1737.   Samuel Urlsperger

Preface

Publication of the First Continuation of the Complete Report on the Salzburger Emigrants who Settled in America encountered many obstacles; but the wishes of so many people for further news on the matter has caused me to give them some satisfaction and to bring out said First Continuation with the assurance that, God giving life, health, and strength, everything not reported will be brought out at Easter Fair 1738, particularly a complete report on the reception, voyage, and happy landing of the third transport in Georgia.

To give the honored reader an idea as to what he may find in the present volume, be it known that it contains (1) the diary of the two patiently working Pastors Boltzius and Gronau which they have sent to me from time to time from Ebenezer and which covers the period from 17 Jul. 1734 to the end of the year 1735; (2) A number of noteworthy and pertinent letters written by said pastors; (3) a double appendix covering the conference and sermon shown on the title page[5] as both were sent to me from Boston by Mr. Jonathan Belcher, Knight, Commander-in-Chief, and supreme Governor of New England, and from Mr. Coleman, SS. Doctor of Theology and First Pastor, accompanied by two important letters written in Latin, of which we promise to give an extract to our worthy reader in the second continuation.

In addition to this, I find it necessary to mention several other matters. First, that on 27 Febr. 1736, the press of the orphanage at Halle printed a few folios for me with the following title: *Reliable Report on the Spiritual and Physical Condition of the Salzburger Emigrants who have Settled in America, how they fared until the 1st of September 1735, as reported to Germany by the Pastors and by some of the Salzburgers themselves.*

Second, that pleasing reports continue to come in of the good work which God has begun in many Colonists, as witnessed by the diaries of the pastors which I have until March of the current year. Yet, as might be expected, Satan is doing everything he can to plant tares among the wheat and to make some members of the congregation dissatisfied through hard trials, just as he succeeded once in making Israel dissatisfied with God and Moses. But the two teachers are making joint efforts against this and, with God's help, have won many and great victories over him.

Third, although the Trustees and the well known and praiseworthy Society continue to assist the Salzburgers, the latter have had to suffer severe trials from time to time, partly because they are working land that is quite wild, partly because they are so far away from England where important decisions must be made.

Fourth, the pastors and most of their listeners have shown through all this an admirable steadfastness, Christian spirit, patience, and devotion to God's will. But also the Trustees, upon hearing of some of the hardships, have offered to furnish relief themselves and have given favorable answers to various requests. I have received a letter dated 19 Jul. 1737 from Mr. Henry Newman, secretary of the Society, which states the following:

P.P.

"In answer to yours of 6 May: As You requested, the Society has turned over to the court chaplain, Mr. Ziegenhagen, the forty pounds sterling of Salzburger money, in accordance with the decision you conveyed to us in your letter of 1 Feb.

Concerning the three points in your letter dealing with the Trustees of Georgia, which were presented to them in full, they have let me know through one of the most worthy members of the Society,

1. How they were in agreement with the first point, that the third group of Salzburgers shall receive the same assistance in regard to livestock, in addition to other freedoms enjoyed by the earlier ones, and that the necessary orders have already been issued.

2. In answer to the second point, the Trustees will continue to give special attention to the Salzburgers, who are confessors of the truth and thus worthy of the love of every good Christian who suffers when Christ's members suffer.

3. To answer your third point, it is true that Parliament has granted twenty thousand pounds sterling to the Colony but has apportioned the sum for certain uses from which the Trustees may not deviate; but, since this sum is destined for the service and protection of the entire land, the Salzburgers and other Colonists will undoubtedly benefit from it.

It gives me pleasure to report further that Mr. Oglethorpe

is preparing for his voyage back to the province in order to do all the things he deems necessary for the good of the colony; to this end, His Royal Majesty has graciously appointed him Commander-in-Chief of all forces in Carolina and Georgia so that he can suppress all hostile enterprises that might disturb the peace, etc."

Fifth, it is hoped that the kind reader will not form a bad opinion of God's work because these people, too, must pass through the narrow gate. Having received the call and having resolved to go to the New World, they themselves recognize that God is concerned with what is best for them in this land, that is, for the salvation of their souls, and that He will always lighten their crosses, physical discomforts, and dark clouds with His help and the light of His Grace.

The SIXTH point is that more than a year ago the Salzburger Colonists, with the consent of the Trustees, left Ebenezer and, because of better soil conditions, built houses two or two and a half hours from there, on the so-called Red Bluff, which has been named New-Ebenezer.

SEVENTH, it is hoped that no one will condemn the two pastors for the occasional inclusion in their diary of descriptions of the difficulties and hard circumstances with which they have to deal from time to time. This is not a matter of shame or cause for reproach for the Trustees, just as it was not to shame and reproach God when Moses recorded in his books how the Israelites, who were His own people and whom He led from Egypt with His mighty arms, suffered from hunger, grief, and other distress (Exodus 16:3, etc.). Besides, such reports are necessary because they help us form a better judgment of the place and also because they encourage the true Children of God to pray and do good deeds for our dear Colonists.

EIGHTH, for the glory of God, we will not keept it a secret that in many ways the wishes of the two pastors and their listeners have been fulfilled. In accordance with such wishes, God has let them have the desired books, medicines, and other things which were sent partly from here and partly from Halle, and the things they are still lacking are now on the way. The Lord has started to move many hearts here and abroad so that they are sharing with this small flock in the outermost part of the world, which has been especially helpful for their schools, their hospitals, and their poorhouses. They have expressed their thanks in letters to me and to others and they will be no less appreciative in the future. Among the good deeds must be numbered that recently a doctor was sent to them from Halle. This the colonists had desired very much. What is still lacking, The LORD will give if He finds it good, so that the shepherds and sheep there will learn: Our GOD is the old GOD of whom it is said: He does what the Godfearing wish, and He hears their cries.

NINTH, no one has cause to be irritated if descriptions of worldly matters in the following reports differ at times from earlier ones, for it is well to remember that it could not be otherwise when conditions are such as the ones in which the pastors must live, where nearly everything can be learned only slowly, through experience.

TENTH, regarding matters of theology to be found in the diary, we ask the kind reader to judge them by the similarity of faith and with the best understanding of which he is capable, in the spirit of Jesus' dictum: Do unto others what ye would that men should do unto you. The reader following this rule, for example, finding an entry on 25 July 1734 about the heart-prayer of a certain Salzburger, will not conclude that the two pastors hold that a prayer taken by a repentant and believing man from a good prayerbook, such as Arnd's *Garden of Paradise,* could not be called a heart-prayer. Instead he will recognize that the pastors are merely relating what the Salzburger told them about his experience; later the Christian reader will see that this good man, who was being tempted, was affected by this prayer no differently than he would have been by one addressed to GOD in his own words, without the aid of a book, in the spirit of truth; at the same time he considered it an aid to rid himself more thoroughly and more quickly of his bad thoughts through prayer.

ELEVENTH, anyone able to give the two pastors and their flock some advice, worldly or spiritual, or anyone wanting further information regarding their situation, may be assured that anything sent to me will be forwarded to its proper place.

TWELFTH, a number of particulars and personalities that seem unimportant to us do not seem that way to others; thus we have intentionally committed to print many such things so that the Salzburgers that are scattered about may get detailed information about their kin and fellow countrymen in Georgia.

THIRTEENTH, although no transport has gone to Ebenezer this year, which was to include some craftsmen which they need very badly, the LORD has provided ways and means for sending them a number of very necessary items this year.

Finally, I pray to GOD that these edifying diaries may serve a good purpose everywhere and that the wonderful examples contained therein of faith that is active through love and Christian patience (which gave those who died a happy and peaceful end), may make a deep impression; also that HE, the LORD, may personally care for His small flock (which should not be afraid because it is small) on the entire earth and, consequently, at Ebenezer, that He may continue His mighty protection of this people, so small in the eyes of the world, against the open and the secret attacks of their spiritual and worldly enemies from which He has protected them so far. May He teach this flock, wherever it may be and when the time comes, to cling faithfully to the words to be read in the prophet Isaiah, Chapter 33, v. 20-24: Look upon Zion, the city of our solemnities: thine eyes shall see Jerusalem a quiet habitation, a tabernacle that shall not be taken down: not one of the stakes thereof shall ever be removed, neither shall any of the cords thereof be broken. But there the glorious LORD will be unto us a place of broad rivers and streams, wherein shall go no galley with oars, neither shall gallant ships pass thereby. For the LORD is our judge, the LORD is our lawgiver! The LORD is our King, He will save us. Thy tacklings are loosed; they could not well strengthen their mast, they could not spread the sail: then is the prey of a great spoil divided; the lame take the prey. And the inhabitant shall not say, I am sick: the people that dwell therein SHALL BE FORGIVEN THEIR INIQUITY. Enough! Written at Augsburg 25 Sept. 1737

Samuel Urlsperger

N.B. The second part of the appendix should be the first. The Christian reader will please consider this in his reading.

Daily Register

Of the two pastors, Mr. Boltzius and Mr. Gronau
From 18 July 1734 to the end of the year 1735

The 18th, July. Recently we had the good news that a fairly large boat could now come much closer to our settlement, but there are still a number of difficulties: (1) It is not as close as had been said but about halfway to Abercorn and, consequently, four English miles away. (2) By water the trip to Abercorn is so long that one can hardly make it in a day even if four persons are at the oars. (3) The routes through the various creeks are so confusing that only those who know the way very well can use them. It is easy for the LORD to eliminate these and other difficulties. He takes care of everything at the proper time.

The 19th, July. A man on a business trip from Carolina passed through our place and stopped with us. We were very happy to become acquainted with this man, for he speaks the Indian language as well as a native Indian. For more than two years he was one of their prisoners and slaves and thus learned the language from his association with them. When he learned that we desired very much to learn this language he was happy. But he assured us that we would not get very far with it: (1) Because there are no people who could teach us and because it is impossible to learn it from the Indians if you cannot live and travel with them constantly. (2) Because there is not a single book from which to learn it. (3) The language itself is very difficult because a single word often has different meanings which can be recognized only with difficulty from variations in pronunciation. (4) We will not be able to accomplish our aim of bringing them to the knowledge of Christ, not only because they never stay in any one place very long, but also because they believe, and have often told him, that each must go his own way and that finally all roads will come together at the place of the greatest happiness and peace. They know nothing about heaven and hell. When he learned that these and other difficulties could not make us waver in our decision, he gave us advice which pleased us very much and told us how to better arrange a number of worldly affairs.

The 20th, July. In answer to our question, said man told us that the Indians have no particular form of worship or service, except once a year, when the Indian corn is ripe. On that occasion all those who live together assemble at a certain place and at a certain time and sit down so that a square is left open in their midst. A man so designated by them goes into this square, sweeps it clean, spreads fresh sand over it, and builds a fire with some ceremony. When it is burning well and strong, all of the Indians, both young and old, throw grains of Indian corn into the fire in place of a sacrifice. Then they take part of the big fire to their homes after first having removed the old fires and all ashes and sand from their abodes.

Shortly before his departure, Mr. Oglethorpe promised our Salzburgers some pigs suitable for breeding. One can see on every hand that the English Nation, particularly the Trustees and the worthy members of the Society, have our best interest at heart and wish to help us in every way possible, which gives us much encouragement in these difficult circumstances.

The 21st, July. Shortly before our morning service mayor Causton and a surveyor arrived to inspect the newly built houses and to inquire into our general condition. He showed great sympathy for our sick, some of whom had contracted illness from the disquiet and the hard work connected with the transportation of provisions and other things. He was exceedingly friendly with all of us, gave good advice regarding our agriculture, granted all of our requests, and assured us that he would help our Salzburgers in any way he could, which was in accordance with the wishes of Mr. Oglethorpe and the other Trustees. Because of urgent business he could stay with us only a few hours.

The 22nd, July. A young woman with a very bad case of dysentery sent a request for medicine a few days ago. Today she tearfully begged for it herself because she knew that God had blessed its use for many people, including her mother and a young boy just a few days ago. Because of her excessive pain we sent her some Essentia Dulci which, thanks to God's blessing, relieved the burning pain in her intestines within a few hours. It was reported to us that she praised God for it with upraised arms, and thanked us for our love. We shall continue to give her other medicines necessary for the case and hope for her recovery through God's blessing.

The 24th, July. As some of our Salzburgers are suffering from scurvy, and as our medicines are not sufficient, we have decided that one of us shall go to Savannah to learn what home cures are used here for this disease. At the same time he shall do a number of errands for the good of all of us.

The 25th, July. Our school, which we hold in our little house every morning and afternoon, has become smaller again because two children have contracted dysentery. We gave them some of our medicine, again trusting in God's blessing. Our listeners have great faith in our medicines and they often consult with us. The sick Braumberger (of whom we have written several times) has reached a very blessed stage as far as his soul is concerned, although his body is extremely miserable. Through the Holy Ghost he has received firm assurance that God has forgiven him all of his sins. Thus he has a great desire to reach his Saviour through worldly death. He was afraid of it when he was well. During his sickness we lent him the late Arnd's *True Christianity*, and with God's blessing through Christ he came to the recognition of his own misery and of the infinite Grace of God. On his difficult sickbed he shows Christian patience and knows that God had to attack him thus so that he would give himself over to Him. He speaks about spiritual things and does not want to hear much about worldly matters. He prays constantly and sends his heart to the place where he hopes to be soon and forever. Among other things, he told us that he had not been able to pray from his heart. And when he used to take a good book, such as Arnd's *Garden Of Paradise,* his devotion would be disturbed by evil thoughts. But now God had given him grace for both his heart-prayer and victory over his evil thoughts. Sometimes he wonders whether he is not lying to himself by imagining forgiveness of his sins; but, when he looks into his soul and presents this worry to his Saviour in his prayers, his heart becomes happy and sure again.

The 26th, July. Some of the Salzburgers went to Abercorn, following Mr. Causton's orders, to bring up the pigs and some other things that were on the boat there. But they made the tiring trip for nothing. People there claimed that the boat was not in.

The 28th, July, Sunday. The two children whose sickness was reported recently have been made well through God's blessing and they attended today's public services both in the morning and in the afternoon. We would have been very sorry if they had died, not only because they are very intelligent but also because they have fine and pliable minds and are being brought up as Christians by their pious parents. Their mother is a veritable Eunice: 2 Timothy 1:5, and these two young plants are most promising.

The 29th, July. The late Huber's oldest daughter had dysentery some time ago. To all appearances it had been stopped, but after a while she developed various symptoms and last night had an attack of epilepsy. Mr. Zwifler was called and he arrived promptly. The sick Braumberger received Holy Communion today. It put him in such a fine spirit that others who attended the ceremony received much edification from it. He is very grateful for even the smallest good deed. From the dedication in the *Household Talks* of the late Dr. Antonius we gave him a certain passage to read, on page 14, which pleased him very much. He said with emotion that he, too, would soon experience these things. God has given such blessing to the medicines we gave him that the pain in his feet has stopped and other things have occurred which we do not consider bad signs.

The 30th, July. Our dear God seems to bless the medicines which we are giving to the deathly ill Braumberger. Not only is the pain in his limbs greatly reduced but he has experienced relief and gathered strength in his entire body. Although he is happy about this divine blessing, he would prefer to die according to God's will because he might again become enmeshed by sin, and the last would be worse than the first, etc. We asked him what he intended to do if God were to let him get up again. He answered that it was his firm resolve, with God's grace, never again to commit a deliberate sin, etc. We reminded him of Christ's wonderful promise in John 10:27-29 and urged him to continue to gather strength and steadfastness through prayer and consideration of Christ's great love while he was on his sickbed. The Good Shepherd would care for the future and would not deny His help. The more he learned to know the unfaithfulness and weakness of his heart the less he should trust in himself for the future but should throw himself with prayer into the guiding hands of the Saviour, just as we pray: "O lead and guide me as long as I live on this earth," etc. He was very much pleased with this explanation.

The 31st, July. The German glazier Rheinländer who has received permission to join us has arrived at Abercorn with his wife and children, and preparations are being made to bring up his belongings both by land and by water. Efforts were made to prevent this man from joining us, but knowing us he paid no attention and put to shame our enemies and those who would slander us by telling them what he knew from his own experience. He assured us that occasionally he had met people that were favorably disposed toward us and the Salzburgers; also Mr. Causton showed him every possible consideration because he foresees great benefits for the land and for our listeners from the skill and the experience of this man. All of his children are happy to join our school, although God let four of them die shortly before their departure from Charleston.

The 1st of Aug. When we told our listeners that Master Rheinländer, whom some of them already knew as an honest and industrious man, would join us, they were very happy and thanked God for it. They are convinced that this man will also be of great help to them with agriculture and animal husbandry as it must be practiced in this country. Because they are fond of him, two Salzburgers left for Abercorn this morning with the sledge to bring up his heaviest things. And tomorrow, God willing, two more will go there voluntarily to help bring the rest of his belongings up by water, despite the fact that they have here much heavy labor of their own. These demonstrations of love and helpfulness by the Salzburgers should strengthen his good opinion of them which he has upheld in the face of their enemies. GOD be praised for having placed such industry into the hearts of these dear people.

The 2nd, Aug. As the building of our houses at the expense of the Trustees was stalled through fault of the carpenters, some of our listeners have declared themselves willing to build a small and well protected house for us in our garden so that we can live closer to them and also enjoy other advantages.

The 5th, Aug. The carpenters promised to lighten the burden of our people.

The 7th, Aug. We were told that a good Indian, who had made his home in Purysburg and had proved himself very useful to its inhabitants, had been bitten by a rattlesnake and died. Some Indians assembled for his burial and interred him, according to their custom, in a sitting position, together with his hunting weapons, household tools, and clothes (he is said to have acquired some fine clothes such as the English have). Even when they kill their enemies they do not leave them lying there but bury them in the manner just described.

This morning the boat with Rheinländer's belongings came up as close as it could. Since necessity requires it, I (Boltzius) will leave very early tomorrow morning for Savannah. May God bless and speed this trip according to His fatherly pleasure.

The 8th, Aug. Master Rheinländer, his wife, and two children are now with us. Only a few things that are still left near the water remain to be brought up. They will live in the little house which we had built in our garden at our own expense until they can build a place of their own.

In accordance with God's will, and in the name of the heavenly Father, I left this morning with three Salzburgers in order to tend to some important affairs in Savannah and to visit Mr. Causton. Although our men worked hard at the oars and we had the current in our favor, we were not able to reach Savannah. As we arrived near Purysburg toward noon, and since we could not continue with our travel because of the very harmful noonday heat, I called on the pious herdsman whose child I had christened a few months ago. His body was miserable and sick, but his spirit was healthy and joyful in the Lord. He spoke edifyingly about his Saviour and related how a few days ago he received such strength from the beautiful hymn: LORD JESUS CHRIST, TRUE MAN AND GOD that he could not sing it enough. There is hardly a house in Purysburg now that does not have one or more sick people in it. The poor people do not have enough food and care. In this respect our Salzburgers as well as other colonists in Georgia are much better off.

The 9th, Aug. We arrived in Savannah before daybreak this morning, and Mr. Causton again received me with great kindness. I told him about the purpose of my trip and reported various matters to him which, with GOD'S help, seem to have had a good effect and will have more, I hope. I had planned to go back toward evening but was prevented from doing so by the outgoing tide and the darkness of the night. May GOD be praised for having helped us to survive this difficult day and for having prevented misfortune through His grace.

The 11th, Aug. I had intended to celebrate Sunday back in Ebenezer, but we were not able to get any further than Purysburg, which is halfway. As I did not like to travel on Sunday, and since the good people of Purysburg showed a great desire for the Word of God, I remained there and was edified with them, in the morning and afternoon, by the words from Matthew 5:1 ff. The dear souls assembled frequently in the house of the sick herdsman.

The 12th, Aug. After much hard labor we arrived in Ebenezer toward evening and, praise GOD!, found everything in good order. GOD be praised for His help.

The 13th, Aug. Today we distributed among our dear people the things we had brought back, shoes and linen among other things, which brought much joy and praise of GOD.

The 15th, Aug. Since the carpenters are not finishing our houses and we have to crowd ourselves in a small hut, I have written a letter to Mr. Causton asking that he give Master Rheinländer the necessary authority. He and some of the Salzburgers will soon finish ours and build the two remaining ones.

The 16th, Aug. At the beginning each Salzburger had been assigned a piece of land for his house and garden and all of the houses were put in very good order. But, with the best of intentions, the Commissioner[6] changed this arrangement and assigned different places to the people. As soon as Master Rheinländer is in better health and stronger, he will go to Savannah to talk this and other important matters over with Mr. Causton.

The 17th, Aug. As soon as Master Rheinländer arrived here, the wondrous GOD struck him down with a bad and dangerous illness. In his right hand, which is swollen very thick, he is suffering unbelievable pain, and besides he is being attacked very hard by red dysentery. Despite all of this pain and miserable circumstance, his spirit is calm and devoted to the will of the heavenly Father. Today I had a letter from a rich captain living near Port Royal in which he announced that he should have sent us, some time ago, twenty cows and as many calves, in accordance with orders left by Mr. Oglethorpe, but that he had been prevented from doing so by various important matters. Instead he was sending us now three fat oxen. The cows would follow soon. At today's conference we announced this new blessing to the Salzburgers and showed them how GOD had given us more than had been received by many other colonists in this land, that He was still doing it, and that they must use this to strengthen their trust in the good and almighty GOD. This awakened them to much praise of GOD.

The 19th, Aug. Our dear GOD is still visiting much sickness upon our dear Salzburgers but He makes it serve for the best.

The 20th, Aug. GOD has so blessed the medicines we gave Rheinländer that he not only seems to be out of danger with the red dysentery, his swollen hand, and his ichor, but he also has got back a good appetite and sound sleep which are visibly restoring his strength. GOD be praised for this blessing. All of us feel the most genuine joy over it. The balsamus cephalicus furnished marvelous treatment for the ichor when the lower part of his body was rubbed with it.

The 21st, Aug. Some of our listeners intend to come to the Lord's Table with us next Sunday. For their preparation they are visiting us this week every noon, and we awaken them to worthy readiness with brief and simple instruction from Luther's *Catechism*.

The 22nd, Aug. The carpenters have finally left their work without finishing four houses, two of which are ours. I gave them a letter to Mr. Causton asking for permission to have our houses finished by Master Rheinländer and some of the Salzburgers. And since the evenings and mornings are beginning to get fresh and cool, we have repeated our request for some bricks, which have been promised, for a fire-place.

The 23rd, Aug. Praise GOD, Rheinländer has recovered from his illness! Yesterday and today he was able to walk about for some exercise. If GOD will only give him more strength then our listeners will soon benefit greatly from his presence. Not only does he himself thank GOD for His gracious help but he asks that all of us praise the GIVER of all good gifts just as we had communal prayer in his behalf.

The 24th, Aug. It has been our heavenly Father's gracious pleasure to bless for us and our listeners the Confession and Preparation which took place today. We based it on Matthew 5:3, 4, 6, 8, which showed all of us anew what kind of preparation is pleasing to GOD. May GOD also give us tomorrow, from the richness of His grace, many blessings from His word and Holy Sacrament.

The 25th, Aug., Sunday. One of our listeners confessed to us yesterday that he wanted very much to have Holy Communion with us; but that he was worried he might still be unworthy and thus commit a great sin, for frequently he still felt unkindness and annoyance over this or that. We urged him not to look upon man but upon GOD and His hidden guidance, to be faithful in the present, and to wait with patience and submission to GOD's will for the proper time and GOD would arrange his physical life so that he would be able to thank HIM for it. We urged him to pray against these evil feelings and to join us for Holy Communion in God's name. He followed this advice, and yesterday after the preparation, and today, he joyfully told us how much mercy the LORD had shown him. At the same time he resolved for the future to follow our advice rather than his own thoughts and judgment.

The 26th, Aug. We have been told several times that this is the month in which terrible and tremendous winds called hurricanes blow and usually do much damage to houses and forests. But so far our merciful GOD has held His hand over us. We are still living in that first hut made of boards which is surrounded by big trees, both green and dead. It is said that these strong winds often uproot such trees, which then shatter anything on which they fall. Our listeners have so much to do that we do not want to trouble them with the cutting down of these trees. Rather, we place our hopes in our Father and trust that He will continue to avert all danger. The new moon has brought almost constant rain and at times the wind begins to blow mightily, but it and the rain soon stop.

The 27th, Aug. Our heavenly Father watches over our present circumstances with such gracious care that our faith is strengthened daily and we can say with the Disciples of our dear Saviour: We have never wanted for anything. The provisions which we, along with the Salzburgers, have drawn from the store house are a particularly great benefit from God and we cannot thank Him enough for it. But our heavenly Father knows full well that in this strange and hot land our weak body needs more care than is given by ordinary provisions, and in His wondrous way He sends us various good things, often quite unexpected and in such quantity that we are able to share with others. May the LORD not let us forget what He has done for us and daily does for us.

The 28th, Aug. Necessity and love for our congregation will force me to make another difficult trip to Savannah so that I can talk to Mr. Causton about the land assigned to them for their houses and gardens. Today Rheinländer and I inspected the various locations and we find it impossible, also unnecessary, that these good people should build their houses and have their gardens in swampy and waterlogged places when there is much beautiful level land on both banks of the river.[7] Besides, the place assigned to each for a garden is much too small. The dear people want very much to be certain that they will have their certain and usable land, because next month a number of things such as turnips, cabbage, parsley, etc. must be planted.

The 30th, Aug. After her husband got well, Mrs. Rheinländer was stricken down by GOD with the same painful disease. Both of them ascribe that not only to the change of climate but primarily to the unrest they had to suffer during the three weeks of their voyage here.[8]

The 31st, Aug. This morning it was as cold here as it usually is in Germany at this time. This appears rather severe now because we have had to live in constant heat by day and night. But the heat we have had here this summer was quite bearable and not nearly as bad as some who tried to scare us would have us believe. It seems to us that it gets just as hot in Germany at times.

The 1st of Sept. Sunday. Mr. Oglethorpe had made the useful arrangement of having mail sent every two weeks on horseback from Charleston to Savannah. And since it frequently passed through our place it was easy to mail letters either to Savannah or to Charleston. But this good mail service has run into difficulties and we hear that it will stop altogether.

The 2nd, Sept. Rheinländer has shown our Salzburgers fertile soil in many places and has given them instructions about sowing and planting. Now that the good people can find so much fertile land around here, which they could not do before because they considered it barren, they are working with renewed eagerness, and everybody who can handle a spade or a hoe is busily working the soil and planting seed. This is the time for white and yellow turnips, cabbage, cress, lettuce, spinach, radishes, etc. Some of them will try rye and wheat.

The 3rd, Sept. Several times recently Mr. Zwifler was sent for by the garrison fifteen miles from here because no doctor could be had that lives nearer.[9]

The 4th, Sept. Thank God, Mrs. Rheinländer is improving very well; and, as she is continuing to improve, her husband has decided to go to Savannah with me tomorrow morning, God willing.

The 5th, Sept. Because a trip to Savannah brings much distraction, disquiet, and weakness of body, I would have preferred this time to remain with my dear flock in Ebenezer. But unavoidable circumstances and my love for their best interest decided me to go along and to report several maters to Mr. Causton in addition to getting some things for them.

The 8th, Sept. After having tended to our business in Savannah we hurried back from there yesterday with the intention of celebrating Sunday in Purysburg. But since most of the people we know and those who want to hear the Word of God are sick in bed; and because Rheinländer wanted to get home quickly because of his sick wife, we rested in Purysburg for only a few hours and celebrated Sunday on the water. As we had not been able to make final decisions regarding the building of houses and the assignment of land, Mr. Causton decided to visit us within four weeks and to bring the surveyor with him.

The 9th, Sept. I have moved into the house of one of the Salzburgers to stay until ours are completed. We will also have our prayer-meeting and Sunday services there.

The 10th, Sept. Today some of our congregation inspected the river and they concluded that it would take a great deal of work but that was not impossible to clear it of the trees that are in it and thus make it navigable. So they have decided, in the name of God, to get started together on the job tomorrow because at present the water is very low.

The 12th, Sept. During evening prayer we read the tract about the Salzburgers who had been in Wernigerode.[10] After that, at the request of the congregation, we started today using the Psalms of David as a basis for our prayer-hours. During our sea voyage GOD gave us much edification through them and, with God's blessing, we hope for the same with our renewed study of them. Because evening prayer can never last much longer than half an hour, we sing a hymn, then give the main content of the psalm, explain the most difficult phrases with verses that come mainly from the New Testament, and then apply the practical truths according to the understanding of our listeners. At school, which can now be held by both of us, we teach the children, nine in number, the most important Psalms in an easy and understandable manner. They are to recite them, sometimes on Sunday during assembly, sometimes on other occasions, for the awakening of the adults. May GOD bestow His heavenly benediction on this simple labor.

The 14th, Sept. The Salzburgers have made good progress with the clearing of the river. But since they need a boat very badly, they have started to build one themselves.

The 15th, Sept., Sunday. For the past week we have had unexpectedly hot weather and all were worried about the seed that had been put into the ground. But last night our dear GOD answered our wish and prayers with a fruitful rain which is continuing today to moisten the dry earth. God be praised for this and all the other spiritual and physical benefits.

The 16th, Sept. Hans Gruber is still plagued with dysentery and continues to suffer greatly. A few weeks ago he had become a little better and was able to perform some light tasks. But he became worse again. His patience and contentment are great, and there are other signs showing that he is not without grace.

The 18th, Sept. Last night the late Huber's oldest daughter had epilepsy. She had had an attack of it once before. Mr. Zwifler tried to help her with some medicine, but it continued all day and, when the convulsions finally stopped, she lay as though dead and completely out of her mind. She is a good child, and the peace of God which surpasseth all understanding surely lives in her heart.

The 20th, Sept. Yesterday evening we heard several loud cannon shots, and today we had news that with them a ship bringing new colonists to Savannah had been welcomed. Whether that is true and whether they are Salzburgers, as we all hope, we will learn reliably within the next few days.

The 21st, Sept. This morning, the oldest daughter of the late Huber peacefully passed away in the Lord and was saved from her great difficulties and from all evil. She had the proper fear of God and was, especially since her last illness, in a state of constant preparation for death. Her love for the Word of God was so great that she was very sad and complained to us with moving words whenever her sisters did not treat prayer and the Word of God with sufficient reverence. Also, at school, in spite of the constant weakness of her body, she worked with all diligence in her efforts to learn to read so that she would be able to make greater use of the Holy Gospel. The fifteenth Psalm was the last she learned shortly before her last illness: LORD, who shall abide in Thy tabernacle?

The 22nd, Sept., Sunday. All of us joined to strengthen one another with this Sunday's Gospel, the 15th after Trinity, from the text about the fatherly care of God. We needed this because of our many trials.

The 23rd, Sept. Today two carpenters returned to us and promised to complete our two houses. May GOD grant that we will at last be able to leave behind us all of this disquiet and distraction. They reported that no ship had arrived in Savannah, as some had assumed on hearing the shooting, but that many cannon had been fired to celebrate the good news that Mr. Oglethorpe had happily arrived in London after a voyage of only four weeks.

The 24th, Sept. Through negligence of the herdsman twelve

cows and four oxen have been gone from the herd for eight days, and they have not been returned in spite of all efforts to find them. The animals had been used to spending the winter in the forest, as is usual in this country, to be rounded up with much trouble in the spring; and people believe that these animals did so from habit inasmuch as fall is approaching. This is bad for all of us because the oxen had been sent us to be slaughtered as needed and now much of our meat supply is gone. But our Father in Heaven knows this and He will provide whatever we need at the proper time.

The 25th, Sept. Our and our congregation's desire to get the books we left behind, which, we hope, were sent to Hamburg before Easter, is growing steadily, especially since we promised them Bibles, Arnd's books on *True Christianity*, and other edifying tracts. We would like to give New Testaments and Bibles to the school children, for they are making good progress with their reading and it is hoped that this will increase their diligence and application. Reports persist that many Germans and Salzburgers are at sea, together with other colonists. Without doubt we will yet be granted our wish.

The 26th, Sept. The carpenters again have left their work to go home because, they say, they do not have enough provisions.

The 28th, Sept. The lost cows and oxen were found in a swamp, a few miles from our place. But it proved impossible to drive them back because they had already become too wild and shy. Meanwhile, all of us will make out as best we can until we get more.

The 29th, Sept., Sunday. A week ago we set aside an hour before supper during which the children are catechized about that part of the Gospel which has been publicly presented during the day. Some grown people joined them and, with God's help, we arranged matters so that old and young can find edification. Already some have been heard to say that divine truths are made much clearer and more impressive to them through such catechizing. May God continue to show mercy on all our work for Jesus' sake.

The 1st of Oct. Last night several letters arrived, sent by the Commissioner[11] from Boston, in New England, which included the continuation of his travel-diary. He makes much of the wondrous kindness and fatherly guidance of God with which he was honored during his entire trip, and he assures us that God never failed to give him the necessary strength to fight and defeat the many temptations he encountered. It is his resolve to reach the point, with the help of his Saviour, of being able to say truthfully after Paul: I have fought a good fight, etc. 2 Timothy 4:7.

He reports that he thinks longingly of Ebenezer and that, with God's help, he hopes to return here to spend the rest of his life. He adds that now and then he met fine people who not only treated him very well but who also showed great interest in our Salzburgers and wished that some Salzburgers and other pious Germans could come to New England, where their good example would be of great benefit to the inhabitants and the Indians. The governor of New England[12] has been gracious enough to send two sloops loaded with boards to be used for the construction of the church and school.[13] GOD be praised for this wonderful news.

The 2nd, Oct. I received a letter from Mr. Causton in which he reports that he is sending a barrel of rice and a barrel of beef to Abercorn, also, that he will make arrangements soon to send us the balance of last quarter's provisions, as well as those for this quarter. Since we do not yet have our own boat and the one in Abercorn cannot be borrowed this week, and since the horses are not fit to carry any load, the Salzburgers have decided to carry what they can on their own backs. They did this today, and it has been reported to Mr. Causton.

The 3rd, Oct. Regardless of the long march and the heavy loads which tired the people very much yesterday, most of them went back to Abercorn today to bring up the rest of the provisions. They are afraid the meat will spoil before they can get the boat because it is in a barrel without salt or brine. May God stand by them with His strength to help them carry this burden.

The 4th, Oct. For several days it has been very cold in the mornings and evenings. This makes us afraid because we have neither stoves nor fireplaces and must make out as best we can with warm clothes. Most of our Salzburgers have no decent beds. There were plans for building two houses, at the expense of the Trustees, in which the colonists that are yet to come were to stay until they could build their own houses. It was our plan to use them for the sick in the meantime, until we could make better arrangements for them, but the construction stopped.

The 5th, Oct. Talk persists that some Salzburgers are on their way to us and have arrived in the vicinity of Charleston. All of us hope it is true. It is not surprising (as we can see now) that these dear people are looking forward to the arrival of their countrymen because they are counting on them for help and a lightening of their burdens.

The 6th, Oct., Sunday. Our three sick men who have been bedridden for more than a quarter of a year seem to get closer and closer to death.

The 7th, Oct. The three orphans[14] whose parents died some months ago in Abercorn are obliged to stay in the common shelter although we have been wanting to give them different sleeping quarters for sometime.

The 9th, Oct. We have had no rain for some time and the land has become very dry. The seed that was put into the ground not long ago will hardly grow and, to all appearances, the people's first crop of turnips and other things commonly grown in the fields during the winter will not be big. That is also GOD's work. May He continue according to His pleasure. Our pious congregation adjust themselves very well to the trials sent by the heavenly Father, and they occasionally speak about this in a very edifying manner.

The 10th, Oct. As the provisions of rice and beef recently received have been used up, I have written to Abercorn to borrow the boat so that we can get some food with it.

The 11th, Oct. Today four of our men went to Abercorn to go from there by boat to Savannah in order to get some provisions. Nothing has been received except the rice and beef that was sent recently.

The 13th, Oct. One of our orphans has become bedridden and we are worried because we lack good medicines. It appears that the children inherited epilepsy from their father.[15] At night they have difficulty in taking care of themselves in the common shelter. As soon as our houses are finished we shall make better arrangements for their care and that of the other sick people. May the LORD grant us His blessing for this. So far, they have had sufficient food, for GOD has so blessed their share of the provisions that they have been able to give some to others.

The 14th, Oct. We learned that Mr. Causton had sent a small boat with a supply of flour, meat, and ship's bread to Abercorn, and this morning the Salzburgers prepared to go there to carry everything here on their backs again.

The 15th, Oct. One of us two could have hurt his foot very badly if our dear God had not graciously prevented a near accident. We cannot give enough praise to God's kindness, which has provided us with constant good health. The LORD be praised for His grace.

The 16th, Oct. The four men who had been sent to Savannah returned this afternoon, bringing with them, in addition to some provisions, a new boat for us. Mr. Causton wants to pay the Salzburgers for carrying provisions from Savannah themselves, because he cannot get anybody to do it there. He would have sent us supplies at an earlier date if there had been some in the storehouse. They also brought the news that two hundred Salzburgers were on their way but that they would go to Purysburg instead of coming to our place. May GOD stand by them with His help during their journey as well as their future circumstances.

The 17th, Oct. Braumberger died in the evening, after seven o'clock. God had put him on a long and hard sickbed. His sickness had been scurvy, which was incurable in his case because it had penetrated deeply and also because we lacked good medicine. We have no doubt that he entered the eternal peace that is for the children of GOD. He longed for it steadily, and we noticed some excellent signs in him before his death.

The 18th, Oct. Our Father in heaven has given us very fruitful weather, with sufficient rain and sunshine. May He be praised for this benefit which pleases our Salzburgers greatly. They wish that God bless their labors and give them a good crop so that they can leave the provisions from the storehouse to others.

The 20th, Oct. According to the new calendar,[16] this is the day on which our congregation left Augsburg last year, and therefore we took the occasion to speak about this in our sermon and to point out to them the wondrous ways and guidance of God. In the evening we found some of them gathered together in praise of God, for He had 1) saved them from the yoke of Popery, 2) provided them until now with the Holy Gospel which they had sought and wanted, and 3) rescued them from many dangers and made the year pass unexpectedly fast; He would continue to help in the future and in the end save them from all evil.

The 21st, Oct. Some of the men of the congregation went back to clear the river today, a useful job which they had not been able to do for lack of a boat. But they found so many large trees in the water and many places were so shallow that it has now become impossible to reach our place by water. It is not completely impossible to do it eventually, but it will take many hands and much time. So they must have patience and spend the winter preparing additional fields. But this is slow and hard work because of the large trees and many bushes. The best and most fertile soil also requires the most work.

The 22nd, Oct. Today our dear people again had to walk a German mile[17] twice to bring up provisions on their backs. They intend to continue with it tomorrow because they cannot finish today. They carry out these and other labors with much patience, but they are sorry that they are so often prevented from continuing with their field work and the building of houses.

The 23rd, Oct. There is in this country a certain root called sweet potato, which grows almost like the potatoes in Germany. But it has a good sweet taste and is very satisfying and is therefore useful in large households that have many people in them. Mr. Causton sent a barrel of them to the Salzburgers, who were very pleased with them. Unfortunately, many of them had become useless because it had been impossible to bring them up fast enough from Abercorn. They grow in great quantity in the poorest of soil. To plant them, seed is not used. Instead, small pieces are buried in the ground. This morning four of our men went to Savannah again in our boat to get the rest of the provisions. May God be with them and bring them back to us in good health. They cannot load very much at one time because the distance is great and the currents run strongly against them.

The 24th, Oct. Last night it was cold as it was a year ago at this time in Germany, when we were preparing for our voyage. We probably would feel the cold much more if we were not surrounded by many tall trees which shelter us from the cold north and northwest wind. A few hours after sunup it was again as lovely and warm as it is in Germany in May. To protect themselves a little from the cold our Salzburgers build fires in their houses which they keep going all night; others in whose rooms that cannot be done build fires opposite the front door.

The 25th, Oct. Since Mr. Causton did not come to see us, the poor people have started to build their little houses according to their own judgment, particularly because they have no protection against the severe cold in the common shelter. They help each other in this, so that no one will find the building of his house too hard.

The 26th, Oct. Hans Gruber, who has been sick with dysentery for a long time, is approaching death. He does not have strength enough left to turn over in bed by himself. Moshammer and his wife, as well as some other Salzburgers, take loving care of him by day and night. May our Father in Heaven reward them for it. At his request, he received Holy Communion today. We saw his burning desire for it, and he gave heartfelt thanks afterwards. Because of his long illness his mental powers also have become greatly weakened. This we must consider when praying with him or when reading him a few Bible verses. He is a simple and honest Christian who loves with all his heart, and within the limits of his understanding, the Lord Jesus as well as his neighbor. Without doubt he will go to eternal peace in the Lord, as he has been wishing for a long time and with all his heart.

The 27th, Oct. This afternoon the carpenters appeared again, and they promise to continue with the building of our two houses as long as the boards last. This worldly affair we have given completely into the hands of our Father in Heaven. If He wants to give us a comfortable place of our own to live in, so it shall be.

The 28th, Oct. For several days we again have been hearing the cannon being fired in Savannah, and now we here received the news that Mr. Pury has arrived in Savannah with a great ship full of people from Switzerland whose destination is to be Purysburg. There are said to be two or three such ships in the neighborhood of Charleston on which there are Swiss and Germans, as well as some Salzburgers.

The 29th, Oct. The Salzburgers derive great pleasure from the Psalms of David, which we are now using for our edification during evening prayer, because they get from them much consolation and instruction for their present circumstances. They frequently comment upon the good fortune of our little pupils who, among other useful and Christian things, are taught these strength-giving Psalms which they recite to their elders' edification, sometimes on Sunday and sometimes during daily prayer, and about which they are at times catechized in public.

The 30th, Oct. The recent cold weather did not last long, thank God, and we now have again warm nights and sometimes rather hot days. The land seems to need rain very badly. We will probably find the climate much more agreeable as times goes on, if our God will preserve our life for a few more years.

The 31st, Oct. Whenever we get news from Savannah, we hope that we will also get news from Germany and from London. But this hope has been in vain so far. We not only have a particularly great desire to get our books and some other things we left behind; but, even more, we hope to get some answers and instructions regarding a number of points brought out in our letters and diaries. We need these badly, for here in this solitude human advice is hard to get and we miss very much what we could formerly obtain so easily and fully. This need, too, drives us to diligent prayer, and GOD has not left us without help and has made our errors turn out for the best. The Salzburgers also want news from their brethren, some of whom are still in Salzburg, others in Prussia. They particularly want to know if some of them have decided to follow them to America. Some land in this region has already been picked out for them.

The 1st of Nov. For some time now we have seen no Indians at our place. Formerly they came rather often to trade the people venison for rice, flour, beans, etc. But today five families appeared at the same time. We are greatly grieved about these poor people, especially because our ignorance of their language prevents us from showing them the way to eternal life. We do what we can for them physically whenever they call at our little house. May GOD himself show us ways and means of helping them more. All souls belong to Him. Occasionally they build themselves a miserable hut; but mostly they live under the open sky, thus not burdening anyone with the problem of giving them shelter.

The 2nd, Nov. As I am still living in the house which two Salzburgers had built for themselves, I read them and any others that may join us occasionally after evening prayer some passages from the two English tracts entitled: *An Account of the Sufferings of the persecuted Protestants in the Archbishoprick of Salzburg.* This makes them remember many things about their previous condition, both before and after they left the Roman Church. For example, many were asked by the authorities whether they would not believe that the saints were praying for the people. Answer: The saints know nothing of us or our misery, how could they pray for us? We will pray to God so that, with His Grace, we will follow in their footsteps. In that way we will surely arrive at the place where they are.

The inquisitors had been very angry at this answer and became threatening. If they noticed that someone could not read, they questioned him closely as to where he had learned such a terrible doctrine, which was quite contrary to Catholic doctrine. And if he confessed the truth, those who had read to him from the Gospel and other edifying books were put to much trouble. In many instances it was the case that the teachers had either died or had already left the country: but the enemies would not be satisfied with such answers. One of them remembered having heard from the pulpit that the Lutherans had only half of Mary's blessing but that the Catholic church had all of it because it asked her to intercede and presented the misery of the people to her: consequently the Lutheran religion could only be false and inadequate. Another added that he often thought of the things he had seen and heard about Popery, and he asked that we all pray diligently for them. What mercy GOD had shown in bringing him and others to the true knowledge! Praise and thanks be to GOD.

The 3rd, Nov. For several days Hans Gruber has been extremely weak, but he retained his full reason and was very happy when we came to him with consoling words, and prayed with him. Today, about eleven o'clock, GOD finally granted his wish and freed him with timely death from his long and hard sickbed. On the sea voyage he had never been sick, being a man with a strong and sound body. But as soon as he set foot on land he began to complain about spells of weakness which increased by and by because, with only one or two exceptions, he would not use any medicine.

The 4th, Nov. Those who went back to Savannah to get provisions again met a Salzburger whom they knew well, together with his wife and children, among the Swiss there. He had settled in Switzerland several years ago.

The 5th, Nov. The mounted post which stopped some time ago is now operating again, going every two weeks from Charleston through our place to Savannah, and from there back again. This means a great deal to us because we can order things from Savannah and other places, as the need arises, and we can also get news.

The 7th, Nov. This week some of our congregation again went to Savannah to get provisions. They will have to continue such trips for some weeks because it is a long way and they cannot load much into the boat because of the adverse currents.

The 8th, Nov. Today the carpenters finally finished building my house and I have been able to have my belongings brought there. Through God's blessing the living quarters I have had to date have not harmed my health in the least. Instead, they gave me more opportunity to practice patience and calmness. The downstairs room will be my living quarters, and upstairs we shall have our services and daily prayer-hours. Our congregation are quite pleased with this because they will find greater comfort and order there than they have had before. We had felt quite certain that Mr. Gronau's house also could be finished. But as there were not enough boards, the carpenters have returned home again. Meanwhile we will use our living quarters as best we can. Our Father has taken care of us so far and He will continue to provide. He does everything at the time of His choosing.

The 10th, Nov. Every time Sunday comes we wish for the things we left behind, together with the hymn books and Bibles we requested, so that we can give them to those of our congregation who can read or who are learning to read, which would contribute further to the edification of all.

The 11th, Nov. A German sent me a letter by special messenger asking me to do him the favor of going to Abercorn next Wednesday. He would be there with his bride and two of her sisters and he wanted me to marry him there. But he asked to keep the matter a secret, saying that he had good reason for wanting to do so. I wrote him in my answer that I would not refuse to serve him with my offices but that I could not comply with his wish until after he had shown in detail and without leaving any doubt that his planned marriage would be in accordance with the Word of God. I told him I would be glad to come to Abercorn to perform the ceremony as soon as he furnished me definite proof of this. In this country such matters are frequently handled in quite disorderly fashion; but, with God's help, we will never be a part of such sinful acts and we have made this very clear to a number of people.

The 12th, Nov. The dry weather continues in this region and the seeds that have been planted are not doing well. The days are pleasantly warm and the nights are no longer as cold as they were some time ago. The present weather conditions appear to be good for our bodily health, and the people who are charged with the transportation of the provisions are happy about the dry weather.

The 13th, Nov. Said German sent another special messenger to me with a letter announcing that he had arrived in Abercorn with a number of friends. He asked that I not hesitate to perform the wedding ceremony since everything was quite in order (as I would see for myself). As I had received assurance not only from the groom but also from a sworn judge that everything about the engagement had been Christian and proper, I performed the marriage according to the Agenda of Augsburg, after first giving them some necessary points from Colossians 3:17. The bride was a native Swiss who had been brought to Purysburg recently by Mr.

Pury. The guests kept themselves within the limits of decency. On the whole, excessive drinking is in this country a common sin which is not recognized as such by most people.

The 14th, Nov. Yesterday it was not possible to go back to Ebenezer, as the wedding could not take place until late evening because of my late arrival. Thus I returned to our place as early as possible this morning. It is no pleasure to remain away a long time and, if necessity did not require it occasionally, I would never leave Ebenezer.

The 15th, Nov. This morning we again had a fairly heavy frost, but the wind changed in the afternoon and all night long we had a warm, soaking rain. God be praised for it.

The 17th, Nov. We have had a great desire to go to Holy Communion together and would have done so if the good people had finished bringing up all the provisions. Last night we again had a heavy freeze, and this morning some ice was found in the water buckets. But toward evening the cold let up, which we consider a gift of God.

The 18th, Nov. Rauner wants to marry a widow-woman from Purysburg and has asked our advice in the matter. He has made inquiries about her and has received testimony of her good character. I have written to a pious man in Purysburg who is said to know this person very well, and have asked him to tell me what he knows about her Christian attitude, her conduct, and general circumstances. We wish very much that such poor people may get a good husband, for they very much need help and advice.

The 19th, Nov. The circumstances in which our dear colleague finds himself now required us to have a house built for him and his wife at our expense.[18] This, praise GOD!, was finished today. We also had recently built a little house to be used as a schoolhouse. In it we also keep our kitchen utensils and victuals, and the woman who helps us with cooking and housework sleeps there.

The 20th, Nov. As we can no longer take advantage of the oral awakening we used to get from our former teachers, our Father in Heaven has given more and more blessing to the effect that their writings have on our heart. We have good reason to thank GOD for having taken with us a number of useful and edifying tracts, otherwise the slow arrival of the books we left behind would be even more painful to us. Also, GOD is so good as to make us remember, for our and our congregation's good, many of the things which used to edify us when we were listening to the Word of God. May His name be praised! Our current consideration, during evening prayer, of the Psalms of David, is frequently sweeter to us than honey and furnishes a wonderful balm for our heart, which often becomes anxious. Trials teach us to listen to the Word. May God continue to preserve His aims within us and to lead His work in us and to His everlasting glory.

The 21st, Nov. For some time we have had no thunderstorm in this region, although the weather has been quite hot at times. This afternoon we could hear some thunder again, but no storm developed because of the strong wind. Those of our Salzburgers who returned from Savannah today brought the news that Mr. Causton has received some letters from England for us and that he will send them on to us by post. This is most enjoyable news for us. They also reported that Mr. Causton had been extremely friendly and kind to them. We all wish that Mr. Oglethorpe would return to this country, for the Salzburgers would benefit greatly from that. His special fondness for them was made quite clear in the short time that he was here before. There are recurrent rumors that he will soon return to America.

The 22nd, Nov. The dear people were finally able to finish bringing up the provisions. Thank God, the hard work has not impaired their health. May God continue to avert all damage with His grace. I had a letter from Purysburg asking me to go there as soon as possible to give Holy Communion to some and to give them comfort and instruction from the Word of God. Some additional important matters connected with my office have made me decide to fulfill the desire of these dear people. Mr. Pury has brought along a Reformed pastor for the French people there, but he is still in Charleston with Mr. Pury.

The 23rd, Nov. Following the thunderstorm, which we could hear in the distance yesterday, a hard freeze occurred last night and again made us rather uncomfortable. We received some letters from our dear fathers in Halle and Augsburg. The letters from Professors Francke[19] and Senior Urlsperger are especially dear to us because we get much from them for our instruction and edification, besides getting renewed assurances of their fatherly fondness for us and our flock. God be praised for this benefit! May He continue to let their prayers bring rich blessings to us poor ones. Next Monday we will try to make the contents serve for the benefit of our congregation, as has been done on previous occasions. Mr. Causton sent an accompanying letter in which he wrote to us in a most friendly and kindly manner. He offers to serve us and the Salzburgers to the best of his ability, having received new instructions from London to that effect. He gives this testimony of the Salzburgers, which translated from the English, reads as follows: "I cannot fail to acknowledge that the conduct of the Salzburgers so pleases me that I am prepared at all times to help and assist them with everything that they consider good."

At the same time he reports that, in a letter to him, Mr. Oglethorpe had written very kindly of the two of us, also, that he had written him the following words of a pious pastor: He (the pious pastor) thanked God that He had done unto the Salzburgers what He had promised in the Old Testament, Psalm 107:13, 14, and 35-38, which words had been particularly impressive to us on our memorial-day festival. God be praised for this new proof of His love and fatherly care. None of the letters mentioned whether the books we left behind had been sent.

The 24th, Nov., Sunday. For tomorrow's evening-prayer I had planned to read the congregation some passages from the letters which I thought would benefit them. But since, God willing, we want to start making preparations for Holy Communion tomorrow, we have used for this purpose today's review lesson, an hour which for some weeks we have kept every Sunday toward evening. God, in His great mercy, blessed this hour greatly for us and for our congregation, and none of us can praise God enough for having led us into a situation in which we can have our services in full freedom of conscience and without fear, and can prepare ourselves together for eternity. The Salzburgers now recognize this benefit better than they did earlier; they consider themselves more fortunate than others, and regret very much that those of them who were left behind but intend to follow them are being prevented from doing so. In all letters, in both those from Mr. Causton and those from Germany, we find a remarkably increased trust in our living God, and we again were forcefully reminded of the words which our Saviour spoke to Martha in John 11:40: Said I not unto thee, that, if thou wouldest believe, thou shouldest see the glory of God?

The 25th, Nov. Since my house has been finished, as reported, it has become necessary to prepare a piece of land for a garden for both houses, which must be protected against pigs and wild animals by a stout fence. In this land no one can have garden vegetables unless he raises them himself. We now have to take care of many things which we would prefer to be spared. For our instruction we are served by the passage Genesis 21:33. In today's regular prayer-hour we made use of Prof. Francke's letter, and our listeners were again very attentive. God sealed everything with His spirit. Last night we had a bitter cold such as we had not expected to find in this land. One of us saw ice two inches thick. At other times it always became pleasantly warm during the day, but today the cold weather stayed and got colder toward evening. We were forced to hold school in the house of a Salzburger, where we could have a fire in the room, otherwise the children's health might have been damaged. The newly built house does not have a fireplace. It could not be built during the summer because then the house itself was not ready. In his last letter, Mr. Causton again made the friendly offer to give us enough bricks, but it is regrettable that the difficult transportation makes it impractical to bring them up now. He also promised to send boards for Mr. Gronau's house.

The 26th, Nov. To take care of some household affairs, Ortmann is taking a trip that will last several days. As soon as he gets back he will help with the instruction of the children, and we have given him oral instruction regarding our methods. He readily accepts good advice and teaching. The cold has lessened somewhat after we had much cold rain on this day.

The 28th, Nov. Because the cold weather remained, we were again forced to hold school in the house of a Salzburger where we could have a fire. There was much smoke and other inconvenience, but one must choose the lesser of two evils. Our benefactors would do a very useful good deed if they were to have a tight house built for us in which the schoolroom could be heated during the winter. I have written to Mr. Oglethorpe regarding a church and a school, but this aspect of it did not occur to me. Perhaps our dear fathers and friends will make the request for us at the right place after reading this. The cold is so severe that we can hardly find protection either by day or by night. This is the case because we were not prepared for a rough winter. Nothing was said about it, quite the contrary. This interferes with our work no little. Charleston is said to be not nearly as cold in the winter. We are situated further north.[20]

The 30th, Nov. Yesterday afternoon we had lovely sunshine, but toward evening a severe cold returned which seems to be destined to stay for some time. This time we based our preparation for Holy Communion on the extract from the *Libri Symbolici* that is to be found in the *Contribution to the Building of the Kingdom of God,* pp. 691 ff.[21] This extract from the testimony of our first converts is most impressive and edifying, and, through God's blessing, it brought both of us strength for our hearts. We hope the same for our congregation, who paid close attention.

The 1st of Dec., Sunday. On this last Sunday of this church year, we and the entire congregation, excepting two persons, went to Holy Communion together. May God let it contribute to the salvation of our souls and to a blessed relationship among ourselves. The cold became more intense last night, and for that reason we have had to make the morning service as short as possible. The cold affects us so much and prevents us from proper execution of our tasks because 1) we did not expect it and, consequently, failed to get many things that are needed for a rough winter. 2) Warm living quarters to which we were used to in Germany are lacking here. 3) Houses here are merely put together from boards and are easily penetrated and filled with the summer heat and the winter cold.

The 4th, Dec. The Lutheran inhabitants of Purysburg have asked me by word of mouth and in writing to visit them as soon as possible in order to give them Holy Communion. As our boat must pass by Purysburg once again, and the severe cold has let up, I have decided in God's name to undertake the journey. May God bless everything. I wanted to arrange the trip in such a way that no one in Purysburg would have any reason for complaint.

The 7th, Dec. Today, through God's mercy, I returned to Ebenezer in good health and found everything here calm and in good order. The Lutherans of Purysburg were very much pleased at my arrival because they had a great desire for Holy Communion. Mr. Pury brought over a French preacher for the Swiss, who intends to practice German as much as he can. A ship's captain related that Captain Frey, the one who brought us across the sea, had suffered shipwreck. May God grant that this report will not be confirmed.[22]

The 8th, Dec., Sunday. In order to keep in step with the Sundays and holy days of the English church, we have celebrated the second Sunday of Advent today.[23] Meanwhile we have used the Gospel for the first Sunday of Advent as the basis of our edification. The cold we had of late has diminished and we now have lovely weather, which does all of us a great deal of good.

The 10th, Dec. Yesterday evening we had, quite unexpectedly, a violent thunderstorm with severe lightning and rain which lasted nearly all night. The people who have lived in this region for some time do not consider this unusual. Instead, they point out that a thunderstorm at this time is usually followed by much rain and cold weather. A German, who with his wife has been living for some time in Philadelphia, brought me a letter from Mr. Siron, of Philadelphia.

The 13th, Dec. The heavy rains we had recently caused our river to rise so much that it flooded several fields and some of the gardens of the Salzburgers. The good people were not prepared for this because nothing of the sort had happened last fall, when the water was said to be at its highest. The cold is increasing steadily and our best protection against it consists of vigorous exercise and warm drink.

The 14th, Dec. Among other things, we have to praise God's goodness for the fact that, in the week just ending, He had given us much awakening of the spirit through the example of the late Dr. Spener, whose biography we have been reading. Our dear God knows very well what we need most under these circumstances, and He has not let us lack in His fatherly care and direction. It would be very desirable if all pastors who want to speed themselves and their listeners toward salvation were to read this biography, as well as the late teacher's magnificent preface to the book on *Nature and Grace*. God doubtlessly would bless such undertaking.

The 18th, Dec. The cold weather has changed again and it is once again warm and pleasant. As far as we can determine from others who have lived in this land for a longer time, last year was not nearly as cold as this year.

The 19th, Dec. From many of our people we hear that they are thankful for God's gracious guidance and for the benefits received so far, and especially for the Word of God. Some of them testify that they are not sorry to have traveled into this foreign land, although they had expected many things to be different. During the daily prayer-hours we have many opportunities to show them, by using the example of the Ancients, the wondrous ways of God and the attitude of the people, especially that of the believers. This does not seem to be without blessing.

The 20th, Dec. The Salzburgers came back from Savannah with some provisions; and again they were encouraged and pleased by the love and friendliness shown by Mr. Causton. They brought me a letter from him in which he again gave evidence of his kind concern for us and offered to serve the Salzburgers to the best of his ability whenever I should send him news about their needs. He will send our provisions as far as Purysburg. There our people are to pick them up, and he promised to pay them for this work. We are becoming more and more certain that the Trustees and other worthy sponsors in England really mean to give fatherly care to the Salzburgers; and if we have had to suffer now and then it was not their fault. We must learn to look to the Hand of God which fills cups of suffering and cups of joy and presents them to us at the right times. Trials and tribulations must also be considered benefits.

The 21st, Dec. We consider it a good deed of God that now our people can come right up to our place by boat. This makes it much easier for them. Formerly they had to carry the provisions a distance of four English miles from where they landed.

The 22nd, Dec., Sunday. As Holy Christmas is nearing rapidly, we make great efforts, with prayer and supplication, to prepare our children and the entire beloved congregation for it during prayer-hour and with our sermons; and we show them what proper preparation is, as demanded by GOD, and how useful it is for us. On Sundays the Catechism, which ordinarily is explained and taught by question and answer during the afternoon, is being left out during this period of Advent. In its place we use some verses for Advent and Christmas, which we expect to continue on Christmas. May The LORD take pleasure in our inadequate and simple work, for the sake of His child JESUS; and may He arm us with His spirit, His strength and His Wisdom, for the praise of His glory and the Salvation of all our congregation. For our own awakening we would like to have all the preparations written by the late Prof. Francke,[24] but we must have patience until the books arrive for which we have been waiting and hoping so long.

The 24th, Dec. Today Mr. Zwifler was married to the person that followed him from Germany, but not until after we drew assurances from both parties that they knew nothing which should prevent them from taking this step. Since Mr. Zwifler had asked the entire congregation to attend the ceremony, and considering that this was very shortly before Christmas, I took the opportunity to give some instruction and preparation with the words from Psalm 45:10-12. Toward the end I applied them specifically to the impending ceremony, then used the entire psalm, in accordance with our plan, for the regular prayer hour.

The 25th, Dec. Again our faith has been strengthened through renewed proof of divine care. Quite unexpectedly our beloved Father has sent us some worldly goods which we can share during these holidays with our poor, and can use especially for the refreshment of the sick. God also continues to bless our regular provisions, consisting mainly of salted and smoked beef, rice, locally raised beans, and flour, so that we are quite healthy. The regular mail passed through our place again today on its way to Savannah, and we posted a letter we had written several days ago to Mr. Causton, asking him to send some provisions soon.

The 26th, Dec. Our beloved God has given us most agreeable weather for celebrating Christmas. We have much cause to praise God, not only because He has let us spend these holy days quietly and in Christian order, but also because He has given us remarkable strength and joy in our preaching of the Gospel of God's infinite grace in Christ and because the services have been well attended by young and old. May He soon fulfill the seventy-second Psalm, which was particularly edifying to us today, so that the earth may be filled with His honor and the knowledge of Christ.

The 27th, Dec. Cold weather has come back, especially at night, but during the days it is warm and lovely. People who know this country have told us that various seeds should be planted after Christmas. Consequently, we are now busy preparing our gardens. Only a small portion of the seed that had been sent to us in large quantity from England came up last fall. I have therefore asked Mr. Causton in my last letter to send us some seed grown in Carolina or Pennsylvania, so that the work of these poor people will not be in vain.

The 29th, Dec., Sunday. During today's private devotion I was particularly impressed by the words of the faithful and truthful witness John, in Revelations 3:14 ff. They encouraged me once again to take seriously my Christianity and my office. And since in my morning sermon I had spoken of the friends and lovers of our Lord Jesus, based on the Gospel of St. Luke 2:33 ff., I took the opportunity to impress the words of our dear Saviour, of the Grace which GOD gives, on the congregation during our review lesson. I begged them in the name of JESUS CHRIST, and admonished them, to leave with the old year all laziness and indifference toward Christianity, as well as everything which otherwise might be contrary to the saving doctrine, etc. May GOD bless this lesson for us all with His spirit.

The 30th, Dec. Today some Indian families again came to our place and aroused in us renewed pity because they know nothing of the great love of God which caused Him to give us His Son and with Him life and salvation, and because we cannot see any means of imparting even a little of that knowledge to them. With the next mail we will send a letter to Mr. Ziegenhagen in order to make some proposals regarding this matter. E. g., A man went to London with Mr. Oglethorpe who speaks both English and Indian. We would like to know if, after his return, Mr. Oglethorpe could not let this man give us some help in learning the language of these poor heathens. We know one other man besides this one who knows both English and Indian.

From the Indians themselves, who like to visit us, we have acquired many words which we have collected in a little book. But this presents a number of difficulties. 1) One can learn from them only the names of objects which can be shown to them, e.g., bread, *appalásko,* meat, *suck-hah,* hand, *tzeuky,* etc. But verbs, adjectives, etc., cannot be learned from them because they know little or nothing about the English language. Thus one cannot learn to put the words properly together without regular instruction from someone. 2) Most of the words they pronounce so low and so far back in their throats that it is often impossible to distinguish the vowels and consonants or to express them with our letters. If one asks too often for the same word, they either become bashful and silent or they start to laugh so long and loud that nothing can be done afterwards.

Several times I have found, on reading some of the words I had learned to some other Indians, that the latter pronounced them quite differently and I did not know who was right, the first or the last. It seems to me that the language of our Indians resembles that of the Wends[25] or Poles in its endings and its manner of bunching consonants. With God's help, we hope to give more definite reports on this from our own experience. At this time I will not go into other methods of learning this language. May God in His love and kindness show us the opportunity and ability for it.

[I. N. I.[26]

The 1st of January of the New Year 1735.

As a prelude our dear Lord has let us experience both joyful and sad things at the same time.] We were delighted with the news in a letter from Mr. Causton which said that day before yesterday, that is on December 30th, forty-nine Salzburgers had arrived who would be sent to us in the next few days, along with the things that had arrived for us. [We shall soon discover who are real Salzburgers here and who are just called Salzburgers through error. The annoying things that have disquieted our minds no little bit in recent days are all sorts of squabbles that have occurred, some of them yesterday and some today, among the people who are not Salzburgers and that make our lives sour, for we must always settle them and advise peace, even though this is usually without much effect. Also, Mrs. Roth was so importunate and shameless towards me in one of her claims that the others who were present were most amazed. Because Roth and his wife are now really beginning to cause us all a lot of vexation and because further disorder is to be feared, we are compelled to ask Mr. Causton again to remove from us the said people, who have already left us once and have been accepted again under certain conditions.]

The 2nd, Jan. Our love for the Salzburgers who have just arrived in Savannah required that my dear colleague, Mr. Gronau, should travel to meet them. This could be arranged easily because he had to go there anyway to get provisions. May God accompany him with His blessing, and may He let him do much good with his service on their souls which probably need very much the comfort and the edification of the Word of God.

The 3rd, Jan. Today it was as warm as we usually find it in Germany in the middle of summer. As much as time permits, the people work diligently in their gardens and in the fields, preparing several acres for planting. The Salzburger named Steiner, who has been ill and bedridden for so long [with scurvy] is sorry that he cannot help with the work. But, in accordance with the advice we are giving him during our frequent visits, he is giving himself over to the guidance of the heavenly Father. The two houses which Mr. Oglethorpe set aside for the Salzburgers yet to come have not been built. For this reason the shelter in which we lived at the beginning is being repaired, so that the good people that are expected from Savannah in the near future can be quartered under a roof immediately. Those who will not have room there will be taken into the houses already built.

[The 4th, Jan. Rauner still insists upon marrying the widow in Purysburg even though we have advised him against it most emphatically because the people who know her in Purysburg give her a very bad recommendation. Someone has put it into his head that we speak against this marriage out of personal feelings. If he were a Salzburger, then we would advise it rather than try to hinder it. We are gradually becoming more accustomed to receiving the judgements of perverse people and no longer let ourselves be so easily discouraged by them.

[The 5th, Jan. This morning a constable from Savannah came to us and brought orders that Roth and his wife and all their baggage should be brought from our place to Savannah and that he would have to comply this same day because it had been resolved to send him to another place in this colony. However, his wife was not at home but, to our annoyance, had gone to Abercorn to go with the boat there down to Savannah, because, for important reasons, we could not let her travel to Savannah at this time in our boat. Now the said constable must change his plans and journey as far as Abercorn in order to catch up with her there. God is an Holy God and reveals in this sad affair various clear traces of His wisdom and Holiness. Because he (Roth) has probably noticed that his impudence will not succeed much longer, he has remained very quiet, humble, and docile since the last report he sent to Savannah about his godless intentions.[27] He has caused us in the congregation the greatest trouble by desecrating the Sabbath; and now God has been pleased to have him taken away from here on Sunday in broad daylight. May God have mercy on his and his wife's poor souls.

[The 6th, Jan. Already last year a fight and violent quarrel began between the Ortmanns and the Rheinländers that wished to take no end, for which reason I was compelled to summon both parties, together with Mr. Zwifler, and reprimand them through God's Word. Unfortunately, I knew that I had not accomplished much with all my representations and had to dismiss them with sighs and warnings. But soon thereafter they thought better of it and promised not only to forget the former insults but rather, as suits Christians, to live in a Christian and neighborly way. Rheinländer and his wife were so heated and angry at Schoolmaster Ortmann that he did not wish to send his children any longer to the instruction-hour. However, because we would not let ourselves be dictated to, and because he would have to keep the children at home, he changed his mind. Also, as he says, he is more convinced of the Salzburgers' honesty and love of peace than formerly. He also wishes that only Salzburgers might be in Ebenezer, for he would get along better with them.

[In this discord many things have been revealed that would otherwise have remained hidden. For example, Mr. Ortmann had given me two letters pro forma to send in my envelope to London but that he had also secretly handed the mailman one with the request to slip it into my packet. Likewise, that his wife damned and cursed me in a most dreadful way because she was of the opinion that I had confiscated letters that had come to her from England, along with the salary. When they were charged with this, they could not deny such un-Christian testimony but testified their remorse for it.]

The 7th, Jan. The Salzburgers who went to Savannah recently with my worthy colleague returned today with some provisions and confirmed the news recently received, namely, that there were Salzburgers in Savannah who would join us shortly;[28] one of these came with them in our boat. They were at sea only seven weeks. Not only in London but also on their entire sea voyage they received many benefits, for by arrangement of our worthy benefactors in London, their ship was loaded with more and better provisions than ours. [They greatly praised Daniel Weissiger, who is at home in Philadelphia and was sent to Germany for collecting, and who looked after them at all times.] No one died, and with the exception of two people who are sick, all of them landed in good health. GOD be praised for hearing our prayers. He does more than we ask or understand. Since yesterday it has been as cold as it was previously.

The 8th, Jan. Today two of the Salzburgers were busy making two additional benches for our church so that everything will be ready upon the arrival of the strangers to praise God the Merciful with one accord for the Grace and good deeds He has shown them and us. Until now the congregation has been assembling in my house, where we used the entire attic over my living room for that purpose. But now that room will be much too small. Perhaps this time Mr. Oglethorpe has sent along orders to build a church and a school as I have earnestly requested in one of my letters. Our beloved congregation would gladly get together and build a large house for this purpose, were it not that they have all they can do with transporting provisions and cultivating the fields.

The 9th, Jan. Since yesterday the cold has become much more severe than we had it some time ago. This also makes us recognize just how great a gift of God fire is, even though we seldom thank Him for it. Yesterday and today, we hoped that the newly arrived Salzburgers would be sent to us, but so far that has not been done. Some arrangements for their housing have been made and they will have this advantage over the Salzburgers who arrived earlier that they can start working the fields immediately and will not have to miss planting time through being occupied with building houses and transporting their belongings and provisions; yet, they too will have their difficulties. They can build their houses after their fields have been planted.

The 10th, Jan. The two Huber orphans are miserably bed-ridden [with scurvy], and [and we know of no remedy against it be-cause the medicines we brought with us are insufficient.] Thank God, both of them are now in a state of mind which gives hope that the Lord Jesus will accomplish His purpose with them and take them into His Kingdom of Glory. One cannot find the least fear of death in them. Instead, they show complete willingness to die. And since Moshammer and his wife have been taking loving care of them during their sickness, they told me today with child-like simplicity what they wanted them to have after their death. Said two people have been chosen by God to care for the sick and they are very good at it. We cannot thank Him enough for this, or pray that He may reward their love with spiritual and worldly goods. We very much need some definite arrangements for the sick and the orphans. May God guide the hearts of our beloved benefactors toward this end. God has made us willing to con-tribute everything we can from the goods He lets us have.

The 11th, Jan. Against all expectation I learned this morning that of the two sick children the boy had died. His death came so softly and quietly that Moshammer's people, who had given him something to drink shortly before, did not notice it. [A few days ago the scurvy was joined by dysentery, which has caused him griping pains; yet the pain ceased a day before his death.] God our heavenly Father be praised for all the good He has done for this boy and for bringing him true understanding of his misery and faith in the name and the sacrifice of our Saviour, [since he, along with his little sister who is still alive, was formerly the naughtiest among the school children]. Even yesterday I reported the said child's physical condition to our doctor, Mr. Zwifler, with the request to supply him with such medicines as suit his sickness, as he had done a few days ago. However, he expressed the opinion that the medicine was being squandered and would not work be-cause we have no warm room here or other good treatment for sick people. Meanwhile he will do his best, he says.

[The 12th, Jan. Mr. Zwifler and his wife give us great pleasure through their Christian behavior. May God strengthen them in this and lay in them a right deep foundation of conversion. The two Rheinländers are full of self-righteousness[29] and become right angry if one tells them that they still lack true conversion and that their hope of being saved in this condition is only imaginary and therefore dangerous. May God have mercy on them.]

The 13th, Jan. Toward evening the dear Salzburgers arrived here by land from Abercorn, awakening in all of us the most heartfelt joy. The Commissioner, Mr. Vatt, was with them, but Mr. Gronau stayed behind with a man sick unto death who will be brought up by water. I welcomed them with the words from Psalm 68:20-21. [In Savannah they were told they would find no fertile ground here around Ebenezer; and, because they saw nothing but bad soil on their way here, many of them became depressed, as the Commissioner reported.] After the people and I had praised God for the good deeds done unto us, I did my best to provide them with shelter and food. Their provisions will be sent after them. I hear that Mr. Causton will visit us soon with a surveyor in order to assign to these people their building lots and fields. [Our dear congregation is still being confused and discouraged by Englishmen who pass through or come to visit us and give the most disparaging judgments about the quality of our region. Meanwhile they all do their best in their diligent work and commend all else to their dear Father in Heaven.] Those who came to America with us have become quite used to the country and the prevailing conditions. They have no wish to go back, especially since they have God and His Word to comfort them during their trials. [Meanwhile, no matter how they are in external matters, God Almighty is our Father, He cannot wish us evil.]

The 14th, Jan. On the given signal, our old and new congregations assembled to praise our God and Merciful Father for His wondrous kindness and guidance. We showed them from the Word of God that our GOD is a hidden GOD who has chosen paths for His children that are hidden and apparently against all reason, and that He continues to do so. They could be assured that it was no accident, nor that it happened according to the will of man, that we had traveled to America. Surely, God has some special purpose to serve with it, and if we remained firm in our faith we would see His glory. And as God always brings trials and tribulations, as we can see by the example of the Children of Israel in the desert, we must not feel strange if our Heavenly Father has made us, and continues to make us, worthy of His punishments, which are beneficial and blessed. We must enter the kingdom of God through much misery. At the same time we encouraged ourselves to praise God with all our hearts for having guided the hearts of our worthy benefactors in London not only toward the newly arrived Salzburgers but also in most unusual fashion toward all of us. They themselves could relate many praiseworthy things in this respect, and we also recognize it in the letters we have received as well as in benefits obtained. The advice given them at the end was taken from Psalm 55:23. Cast thy burden upon the Lord, etc.[30]

My dear colleague and some Salzburgers arrived by water [and brought Mr. Weissiger with him, who has been in Germany for some time to collect for church and school construction in Pennsylvania. He just wishes to look our place over and depart again already tomorrow.] One man, sick unto death, could not be brought any further than Purysburg. There a Christian man, Tullius by name, volunteered to take him into his house and to care for him like a brother. The name of the sick Salzburger is Glantz [and he is said to find himself in a very fine frame of mind.] Because our boat will go back to Abercorn tomorrow, my dear colleague will go to Purysburg once again to see if he is still alive or whether to arrange his burial. The letters received from London and from Germany have been most edifying for us, and very useful in our instruction as well as other matters. God be praised for not rejecting our prayers and for not turning His kindness away from us. May He repay the Praiseworthy Society a thousand times for all the benefits we have received this time, in addition to our salary, and may He continue to make us better prepared to render service in the praise of His glory.

[The 15th, Jan. A man by the name of Dietzius, who came across the sea with the Salzburgers, wrote me a longwinded letter and violently accused Commissioner Vat therein of having deprived the Salzburgers on the sea journey of much of the provisions and benefits that were destined for them and having given part to the Englishmen and confiscated part. However, it is obviously all false and I was well informed of everything before the arrival of his letter. What he calls confiscated, Mr. Vat has brought well preserved and will distribute here among the people. He would not have acted as a good steward if he had given it all out at one time, since they were lacking nothing. The man Dietzius himself stands in bad credit with the Salzburgers and often gave offense by his disgraceful accusations. I do not only hear people praise the Commissioner but I also recognize a great honesty and love for the Salzburgers in him, even though he could not please them all well on the way, especially since the people let themselves

be incited by the said Dietzius, who has a good gift of gab. Mr.
Weissiger journeyed back to Savannah today to get ready for
his return trip to Pennsylvania. Yet he came back with a new
pastor. . . .]

Today the English pastor, Mr. Vollerton, who is being sent to
a congregation near Charleston, came to see us just at the time
when the Salzburgers were arriving for evening prayer. This not
only pleased said pastor very much but also made him express the
wish that he would be able to accustom his congregation to frequent assemblies for prayer and study of the Word of God. And
when he saw that our children have school with us and learned
how we deal with them, he wished that some arrangements would
be made for the good of the English children in this colony
[which for the most part grow up wild and in disorder, as he himself has observed in the short time he has been here. He himself
will write his ideas on this subject to England.]

The 16th, Jan. The cold weather continues, especially at night,
but not as severe as formerly. However, it is still cold enough for
ice. [For the most part the newly arrived Salzburgers have their
troubles with diarrhea and swollen feet, just as the first who came
with us to this country did. The water, which does not appear as
healthy here as in Germany, may contribute to this. The best that
we can recommend to them from our own experience is to remain
warm and quiet and to drink something warm instead of cold. In
this case a few of them have been well served by our balsamus
cephalico—neroing[31] for want of other medication.] Two unmarried persons among the newly arrived Salzburgers announced to
me that they intended to enter the state of holy matrimony. The
man's name is Andreas Resch, from the district of St. Veit; the
woman's is Sibylla Schwabe, from the district of St. Johann. After
having made thorough inquiry into their circumstances, and having instructed them from God's word in the proper meaning of
their intention, I promised to marry them as soon as possible, in
accordance with their wish.

[The 17th, Jan. Commissioner Vat treats the Salzburgers whom
he brought here in a very fatherly way and cares for them as best
he can. We find in him great honesty and wise reflection, and we
enjoy his company with profit.]

Mr. Zwifler's spirit is so deeply moved at the presents that were
made him by the very praiseworthy Society in the form of money
and instruments, herbs, etc., needed for his profession that he will
draw himself still closer to Christ through this divine love-bond,

as he told us with great emotion [and moist eyes]. The day of final reckoning will show how the kingdom of our Lord Jesus Christ was built and augmented also by the worldly gifts of the worthy Society. May He give them His blessing for these, both here and in eternity. We are amazed when we consider the expenditures of the Society and that, through God's blessing, it has not become tired or incapable of giving. God's spring has water of plenty.

The 18th, Jan. The cold increased terribly last night, but it grew milder during the day. The Salzburger who had to be left in Purysburg because of his great weakness had died and been buried upon the arrival of my dear colleague. Some of those who had grown a little sick after landing are getting better now and the Commissioner takes every care of their health.

The 19th, Jan., Sunday. The English Pastor, Mr. Fullerton,[32] [Mr. Weissiger,] and a merchant from Hamburg left today for Purysburg after first attending our morning service. The Pastor as well as the others love our Salzburgers very much and take great pleasure from their eagerness in their divine service. But all of them regret that they not only have been settled a long distance from Savannah but also have been assigned very poor land. The dear people are told constantly that they will not be able to subsist after the time has passed during which they receive provisions. [Therefore we have enough to do to raise their spirits and to encourage them to trust in the Lord Almighty.]

The 20th, Jan. The books destined for our congregation, Bibles, New Testaments, hymn books, Arnd's books on *True Christianity*, etc., were delivered to us today. This filled us with great joy. May God give this much blessing so that our worthy benefactors may rejoice over it in eternity. The Reverend Senior Urlsperger has written a very edifying and impressive letter to the first group of Salzburgers, which we read to them with care. We would like to have more such letters because GOD always blesses them.

The 21st, Jan. The cold continues to be severe, prevents the people from sowing and planting. Many English people whom we consulted earlier about the proper time of sowing and tending of gardens named the twelve days after Christmas for planting time, but this is impossible because of the severe cold. Andreas Resch and Sibylla Schwabe were married this morning, in the presence of the Commissioner and some other persons who had been asked by the bridal couple. For these and similar ceremonies we like to assemble the entire congregation, but that was not possible this time because the people are busy with much work, especially the transportation of provisions and other things.

The 22nd, Jan. Mr. Zwifler told us that, having received medicines and presents from London, he feels obligated to concentrate all of his efforts on the patients without accepting any pay whatsoever as long as provisions are furnished. [We hope that this will be useful to the Salzburgers, who formerly, in order to save their limited money, did not wish to make use of Mr. Zwifler's services but helped themselves with household remedies and made their ills even worse.]

The 23rd, Jan. Schoppacher's small child that had been baptized shortly before the departure of the ship from Gravesend died last night and was buried today. It had arrived here sick and miserable. [Mrs. Roth received permission from Mr. Causton to return to Ebenezer for several days and to put her things here in order. The Salzburgers have claims to make for provisions they have loaned and for wages for their work; but she makes many excuses not to give the people their due. This is her old method: through unrighteousness and squabbling they have done little for themselves.]

The 24th, Jan. The newly arrived Salzburgers are insistent with the Commissioner that they want to be settled at a place with fertile soil. He is making every effort to persuade Mr. Causton and other officials to grant the request of these people, particularly since everyone who sees our region expresses a very poor opinion of it. May God himself show us what is to be done in this matter. The dear people fit in well with us.

The 25th, Jan. The Commissioner has gone to Savannah because of said matters. He would have gladly taken me with him to see what I could do in the matter with Mr. Causton and others. But circumstances did not permit me to leave my congregation for several days. [He is a very honest man who avoids no effort or discomfort and even makes his weak health even weaker through many kinds of rough work just to further the people's good.] The cold weather seems to have gone completely and now it is warm and agreeable even at night. [The new Salzburgers wish very much to be finished soon with bringing up their things and provisions in order to be able to get started with their field work. In this regard they have a great advantage over the first ones in that they have been lent a fine periagua[33] in addition to our boat.]

The 26th, Jan., Sunday. Today, following the afternoon service,

Christian Steiner died after long illness. He had been a good worker, and on his sickbed he sometimes worried that his sickness prevented him from doing field work and other labors, thus making him a burden to the others; but he always patiently submitted to the will of God. God's mercy was more evident in him after he had the last Holy Communion on his sickbed. Since that time his body had grown weaker and weaker. We have no doubt that he has entered the peace of the LORD.

The 27th, Jan. The books, Bibles, hymn books, etc., that were sent recently, were distributed yesterday and today to those who did not have any. There is general joy over this. The longing for GOD and His word is still, thank God! very great in our congregation. This serves us for our own awakening. Mr. Costerus of Rotterdam [who has already been mentioned in our diary] sent us some letters to which he added some others which he had written from time to time to Germany. He is happy that here we have the opportunity to make known the Name of Christ among many different people. [This good man has a really good heart, as we ourselves already observed in Rotterdam, but a weak judgment, to which his great age must contribute much. Therefore we found in his letter all sorts of far-fetched things, which are largely difficult to guess. In Rotterdam he showed us much love and courtesy, for which reason we recently felt obligated to write to him.]

The 28th, Jan. The new Salzburgers are very anxious to get started with their field work, especially because planting time is coming closer and closer. At present they are still busy with transporting their provisions, which is slow work partly because of the distances involved and partly because of the strong current. Some who can spare a little time help others with their field work. Similarly, the first Salzburgers give evidence of their great love for the new arrivals. May GOD keep them in a community of spirit, and may He continue to remove all stumbling blocks from their path.

The 29th, Jan. [Because the lack of provisions is very great again among the first Salzburgers, we have been compelled to send an express messenger to Mr. Causton to advise him of our plight, even though it had already been done. He is probably unable to get anyone to bring it to Purysburg; and even if we send our boat down to Savannah very little can be loaded into it. Therefore the poor people, of whom there are so few anyhow, have to travel down much too often and consume their energy and time. To be sure, the people have received some money for the previous work of bringing up the provisions; but, contrary to our expectations, it was very little. This is a great hardship in which we are. May God stand by us and give the people a large amount of patience, as He heretofore has done, as we must acknowledge to His glory.] The cold has again become fairly severe. This was quite unexpected.

The 30th, Jan. Mr. Causton, the Commissioner, and the surveyor[34] arrived here unexpectedly. But they stayed in Ebenezer only a few hours and then went to a certain location, several hours from here, to select some good land for the Salzburgers there. [To be sure, the new Salzburgers have asked permission to settle at another place, where good land is nearby; but this will not be permitted them, but rather Ebenezer will be steadily built up right where it is.] As soon as Mr. Causton returns to Savannah he will send us our provisions. [Meanwhile Commissioner Vat is to advance some of the first Salzburgers' provisions.

[The 31st, Jan. It troubles us very much that our poor Salzburgers are sometimes reproached for being lazy because they could have done more field work than they did in the time they have been in Ebenezer. But we can truthfully testify that they could not have cultivated more land in that time than they already have and we are amazed that they have been able to accomplish so much. Almost all last summer they had to drag their provisions and things from Abercorn the whole way here with worthless horses and partly on their backs over paths which they had prepared. And even though a passage by water has been discovered for sometime, the way is so far and difficult that they must expend much time and energy in bringing up their provisions, especially since not much can be loaded into the narrow boat at one time. Also, it cost no little effort to clean out our Ebenezer Creek as much as was possible. In addition they have had to help the carpenters who built the public houses and therefore neglected their own. They were not adjusted to this way of life, and the severe diarrhea and the aforementioned hard work have greatly diminished their strength so that they cannot work as they could in their fatherland. And if they had not occasionally spared themselves at our warnings, surely more of them would have died.]

The 1st of Feb. The books which Mr. Urlsperger had sent along for the congregation were delivered, unpacked, and partially distributed today. How happy these dear people are to be provided with the Word of God, hymn books, and other wholesome works! With these, the good that is in them will increase, with

God's blessing. May GOD reward this good deed a thousand fold. During evening prayer we strengthened each other in our trust that God, who gives us the greatest goods with His word and thus cares so well for the noblest part of man, his immortal soul, will also give the lesser good for the care of the body, just as He promised through His only begotten Son in Matthew 6:33, But seek ye first the kingdom of God, and all these things shall be added unto you. We took the occasion also to impress upon them the words from I Timothy 6:6, Godliness with contentment is a great gain, etc. As we hear, God has blessed this especially in one married couple, and we hope in others.

Our old and new congregations please us very much with their uncommon good behaviour and their great love for the Word of God. The Lord be praised for this. May He make them more and more hungry for the good and pure milk of the Gospel. During Saturday's evening prayer it is our custom to leave out the thorough study of the Psalms of David, as we have it ordinarily. Instead, we have a brief review of the subjects that proved most edifying during the week. At this time the children are catechized with care, they are asked to recite some of the verses they have learned, and, in the presence of the congregation, they are given good reminders, or are lovingly chastized for faults that have been noticed in school or otherwise, all of which contributes to their betterment.

The 2nd, Feb., Sunday. We would have new reason to praise God greatly if our benefactors should decide to have a church built here. Whenever public service is held no one likes to stay away. They frequently assemble in my living quarters, but as the congregation has become larger they must sit close together in the small room. This will cause much discomfort, especially during the hot summer. Morning and afternoon school also must be held in my house because the little house where it was held formerly is now too small, [but this greatly disturbs me in my work.]

The 3rd, Feb. The new Salzburgers often talk with thankful spirit and in praise of God about the goods deeds done unto them in Germany and in London, and they beg us to offer humble thanks in their name, which we are doing herewith. May the God of all blessings spread His goodness over these benefactors like a cloud of dew, and for all the refreshment they have given to these good people, may He refresh them in turn during their lifetime, on their deathbed, and before the throne of the Lamb. This I can state with certainty: these dear people never forget their benefactors in their prayers. When they have to suffer severe trials, they do not ascribe them to people but believe that the heavenly Father considers them more salutary for them than good days, and they remain patient and happy.

One man, Madereiter by name, grew weak and miserable in body soon after his arrival, but in his spirit he is so happy and satisfied with God that it is refreshing to everyone to hear him speak and testify of the love of his Saviour which he is tasting so sweetly in his heart. He had never been sick in his life but knows how to adjust himself to it. That is so because he has learned to be satisfied with everything God does, and to take everything from His hand, so to speak. Now he thanks God for having sent him into this wilderness where the Gospel is particularly satisfying to him and where he cannot see as many bad examples as elsewhere. O what a noble thing is Christian simplicity, and how the work of the Holy Ghost shows itself in those souls that submit themselves simply and humbly to its punishment and purification! The oldest girl of the two orphans that are still alive has been sick for some weeks and death seems to be coming closer. May God continue to prepare her for a blessed passing away, as He has begun to do already.

The 4th, Feb. Today we have nearly finished our letters, which are to be sent to London at the first opportunity. Among others, we are writing to Mr. Oglethorpe, Mr. Vernon, Captain Coram, and Secretary Newman, thanking them for ourselves and for the Salzburgers for all the good deeds that have been done for us. The Salzburgers themselves have brought us many letters with which they want to offer their thanks for the benefits received. Many duties prevented us from bringing our letters and the diary in order at an earlier date. [We are at a disadvantage in being so far from Charleston and having to give our letters to the mounted post without knowing when they will be dispatched.] Commissioner Vat will write a few lines to accompany our letters, so that the report on the condition of the soil in this region may be taken under consideration as soon as possible.[35]

The 5th, Feb. Contrary to everyone's expectation, a new cold wave appeared. We are told that a number of very cold nights had been experienced here at other times, but that the present severe and lasting cold is very unusual. We find it impossible to protect ourselves from the cold except near the cooking fire. This interferes with our desire to work, especially during the morning and evening hours.

[The 6th, Feb. Commissioner Vat is prevented by his weak eyes from sending many letters to London and Germany, yet he considers it necessary to accompany our letters with a few lines in order that the report of the nature of the soil in our region might be taken into consideration all the more.]

The 7th, Feb. As Mr. Oglethorpe had been earlier, so Mr. Causton is now very insistent that the people should work the fields together and divide the harvest. Although such an undertaking presents many difficulties, we called the new Salzburgers together this evening, told them that there were some important reasons for their communal labor, and listened to their objections. They promised to follow this advice and to make an honest attempt at it, because they did not want to be accused of disobedience by their benefactors. We have always found it very useful to discuss with the entire congregation the things that should be done; and, although many problems arose during the early, difficult days, not a single Salzburger had to be urged sharply to do his duty, as far as we know. The words of Matthew 21:29 were literally fulfilled in some of them.[36]

The 8th, Feb. The severe cold has been followed by a warm day, with strong winds. So far we have experienced what we have been told by others to expect, namely, that the weather in this country is very changeable. The new Salzburgers wish very much to finish with the transportation of their provisions and belongings so that they can begin to work the land, especially since Mr. Causton wants them to plant Indian corn and beans by the middle of this month, not at the end of March or beginning of April as is done by other people in Carolina. As the men will all work together, the women have decided not to be idle and have been assigned a piece of land for a number of gardens. [Our letters have been sealed along with the diary, and one of us will have to travel in person to Savannah in the next few days in order to see whether we can find a safe opportunity to send them to London. Perhaps the minister in Savannah, Mr. Quincy, can help in this.]

The 9th, Feb., Sunday. Until recently the hymns to be sung during our services had to be recited to the congregation. But now that a goodly number of hymn books have been sent us through God's fatherly care, and since most of the members can read, we no longer have to recite them. This seems to be much more agreeable and edifying to the congregation. Perhaps the few people who don't read very well yet will be encouraged by this to apply themselves more and to take advantage of our private lessons, for which we have saved a few of the books.

We have made it a habit to practice all week in school with the children those hymns which we want to sing the following Sunday after the sermon. They learn them so well that even the smallest children can join in the singing during services. During evening prayer we still have to recite a great deal. How happy these dear souls are to have Bibles now! They always bring them to the services to read along in the chapters that are read to them before and after the sermon, and they mark strength-giving verses so that they can read and review them again.

The 11th, Feb. Schweickert, Baron von Reck's servant, wrote me a letter from Boston, in New England, saying that he had been employed there by a German major named Lackner. But as he had no opportunity to strengthen himself with the Word of God, he begged that I send him a Bible. I shall send it on to Charleston in a few days. There are a number of people who have expressed their desire for edifying books, especially the Bible. Now that we have received a good supply from Halle and Augsburg, praise God!, we shall do our best to serve them in the hope that, as our congregation grows, GOD will awaken benefactors who will provide us with additional Bibles and other spiritual works. Some of the Englishmen also show a desire to read Arnd's books on *True Christianity,* which have been translated into English.

The 12th, Feb. Today our boat arrived with the provisions requested, which pleased us very much. Now the first Salzburgers have received provisions for an entire year. We hope that these benefits will continue until they have made their first crop and can take care of themselves. God be praised for His care. May He give rich rewards for all the benefits received.

The 13th, Feb. The Huber girl that had been sick died this afternoon. Even before her sickness she had been a pious child, but her long and difficult confinement has increased the good in her.

The 14th, Feb. Mr. Causton is now very serious about finishing the three communal houses. He has sent us two board cutters who are to be followed soon by the carpenter from Abercorn who built the first three houses. Until now my dear colleague has had to put up in a very poor little house. Thank God this has not harmed his health.

The 15th, Feb. Mr. Causton came to see us with the surveyor and Captain Dunbar, who brought the last Salzburgers to America, in order to inspect our land once again. They departed together after lunch.

The 16th, Feb., Sunday. In performing the duties of our office we have learned that edifying examples have been particularly impressive to our listeners and have served to better explain some truths presented to them, and therefore we have retained the practice of telling and reading them such examples during evening prayer as well as during the review lessons on Sunday. In today's review lesson we attempted to make meaningful to our congregation the report on the great awakening which has been taking place for some years in the congregation of Pastor Beyer, in Zezeno. This fitted particularly well the sermon we delivered on the Gospel of the Sunday Sexagesima. The good spirit which shows its salutary work so strongly in that congregation also shows itself strongly in our congregation, as we must confess to the Glory of God. These dear souls not only appear at the services hungry for the good and pure milk of the Gospel, but they are so eager that neither eating, cooking, nor any other worldly care can detain them. And most of them spend the entire Sunday as a day of the Lord, praying, singing, and reading, so that we are always very much edified whenever we visit them. May God keep and strengthen them in this spirit, and may He be praised for His everlasting faithfulness, always and eternally.

The 17th, Feb. Commissioner Vat is so weak in body that he has not been able to leave his bed for several days. God be his physician and helper.

The 18th, Feb. It has been so cold on two successive nights that some of the plants in the garden, which had been planted too early, were killed by frost. The days, on the other hand, are comfortably warm, sometimes even fairly hot. We all are pleased with the blessing of God that was given us with the provisions received last, not only because our needs were filled by them but also because everything was done according to our wishes. This testimony we can again give about our listeners: they heartily praise our dear God for all benefits, and they never cease being surprised at the love and kindness shown by their benefactors. Their intercession for these will not be unheard by our Father in heaven.

The 19th, Feb. Mr. Causton has promised to send some black slates for our pupils. As soon as they arrive, the bigger children, who are well founded in reading, will be started in writing and arithmetic. In order not to neglect the bigger ones for the smaller children, we have had to divide them into two classes. All of the children are together in the two religion classes we have in the morning and in the afternoon. In all other lessons the smaller children are taught by Mr. Ortmann while the two of us continue with the bigger ones. The parents continue to send their children to school regularly, and the children themselves come to us eagerly and joyfully.

The 20th, Feb. One of our first Salzburgers had to go to Pallachocolas (a small fort on the Savannah river)[37] for business reasons. When he returned today he had much to tell of the disorderly and shameful behaviour of the Indians there. At that place there is for sale rum (a sort of brandy made of sugar cane), which drives the Indians to terrible excesses and makes them drink themselves to death. Toward evening some of the Indians from Pallachocolas came here. They had apparently brought with them some of the strong drink, for they got drunk here and caused some trouble. When they are drunk they are very rough so that one's life is in danger. I had considerable trouble in my very house, shortly before the evening prayer-hour. But God saved me from all distress and discomfort. So far we have failed to find in any of them the good traits they were said to have when we first arrived in America,[38] although they are much easier to deal with when they are sober. Today one of them repeated many times, in an insolent and surly manner, that he was the prince and that the king who had returned from England recently was his father's brother. He spoke English fairly well and, like some impudent Christians in this country, knew how to swear so terribly and to misuse the name of God, whom he does not know otherwise, that I was amazed. May GOD have mercy upon these miserable people.

The 21st, Feb. As we had heard that a great many peachtrees were to be found not far from here, and as a certain Englishman had given the necessary permission, some of the Salzburgers have brought a considerable number to our place. They are said to bear quickly and plentifully in this country. Except for these, there are no fruit trees to be found in this colony. The reference to various fruit trees in the printed description of Georgia must have been meant for Carolina, particularly Charleston, where many good and rare trees are said to be found in the orchards of prominent Englishmen. Today it was as hot as is rarely the case in Germany in the middle of summer; but the nights are so cold that some of the garden vegetables that had been planted early have been killed.

The 22nd, Feb. All of the first Salzburgers are now, praise God!, in good health, and they hope to get more and more used to the land and the food. The last group, on the other hand, is still made uncomfortable by various weaknesses, but these do not occur as often nor are they as severe as those suffered by the first group after its arrival.

The 23rd, Feb., Sunday. Today the banns were published for the first time for the marriage of Rauner and the widow from Purysburg. But he may not bring her here until after the third publication. As the Catechism has been finished in the afternoon lessons, we based this afternoon's lesson on part of the Passion story and impressed its truths upon the children with questions and answers. With God's help, we will continue with this throughout this period of Lent. The cold weather has left us again, and this afternoon we had a warm and fruitful rain which may well last through the night.

The 24th, Feb. Last night I was called by Geschwandel who asked that I hurry to his house in order to baptize his newly born son who was very weak. It was high time, for the baby died within an hour after having received Holy Baptism. The parents as well as those attending the ceremony praised God with me for having let this weak child experience the bath of rebirth. We find it very necessary to insist that our listeners not try to spare us but take advantage of our office by day and night. We hear that some of them do not want to cause us any inconvenience because of their sincere love for us.

The 26th, Feb. The Salzburgers have not been able to start on their communal field work, partly because they have been busy transporting their provisions, and partly because they wanted to prepare several pieces of land, close to our place, for use as gardens. We ourselves strongly advised them to do the latter. All this having been done, they started today to look for the best big place they can find. In the next few days they will all work together and prepare it for the planting of corn and beans. These dear people are all very eager to work. If only the land could be as good as they wished, they would spare no pains to accomplish much that is good, with God's blessing and to the joy of their benefactors.

The 27th, Feb. The cold nights we have had a number of times have disappeared and the land has been refreshed with a warm and fruitful rain. Commissioner Vat had brought with him a good supply of seeds which was distributed to the Salzburgers that he brought here. But they have given some of it to the first group for their gardens. The seeds that were sent us from England in large quantity were partly spoiled aboard ship and were delivered to us too damp. Therefore, with few exceptions, they would not come up although they probably cost our benefactors a great deal of money. We have tried to have some from Charleston or Savannah sent, offering to pay money for them, but we have not been able to have this wish granted. Meanwhile, the people now have the best and most necessary seeds; and, since some of them have come up already, they hope with God's blessing to get some garden vegetables, which they have had to miss completely until now.

The 28th, Feb. Mr. Zwifler is proving himself very faithful to his profession. And as he is getting much practice in matters about which he knew nothing previously, he is becoming more and more useful to us.

The 2nd, Mar., Sunday. Excepting Mrs. Geschwandel and a few others, all of the Salzburgers are now in good health, thank God! Sundays as well as on other days they diligently and eagerly cling to the Word of God.

The 3rd of March. Today the Salzburgers started, in the name of God, with their communal field work and we were surprised to see how many trees they felled and partly burned. They start their work at the break of day and when the sun gets very hot they go home and stay there until afternoon.

The 4th, Mar. The first Salzburgers have prepared several acres for the planting of corn, but they still lack the seeds. As Mr. Causton has promised them seed corn, beans, and sweet potatoes, I wrote him a letter today reminding him of his promise and telling him of the need of the Salzburgers. Mrs. Geschwandel has become so sick and miserable of body that her recovery is very doubtful. She has great faith in her Saviour and can say for the strengthening of her faith that He has always heard her prayers, yet with all of her joyful faith she remains of humble spirit. She does not take lightly even the smallest fault or weakness but makes them serve herself in presenting her heart humbly to God and, as a great sinner, to flee deep into the wounds of the LORD JESUS. It is a great pleasure to talk with her.

The 5th, Mar. The climate in this country is extremely inconstant. A few days ago it was fearfully hot, but now it is cold again by day and by night. It appears that this cold will kill or retard the growth of the garden vegetables that have been planted too early. Besides, the wind is often so strong that we must fear that the houses, which are built on bad ground, may be blown over by it. But it cannot hit us too hard because we are protected by forests on nearly every side. If a strong wind rises while the land is parched and dry, it hurts the sandy soil very much; for it blows the sand away and thus interferes with the growth of the plants.

The 6th, Mar. Everyone who passes through our place sees that the good people are working with all their might, from morning till night, felling trees and preparing the fields.

The 7th, Mar. Twice in succession we have had the bad news from Savannah that some servants there, who for some misdeeds had been sent from England to be slaves in this province for their punishment, had plotted with a colonist from Abercorn to burn the city. We cannot thank God enough that we do not know anything about such insolent riff-raff in our place and are able to fill our offices in the service of God with pleasure and in peace. May our Father in Heaven continue to hold His hand over us.

The 8th, Mar. The cold weather that we have had for some days has become milder during the day time. But at night it is still not as warm as expected, or as warm as it appeared to us a year ago when we arrived near Charleston on this day.

The 9th, Mar., Sunday. As it has been one year this week since divine providence let us land here safely after a difficult sea voyage, we have announced to the congregation that we will hold our memorial service next Saturday, at which time we shall recount the many instances of divine help and the rescues from much misery and danger, to the glory of God. Toward this end we shall read from our diary about some special instances showing how divine providence operated amongst us so that they will be recalled to our memory. We have had to choose Saturday for this because the dear people are overburdened with work on all the other days, this being sowing and planting time. On Saturdays they usually leave their regular work earlier to prepare themselves for Sunday. Thus the celebration of our memorial service is best held on this day.

The 10th, Mar. All of this day we have had a cold rain which caused us more discomfort than the freezing weather we had some time ago. It is our intention to have Holy Communion also during our memorial service, for which purpose we began today to prepare with the congregation for this important undertaking. I continued with the discussion of the great inner suffering of the LORD JESUS, some of which had been read and catechized, as much as time would permit, in yesterday afternoon's regular lesson on the Passion story. For the better and clearer understanding of this most important matter I referred to the 18th, 69th, and 88th Psalms and also read them the first part of the hymn: My friend melts away with love, etc. Explanation and application of this was blessed by God in my heart and, I hope, in others as well. In the hours of preparation I intend to continue, in God's name, with the consideration of the inner suffering of Christ and to apply it to the listeners in such a way that they will learn to recognize and truly regret the atrociousness of the sins for which the Son of God had to suffer so terribly, also that they will accept in faith the inestimable Grace of Christ we have received through it, and in proof of this will honor and please Him by leading a pious life, for He was shamed, grieved, and martyred for the sake of our sins.

The 11th, Mar. Important matters had made it necessary for my dear colleague to make the difficult trip to Charleston. Today GOD brought him back to us in good health, for which His name be praised with joy. Some of the things he purchased to fill our needs have been brought up from Abercorn by the dear Salzburgers who carried them on their backs. The rest they will bring up by boat from Savannah.

The 12th, Mar. Last night we again had an unexpected and heavy freeze. This climate seems very strange to us, especially since last year at this time, when we arrived in Savannah, it was comfortably warm by day and by night. A cloth tent was put up for the Salzburgers after landing, and they could not have survived in it had it been as cold then as it is this year. The changeable weather probably contributed a great deal to the sickness of several people amongst us, all of whom are made very uncomfortable by the cold. Today Rauner brought to us the woman he wants to marry, and the marriage shall take place tomorrow. Their banns have been published for three successive weeks and no important objection has been raised.

The 13th, Mar. Mrs. Eischberger, the wife of one of the last group of Salzburgers, brought two girls into this world last night who had to be baptized shortly after their birth because they were so very weak and poor; and one of them died a few hours later.

Mrs. Eischberger is a true child of God and knows very well how to bear the cross which our beloved God has sent her in this period of Lent.[39]

The 14th, Mar. Of the two weak babies who were baptized yesterday, one died yesterday and the other one today. They will be buried toward evening. It has been our custom to arrange burials as follows. 1) The signal for the burial is given with our small bell. 2) We usually choose for it a time when the listeners have finished their day's work so that all those whose circumstances permit may be present at the interment. 3) After our school children and some of the people have assembled at the place where the body is, we sing a funeral hymn which is followed by the reading of a passage from the Bible which deals with dying. 4) The bearers are followed by the school children and the schoolmaster, the rest of the people following them. We do not sing on the way, but as soon as the body is interred, we all sing: Now let us bury the body, etc. 5) After the burial we give a brief reading from the Word of God to the assembled people, and then we close with prayer and a few verses of some hymn.

The 15th, Mar. This day was set aside for a memorial and thanksgiving day on which we want to remind each other of the spiritual and worldly benefits received so far, and to encourage each other to praise God and His eternal mercy. The morning lesson was taken from Psalm 50:14-15, and the afternoon lesson from Psalm 116:12-13. For their own and for the congregation's edification, the children had memorized two psalms, the ninety-second and the one hundred sixteenth, which they had to recite in public, as is usually the case on Sunday. Our beloved congregation assembled frequently for public worship, and we hope that our heavenly Father will be pleased with our devotion and the offering of praise we made in Christ.

Important considerations caused us to postpone Holy Communion until tomorrow. The people who during the last few days had announced their intention of doing penance and making confession came to see me this evening. We usually handle this in the following manner. 1) The communicants come to me during the week preceding the Sunday which has been set aside two weeks earlier for the celebration of Holy Communion. We speak with them according to their individual needs and pray with them. 2) We have hours of preparation for an entire week, which are attended also by those who do not intend to go to Holy

Communion. 3) On Saturday, at a given time, they all come to the room in which we have our services. After a lesson from the Word of God and after singing a few hymns, we all kneel and pray. The pastor recites a prayer of penance and confession which the bearers pray silently after him. 4) After this prayer is finished the congregation moves closer to the teacher and answers with a firm YES three main questions aimed at the recognition of their miserable sinfulness, their true repentance, their faith in Christ, and their renewed obedience. Then this YES is included in a prayer, after which absolution is given them. This is affirmed by the entire congregation with an AMEN. 5) At the end comes a short hymn or a few verses.

The 16th, Mar., Sunday. The persons who partook of the Holy Sacrament this morning numbered fifty-five. All of them showed heartfelt devotion and great respect for the Holy presence of God, and our beloved heavenly Father granted us particular joyfulness in proclaiming His Gospel. After Communion we were able to sing several Lenten hymns, for most of the people now have hymn books and we no longer need to recite the verses to them. We start and end this holy act with prayer and, through the Grace which God gives, arrange everything in the most edifying manner. There are several sick people who had a great desire to take Communion with us, but they were satisfied when we told them that Holy Communion would be had again at Easter. As the congregation has grown, we intend to have it every six weeks.

The sick Mrs. Geschwandel received Holy Communion the day before yesterday, much to the comfort of her soul. Her love for her blood-bridegroom Christ JESUS is very ardent, and she wishes nothing except to be saved from her painful sickbed in order to be with CHRIST. The last time she took Holy Communion she was so impressed by the verse: Christ has taken death's power away and has brought life and immortality, that she has taken nourishment from it all of this time. And even in her present circumstances she richly experiences the power of the holy Gospel. In associating with her, one can learn from her living example what the words mean: The kingdom of God does not consist of words, but of strength. She is one of the simple and minor children to whom the Lord promised to reveal His kindness and who will succeed before others.

The 17th, Mar. Last night we heard the first thunderstorm of this spring, but it soon went away. For the past three days it has been very warm during the day and fairly warm at night, following the freeze we had earlier. Today we had uncommonly strong wind. Also today, we started the bigger schoolchildren on arithmetic and writing, for which they showed great eagerness.

The 18th, Mar. For a short time we shall omit the Psalms of David from evening prayer. Instead we shall read and relate incidents from our early diary to remind ourselves and each other of the guidance of God, and how He has gone with us in earlier times. We hope that this will awaken us to renewed praise of God for His fatherly rescue from many miseries.

The 19th, Mar. Mrs. Geschwandel is still being subjected to much pain and weakness of body, although Mr. Zwifler gives her every possible care and faithful service. In spite of all her pains she remains calm in her faith in the wounds of her Saviour. She cannot give enough praise to His love. Visits to her are always very edifying for me. She often praises the LORD for having considered her worthy to suffer in Salzburg for the sake of the Gospel and for finally leading her away so that now she can without hindrance strengthen herself, in days of health and of sickness, with the pure Word of God.

The 20th, Mar. On visiting a sick Salzburger this morning I found him in his bed, reading Arnd's *True Christianity*. He tearfully told me about the great edification he was deriving from this beautiful book which he had not been able to buy in Salzburg for any amount of money. He thanked God for leaving him enough strength during his sickness to comfort himself from the Word of God and other good books. For the rest, he did not care what happened. With God's blessing, the books recently received are doing much good in the congregation. May God himself make the reward for them.

We also try to encourage spiritual growth among the Englishmen with the English books and tracts that we received from the pastor in Savannah, Mr. Quincy, at the request of the Society. Some of them take them very eagerly. Many people in this colony do not hear any sermons for long periods of time because they live too far away from Savannah. Some of them, therefore, make good books and printed sermons serve for the edification of their souls. The cool nights which we again had yesterday and the day before, were unexpectedly followed today by a violent thunderstorm. Among other things, we heard one thunderclap so loud that we have never heard its equal before. A tree just back of our schoolmaster's garden was struck, but our Father has let it pass without damage.

The 21st, Mar. Last night was very cold again, but it did not freeze. People who have lived in this country for several years have told us we shall still have cold nights but do not need to worry any more about a freeze. Thus various seeds can now be safely committed to the earth. Some Englishmen have sent us various fresh seeds, some voluntarily and some because we asked them. With them we can be of service to those members of the congregation that do not have any.

The 22nd, Mar. My dear colleague does not intend to come back from Purysburg until next Monday because the Lutherans there have a great desire for Holy Communion. Grant GOD that many of the souls who will hear the holy Gospel on this occasion will be led to our beloved Saviour.

The 23rd, Mar., Sunday. Our sick people, including Mrs. Geschwandel, have recovered so far, praise God!, that they seem to be out of danger. Mr. Zwifler is making every effort and he gains more experience all the time. The proper working of the medicines is interfered with by the fact that the sick people are lying in huts through which the wind can pass easily and which can even be penetrated by rain. Last summer time did not permit the building of better houses, and no one expected such a severe winter with its changeable and frequently violent weather. And as the people are now busy with sowing and planting, and as they still have hope to move from here to a more fertile region, they cannot and will not build better houses.

The 24th, Mar. Schoolmaster Ortmann is proving himself to be diligent and faithful in his schoolwork. His work with the small children is not without profit.

The 25th, Mar. Toward evening, my dear colleague returned from Purysburg.

The 26th, Mar. A sick man opened his heart to me and requested advice from the word of God. When he was still a farmhand in Salzburg, his master had ordered him to build a fence which, unbeknown to him, went too far on the neighbor's land. When the two farmers talked about it, they decided it was his fault. At the time he had not rectified the matter but, rather, he had excused himself on account of his ignorance. But now he was fearful over it for he had learned from a recent sermon, and by reading Arnd, that it is a great sin to narrow a neighbor's boundaries. The man's Christian attitude is excellent, and we took the occasion to point out to him the free spring that washes all sin and uncleanness, namely, the wounds of Christ. He accused his desperate and wicked heart of liking to stray away from God and to take the wrong paths, in which connection the two verses from Jeremiah 2:12-13 and Isaiah 1:3 impressed him greatly. Also Psalm 95:10-11. In our sermons, catechizations, and evening prayers it has been our chief aim, with the Grace given by God, to bring our listeners to a thorough understanding of the fact that their hearts are by nature very much corrupted by sin, and also to give them a thorough understanding of the ineffable Grace of God in Christ, which is offered through the Gospel to the repentant and divinely saddened souls, for on our part we have learned ourselves that this is the safest road to heaven.

The 27th, Mar. Everyone is surprised at the fact that the cold weather is staying so long. The days are warm enough, to be sure, sometimes even hot: but at night it still is frequently so cold that thin ice is formed. The first Salzburgers have asked us to give their thanks to Mr. Schauer for all the good he did for them earlier,[40] and also for the balsam which he had recently sent to them by Mr. Vat and which was distributed to them today. They know many cases in which it has proved very useful and healing for them in different ways, and for that reason they esteem it highly.

The 28th, Mar. The mounted post brought us letters from Savannah which had come from London and Germany in a boat that arrived last night. Some medicines and other things also arrived for us.

The 29th, Mar. This morning we again had an emergency baptism, for Mrs. Schweiger had brought into this world a weak and premature boy. In all of their misery, our beloved people find comfort in the fact that God has found them worthy of receiving His word and the Holy Sacraments in this wilderness, and that even the weakest of children can get Holy Baptism by day or by night. They often say: Praise and thanks to God, we do not know how much good we have here, and we do not recognize it enough. The little boy who came into the world today died about noon and was buried toward evening.

The 30th, Mar., Sunday. I visited the sick Mrs. Schweiger and found her strengthened in body and soul. As Adam Riedelsperger and his wife (a truly pious couple) were there, we all spoke about the many miseries which man has to suffer because of sin. New proof of this was given us by the child that was born and died yesterday: but it is a very great Grace of God that Christ has taken over our sins and has done penance for them, through which all people, including said poor child, had acquired eternal glory that is important beyond measure. What a great pity it would be if this child not only had to be brought in this world with pain and much difficulty, but if it also had to suffer eternal damnation because of God's wrath over the world's sin. As it is, it was cleansed by the blood of Christ in the bath of rebirth and thus was freed of all present and future misery. O what a great thing it is for us to have such a Saviour! The confined woman told us that she already had thanked God many times for letting the poor child have the benefit of Holy Baptism and that she was not sad over the cross that had now been put upon her, because she had submitted herself to the will of the Lord who had always done what was best for her. This lead us to the beautiful and comforting song: God cannot mean any harm, etc., which I read to the people present and, for the strengthening of their faith, explained briefly with Bible verses and examples.

Mrs. Eischberger is almost completely well, although she still suffers discomfort from swollen feet. She is very pious and speaks about divine matters with devotion and inspiration. She often thinks of Pastor Riesch in Lindau, on Lake Constance, and cannot praise his special love for her and the other Salzburgers enough. I promised to write to him when I could. As several people are living in this small house together, I showed them how they could best spend their time, especially on Sundays. They all esteem Arnd's *True Christianity* highly, and I showed them how they could find in the index those chapters and prayers that fitted the Sunday Gospels especially well. They liked this very much.

The 31st, Mar. We led an old honest man, who is weak and miserable of body, to see that God is Love and that He remains a good Father and Love itself even when He lets His children fall into distress. He likes it, we told him, when people give themselves over to His will and into His loving hands with Christian patience, just as parents are particularly pleased with children with whom they can do what they wish, etc. To this he answered: The adults must learn, not only from the children but also from the birds and the flowers, that they must not worry, etc. Thereafter he recalled the many and great sins of his youth and testified tearfully that he could not marvel enough about God's love and patience, for He had not punished him when he was living in his terribly sinful ways, but instead had brought him to the

Gospel. For that reason he was particularly refreshed by the two verses from the prophet Ezekiel, chapter 18, v. 32 and chapter 33, v. 11, which he could find in the Bible by himself. He tearfully bemoaned the fact that many people in Salzburg led wicked lives, more wicked even than the heathens, and in many instances did not know right from wrong because they never heard a good sermon. Now, whenever he is afraid because of his sins, he thinks of the verse (which he recited with tears of joy): Yea, the Lord has not cast you out as a sinner, but has done untold good unto you even though you have not yet asked for it: Should He not now do the same, etc. This always lightens his heart. I recited the verse for him: I have loved you always, etc., also the beginning of the one hundred and third Psalm, and gave him a brief talk designed to bring grateful remembrance of the benefits received so far, and to further strengthen his childlike and sweet faith in His help.

The 1st, April. Mrs. Geschwandel's illness has become so much worse in the last few days that there is hardly any hope for her recovery. She has dysentery and complains about terrible fear in her heart and cutting pains in her body which often weaken her so that she cannot even talk. Necessity requires us to put up a well built hospital, but there are a number of difficulties to be overcome. We will present the matter to GOD and think about it more among ourselves. Last Sunday, Palm Sunday, we admonished our listeners to turn with all of their faith toward our good Saviour and not to put trust into their own strength or the help of others, but to expect in all faith help and assistance from the LORD, for He has the key to the hearts of all men and, so to speak, to their storehouses. If it is His will to provide for us, benefactors will be found who will fill our needs from their abundance or own stores; this we showed and made clear to the congregation with a fresh example, telling them that the worthy court chaplain Mr. Ziegenhagen had sent us ten pounds sterling for the box in which we have started to collect some funds for the use of the needy and poor in our congregation. This cheered the dear people very much. One of them said: Since the people in England mean so well for us, I believe they will surely transfer us to some better soil. As we do with others, we advised him to pray and told him that God, who can guide the hearts of men like courses of water, would surely accomplish this. For several days God has been giving us very fruitful weather. It is warm by day and by night, but not too hot, and today we had a very fruitful rain. We are now much worried with snakes about our place, and one cannot be careful enough of them. They crawl into peoples' houses and go after the baby chicks.

The 2nd, April. Mrs. Geschwandel died this afternoon. It was GOD's pleasure to impose upon her a long and difficult death-struggle. She made good use of this week of martyrdom by re-calling the suffering of her Saviour. We would have liked it if God had granted her for her death day next Friday, the day of death of our Redeemer, for this day she always took special care to remember the love of the LORD JESUS. The LORD JESUS and His merits meant everything to her. Not only was she always very happy when I visited her often, but she also waited to hear much good predicted for her from her good LORD, as she used to call Him. On her sick-and-deathbed she made good use of the hymn book which we had given her shortly before her illness and which she had accepted with childlike joy. As I found today, she diligently marked those hymns that speak of the LORD JESUS and His Grace, and of earnest Christianity. For example, Enlight-en me, LORD, my light, etc.; LORD JESUS CHRIST, true man and true GOD, etc.; O GOD, how much woe overcomes me at this time, etc.; CHRIST is my life, death is my gain, etc.; I will not leave GOD, for He does not leave me, etc.; O GOD, I have been much corrupted, etc.; Jesus shall be and remain my comfort and my Saviour, etc.

She was a very patient and gentle sheep of the LORD JESUS. We never heard her complain and, when we noticed her distress and spoke about it, she always answered: Our LORD means well for me, it will change if it is His will; more I do not want. She knew very well the dangers facing a Christian until the last mo-ments of his life, and that a great and serious struggle was neces-sary if one did not want to lose Christ, and with Him all salva-tion. Until her last moment, and during all of her bitter struggles, God gave her much heavenly refreshment. May God never let me forget what I have learned during the time of her illness, and may this example of a truly devoted Salzburger woman bring much blessings to our congregation. Today we received from Sa-vannah the box of medicines which Prof. Francke sent to us. God be praised for it, and may He reward this good deed, which is very useful to our congregation, with thousandfold blessings for body and soul. Mr. Zwifler is convinced that these medicines will be the safest and most successful for the patients, and he asked permission to get some of them for his difficult cases. He made a start with that today, and at the same time we made him a present of a copy of Dr. Richter's *Instruction in the Human Body and Life,* which we have in duplicate.[41]

The 3rd, April. From some swampy place someone brought us a yellow flower to be planted in our garden which could be called an American Tulip, for it very much resembles the tulips in Germany. Its smell is bad, but the color and entire shape of the flower are so remarkable that flower-lovers in Germany would be surprised. We had reason to talk to a man about the fact that a Christian should control himself and should not permit himself to lose his temper through anger or rashness, etc., which could only lead to the commission of sins while at the same time burdening his conscience and bringing trouble. To this he answered that he often recalled the verse: Who shall separate us from the love of Christ, etc., but that he also felt himself still far removed from the spirit of Paul and other children of God, which made him very sad, etc. Sometimes he forgets, he said, that he did not control himself as he should have in a certain place in Germany, where at the beginning people caused him much vexation and heartache. Now he is thanking our beloved God that He has led him from Germany into this lonely place where he can have the Word of God, where he can live undisturbed and in peace, and where he does not have to see such bad examples. In the place where he had been, wickedness among young and old had been very great; and, since his conscience and God's word moved him to chastise this badness occasionally, he had had to suffer many bad names as well as other disagreeable matters. At times he came close to convincing them with a single verse, but afterwards they always were that much more malicious. To be sure, the voyage made his child so sick that it will probably die, and he often thinks that it is his fault because he went on the voyage; but he consoles himself with the thought that he made the trip according to God's will and that he can send his other healthy child to school here and bring it up without having it seduced by this band of evil people.

The 4th, April. As long as he has been with us, M. has been suffering from scurvy. I visited him after the morning service to revive his spirits on the occasion of this day of death of our most beloved Redeemer. He very much bemoaned his lassitude and indifference toward the good, saying that he no longer felt the zeal that he had in Salzburg, all of which caused him much grief. God had loved him and all people so much that He had given His own Son over to suffering and death. If a king were to do this with his son, what a great thing that would be. But what God did was much greater, only he lacked the proper zeal and love in return, etc. He knows a beautiful chapter in Arnd's *True Christianity* in which it is said that, for Christ's sake, we should be like angels, even like Christ himself. That is a very great thing, he said, but his zeal to thank God and to love Him for it was still so small that it did not seem like a fair trade to him, etc. As this man is a true lover of the LORD JESUS, we set him straight saying that God would have patience with his weakness and would not hold against him his indifferent love and indifference toward GOD, etc., for Christ's sake and because it made him suffer. We added that much of this was caused by the weakness of his body, and this was confirmed by a Salzburger who was standing by, and who had had the same experience.

The latter told me that for several days the verse from Romans 12:1-2, which just yesterday had been impressed upon the congregation in the sermon about the doctrine of Holy Communion, had been particularly impressive and edifying to him. He added he had personally experienced that no man can ever participate in real worship of God as long as he continues to let his heart and body cling to worldly or even sinful matters, instead of renouncing everything. Without doing so, he will never get any benefit or divine blessing from his worship, and the main issues of Christianity as well as the treasure of Grace will remain quite unintelligible and inconceivable to him. But if a man simply follows the instructions of the Holy Gospel, he will soon find the right way, on which even a fool cannot err. He remembered (as other people present confirmed), that in Salzburg God had shown untold mercy to the simplest people who had gone to secret places in the mountains to sing, pray, and read the Gospel even though suffering from hunger and thirst.

This story again reminded the people of all the good that God had done for their bodies and souls in this wilderness, and they did not know how to thank Him enough. One of them cited the verse from the 119th Psalm: Incline my heart unto Thy testimonies, and not to covetousness, and he explained that God denies us worldly things to which our heart likes to cling and trains us in bearing the cross, so that our heart will enjoy all the more the testimonies of the Lord. It was related also that a German shoemaker, who had come over from Purysburg in order to help the Salzburgers with his handicraft, had told one of them that they should always keep in mind the great mercy God is giving them through the frequent preaching of the Gospel, for they could not know how those people felt who did not have this privilege. This is said to have moved them very much.

In our morning service today we had sung the hymn: Lord Jesus Christ, light of my life, etc, but when they wanted to sing it once again they could not agree on the tune, so I had to sing it for them before leaving. God gives them much pleasure from the beautiful Halle Hymn book[42] I am sure our Heavenly Father will bless for our benefactors what we have often expressed: May God reward them thousandfold. Schoppacher's youngest girl, aged three and one half years, has been sick ever since the sea voyage was finished, and she died this morning before sunrise. Old Schoppacher himself thinks that he may follow her soon because he is confined to his bed with scurvy too. On this the deathday of His son, God has put into our heart much comfort and edification. In the morning we talked about Christ's death, according to Matthew 27, and in the afternoon about His burial.

The 5th, April. Toward evening, on the given signal, our congregation assembled in order to prepare themselves with us for Easter from the Gospel as well as with song and prayer. God's favor was with us when we preached about the great mercy that is given us through Christ and about the means of obtaining it, so much so that toward the end we all knelt down in prayer and concluded this preparation with pleasure and, we hope, with God's blessing. The words which we singled out for the consideration are written in Psalm 22:27:

The 6th, April, Sunday. A Major from Purysburg came to see us yesterday. He attended today's morning service and was very much pleased with it. He expressed surprise at the poor quality of our soil and he intends to write a letter about the needs of the people. When visiting the sick, I found some of them worse than they had been on previous days. The cold air which moved in last night probably contributed to this, especially as the people must lie in poorly protected houses. They are all very sad that they could not benefit from the sermon this Easter, like the healthy people. But we showed them that Easter can be celebrated

not only in church but also on the sickbed or in any other circumstances into which God might lead us. The important thing
is to get to know the Saviour and His gifts of salvation intimately
and to continue to strive for a better understanding of them
through prayer and supplication.

Mrs. Schweiger's body seems to grow more and more wretched,
yet her mind is filled with nothing but thoughts of her Lord and
Saviour. We asked if she were clinging to a particular verse of
the Gospel, and she quoted this one: "This is assuredly true and
a dear and beloved word, etc." She added that she prays constantly:
"My God, for the sake of Christ's blood, give me a happy end."
The sick Schoppacher lives in this neighborhood, but I could
speak with him only very briefly because I had to hold the review
lesson. A young Salzburger was with him who was reading him
an Easter sermon from Moller's book of sermons,[43] a book which
is highly esteemed by some of the Salzburgers. I had read to him
1 Corinthians 15 as well as the hymn: Where is the lamb I love,
etc., and I talked with him briefly about both.

The 7th, April. For some days the sick Schoppacher has been
asking for Holy Communion, which was given to him today. His
Christian spirit is in good condition and he looks for mercy and
comfort only in the wounds of his Saviour. This time he again
recalled the sins of his youth which he had committed in Salzburg. They still depress him very much and he cannot thank God
enough for having brought him to the true gospel, since it is not
from the saints or from the Virgin Mary but Christ, our only
Saviour, that good is predicted for him in his sickbed, and this
alone brings him comfort. We took this opportunity to prepare
him for Holy Communion with a talk about Hebrews 7:25. God
has shown us the favour of letting us celebrate this Holy Easter
in outward peace and calm. This was very agreeable and impressive even to some strangers who are here. May GOD be praised
for it. And may He let us commend to His divine blessing everything we have endeavored to do with His word for both the young
and the old.

The 8th, April. Mrs. Schweiger died soon after lunch. Mr.
Zwifler thinks that she had internal gangrene. With all of her pain
she submitted calmly to the Will of God and wished nothing more
than to be saved and taken to her Lord and of this she had no
doubt. Besides always coming eagerly and regularly to our public
worship, she was an ardent reader of the Bible and a lover of

Arnd's *True Christianity*. She led a quiet life, talked little, and was always content with the guidance of God.

The 9th, April. When visiting the sick Schoppacher I found him in very low spirits, lying on his bed in deep thought. I soon took the opportunity to speak about our beloved Saviour, of whom his heart and mouth had always been full to overflowing, and showed how one can be sick and die easy in His wounds. Then I read him the beautiful hymn: My soul, come into the wounds, etc., and made some explanation and application of it. All this he acknowledged, more by nodding his head than with words, and at last he sighed: "O Thou gracious and merciful GOD!" Whereupon he moved his face closer to me and testified that the taking of Holy Communion had made him experience terrible struggles and that the same had happened to him that had happened to the Saviour in the desert after his baptism. He was tormented by the sins of his youth, saying that the devil was taking advantage of them and was trying to rob him of his Christian religion with all of its grace.

He had learned more and more, he continued, how man accounts for nothing, how great an evil sin can be, and how necessary it is to accumulate a large treasure of the Grace of God and of beautiful Gospel verses. "O what a favor it is," he exclaimed, "to have Christ and the Gospel; we do not recognize that enough!" He expressed sorrow that many thoughts came to his mind which dispute God and His Word, and he said he prays against them and hopes that God will not try him beyond his endurance. Since he made no specific mention of the temptations, which we could guess from his expression and from his words, we did not consider it necessary to inquire into their nature. Instead, we explained to him that the very feeling he had over the sins of his youth should show him the abomination of sinning and its unholy effects.

Surely it is terrible, we told him, to insult God with deliberate sins and in expectation of mercy, in the false hope that God will be merciful and forgive your sins if only you will pray with the publican: God, have mercy on this sinner. This thinking, we said, leads thousands to hell. But even if the eyes of some people are opened so that they turn to God with sincerity and achieve forgiveness of their sins in accordance with their faith in Christ, God often reserves the right to let the former sinner feel what it means for him, in terms of misery and woe, to leave the Lord, his God, instead of fearing Him. But now he knew, we said, that he belonged to God's order, in which he received Holy Communion two days ago after first recognizing and confessing his sins and receiving absolution in the name of the Holy Trinity. Therefore it behooved him now to pay more attention to the word and the promises of God than to the ideas of his reason or the reproach of his conscience.

We told him that God forgives and forgets all sins, that He destroys them like fog or clouds, and that He throws them into the depth of the sea. Where is there a God like Thee who forgives sin? etc. But perhaps he would know better the verse from 1 John 2:1-2, and if any man sin, we have an advocate with the Father, Jesus Christ the righteous: And He is the Propitiation, etc. "O my God," he answered, "this verse is being much abused in the world, and may God have mercy!" I answered that it was written for the poor and weak souls as well as for those who suffer from temptation. This made him a little happier and he said, "God so, so (he repeated this word twice in his great emotion) loved the world that He gave His only begotten Son, so that all who believed, etc." I said, "This is certainly true, and a dear and precious word, that Jesus Christ has come, etc." He confirmed this and added, "Yes, Christ the Lord has called all sinners to come unto Him: Come unto me all ye that labour and are heavy laden, and I will give you rest". To that I added this one: "They that are whole need not a physician; but they that are sick. I came not to call the righteous, but sinners to repentence, etc."

He said that insolent and frivolous people were apt to come running up to take advantage of Christ and His merits without being converted, but the miserable and low spirited sinners must He call, etc., and when they did come to Christ to achieve salvation in all seriousness, then the tempter would come in order to deprive these people of Christ and His grace. But one can get consolation from Christ and His merits, for He is the A and the O of Faith, and it would be contrary to His honor to leave His work unfinished. He will help gladly, He will not abandon the soul because He loves it too much. The devil and his cohorts have already been defeated, and it redounds to the honor of the faithful that they shall be soldiers of Christ and victors through His strength. And it will hurt and shame the devil all the more to be defeated by such weak tools as the believers must know they are.

After this we gave him encouragement from Ephesians 6 and

also from 1 Corinthians 16:13. Watch ye, stand fast in the faith, etc. We told him to continue to struggle actively and to pray, and to fight his way more and more into the wounds of Christ even though he might have no feeling of success, for once there neither the wrath of God, nor sin, nor the devil could find him and harm him. The last verse, in which Paul admonishes the believers to be serious, gave him much food for thought. And to make him understand even better that such suffering is always the lot of those who are working for their salvation in all seriousness, I recited for him 1 Peter 5:9. He was particularly impressed by the verse from Micah 2:13: The breaker is come up before them, especially as it was made clearer to him from the 1st book of Samuel 14:1 ff. by the story of Jonathan and his armorbearer. After praying with him I took leave of him in the hope that God would give His blessing to him for all of this, although the load did not seem to have been removed from his heart.

Moshammer is a man well versed in the ways of Christianity and useful to us in many cases. I believe it will be advantageous for him to visit Schoppacher and to talk with him about his problems as he has promised to do. He has spent a long time in the school of temptation and trials of all sorts and appreciates very well what a benefit it is under such circumstances to have the encouragement and advice of an experienced Christian. He says that, for lack of these, he himself had been in darkness for a long time. He took many a wrong path until at last God drew him away from wordly company with physical hardships, leading him more and more toward an understanding of His word so that the light had come to him gradually through the Grace of God. He regretted nothing more than that many years of his youth had been spent in the ways of this world. What bliss it would be if he could recall having spent his entire life in accordance with the admonition of Tobias: Have God before your eyes all of your life, etc. This reminded me of the advantages enjoyed by the students and pupils in Halle over many others in Christendom. They can always view Christianity with the advice and guidance of experienced fathers and men. It is to be hoped that no one will think little of this benefit.

The 10th, April. Last night at one o'clock I was called to see the sick Schoppacher because he felt very weak and miserable and thought that he would die soon. This time his heart was much more confident in Christ than it had been yesterday. And since the words from St. John 3:16, "should not perish," had been so refreshing to him, I spoke briefly about them in simple fashion, and prayed with him. I also read him the hymn: O Jesus Christ, your manger is my paradise, etc. because it had been very edifying for me and others during yesterday's evening prayer. A certain passage from our travel journal, the most important points of which are still being read, led us to this hymn during said prayer hour.

When I visited him again this afternoon, his mind had been consoled and much strengthened with God's promises, for which he could not offer enough praise to the Father of all grace. He said that, whenever a verse was recited to him or remembered by him during a period of trial, he began to feel much better about his labors (by which he meant his struggle), only the Enemy had soon misled him again. He was sure that God meant well with these trials, for without them no one would really know what joy or suffering is, just as in nature, if the sun were to shine always and we never had bad weather, people would not long for sunshine and lovely weather but would think very little of them. In our prayer we presented to God, among others things, the verse from Isaiah 42: 1-2. I left this with him at the end of our prayer, just before leaving, and he was very much pleased with it.

On visiting the sick Bacher, I found him reading in Moller's book of sermons. As he was just reading aloud the verse: The days of our years are three-score years and ten . . . are labour and sorrow, we spoke with him about the frailty of human life and about the many miseries with which we are surrounded from birth until death. He said that the children of God on this earth had never lacked misery but had never lacked divine comfort either. Hereupon I opened up for him and his pious wife's edification the beautiful words from Genesis 5:29. I showed what had been the comfort for all believers in this vale of tears, namely, the Lord Messiah, our Saviour, and that God's purpose in sending us suffering is none other than to make us recognize sin as the root of all evil and, at the same time, to recognize Christ as the Giver of all salvation, thus making us more and more eager in our desire to go to heaven. The words contributed by these two righteous people were filled with vigor and virtue so that is was a pleasure to be with them. They bear up well under all of their misery for they have God's word that their souls shall be refreshed through it, which makes them quite satisfied with the guidance of God.

As he promised, Mr. Causton has sent the Salzburgers some sweet potatoes, or a certain kind of elongated potatoes, which are to be planted. They had been very anxious to get them because they had often heard that, if nothing else would grow in this sandy soil, these potatoes would still grow well because they liked dry sandy soil. Now they still have to wait for seeds for corn and beans. Moshammer came to see me about some of his worldly needs. In the course of our conversation we spoke about Schoppacher, in whose heart our dear God has let the light of His Grace penetrate the darkness of temptation. He related that at the beginning of his conversion he had been subjected to much anxiety of conscience. Then he had happened upon some chapters in Arnd's *True Christianity* in which denial and sanctification are urged in great earnest. God made his body so miserable that he could not work; yet he had strength enough to read diligently in the Bible and in Arnd's *True Christianity* until he came upon . . . chapters which led him to the free and open source of the power against sin and uncleanness, namely, Christ and His abundant grace. If, through God's grace, such people are brought into the company of pious Christians very early, they always build a firm foundation for their Christianity; but, if they come into the wrong hands, they often incur great danger. In the fire of such temptation the love of self is badly burnt and one gracious glance from God is more magnificent and desirable than all the treasurers of this world. In Arnd's *True Christianity* the heart is ground finely, he said, that is why he continues to get much refreshment from it. He can see that our Father in Heaven has for some time been giving him increased faith; and along with other things, he thanks God, for having led us away from the world, so to speak, and for having brought us into this wilderness.

A Salzburger woman asked for some of our medicine to help the weakness of her body, and in doing so she assured us that she and her husband had prayed to God many times to give us more of this good medicine, for it had previously helped her condition very much. She added that God gives us one thing after the other and everything that is useful, but she admitted that she recognized His Grace and care far too little. God has given her unspeakably great edification from His word, and she as well as others are very much pleased to be reminded of God's earlier ways when we read from our diary during evening prayer. During the sea voyage and in periods of hardship she had prayed to God many times to give her to the faith she formerly had, when she was as sure of God's Grace in Christ as she was of her own life. But this joyous certainty had been lost, partly in N. and partly on the voyage. This had been her own fault because she had been lazy in prayer and other important acts of Christianity, and consequently death had meant no joy to her. But, since she landed, God had heard her insistent prayer and had given back to her such certainty of faith in His Grace that now she looked forward to death with joy and believed that God would soon lead her out of this vale of tears. Such simple and truly honest talk often reminds me of the verse from Matthew 11:25-26.

The 11th, April. The man whom Mr. Causton had sent here to cut boards got lost in the woods, together with a helper; but a Salzburger who met him accidentally put him back on the right path. Upon his return he announced that while lost he had seen several thousand acres of fertile soil and he expressed surprise that this place was not known here in Ebenezer, especially as it was only one hour away from here. In order to learn the truth, the Commissioner and I went to that region, together with two Salzburgers. But we found everything to be so wet and swampy as to make it unfit for agriculture. Besides, it was a very narrow strip, just as it had been described previously by some Salzburgers who had explored the entire region and picked out the best land here and there. Now and then the people have found a good piece of land near the river, but seeds do not do well in it because there is too much sand under it.

The largest of the pupils of both sexes, eight in number, have learned to read well enough so that now they can go home during the reading lessons in order to help their parents as much as they can with their work. During the reading lessons two of the girls are being instructed in knitting and other feminine occupations by Mrs. Zwifler, who has agreed to do this. After classes in religion, the smaller children go to Mr. Ortmann for spelling and reading, but the larger ones get instruction in arithmetic and writing from my dear colleague. The children come to school willingly and with pleasure, and we are trying to make everything as easy and pleasant for them as we possibly can.

Mrs. Schweighofer has taken over the office of mid-wife here in Ebenezer, in God's name, and everyone is very pleased. She refuses to say how she is to be compensated for her troubles. Instead, she will be satisfied with whatever people want to give her after she has given the lying-in-women every possible attention and care. Her attitude toward God and man is so honest that we must consider it a divine blessing to have this good woman, who has the necessary piety and experience for such matters. May God have mercy upon all of our circumstances and give His physical and spiritual blessing to this good institution, as He has done to all others. Toward evening, a special post rode through our place in a great hurry in order to call the captain of Fort Ogeechee[44] from his estate in Carolina, for news had been received that the Spanish Indians are again making hostile moves against this colony. It so happened that in today's prayer hour the passage to be read to our congregation according to our plan was the one entered under date of March 10th, which fitted this news extremely well.

The 12th, April. For some nights past it has been quite cool, while the days have been hot. Yesterday morning we had such heavy fog that one could neither see very well nor tend to his business until eight o'clock. We do not notice that it is harmful to people's health. In this country we are not well off in this respect. We do not have glass windows but only openings in our houses so that, when we have heavy fog or rain, we must either close the shutters and burn the lights, or we must suffer discomfort inside the rooms with the windows open.

Adam Riedelsperger is still weak and feeble in body, but he is strong and joyful in his Saviour. With all the sufferings of this life he draws much comfort from the fact that God has been thinking of him since eternity and has decided upon many good things for him in Christ. He says that his days have been counted by this kindly Father for as long as he shall live in this world in sickness and in health, and that it would be foolish to worry and not to let GOD do with him what He wants, etc. The strength that God still grants him he applies to diligent prayers and sighs, and he considers it no small benefaction that he can speak with his Father in secret and commend his circumstances to His good and gracious will, etc.

The very weak Schoppacher shows just as fine, a spirit as we can see with great edification from all of his expressions and words whenever we visit him. He bows before God as the greatest of sinners and wants to hear about nothing except his beloved Lord Christ whose superabundant grace he has fully experienced in previous times and at the present. He gets much comfort from the verse: My power is great in the weak, and he believes that GOD will never leave him alone, but will surely lead him to the right goal for which his spirit continues to long. He is still far from that goal, he says; and at times he still is subjected to the meanness and the temptations of Satan, and this worries him; but his fantasies are no longer so frightening and he thanks God for that with upraised hands. He is learning more and more that nothing holds good except Christ and His grace, etc.

Hereupon I led him to the words of Jeremiah 3:23, Behold we come unto Thee; for Thou art the Lord our God. Truly in vain is salvation hoped for from the hills, and from the multitude of mountains: truly in the LORD our God is the salvation of Israel. This verse pleased him very much. And since our conversation also recalled to me the hymn: Be contented and be calm, I read it to him in its entirety. At the end he called out to his wife that she should remember this hymn because it was very edifying to him.

In addition to the seed potatoes Mr. Causton has also sent some provisions, part of which have already been brought up by some Englishmen, the rest to be fetched from Purysburg by the Salzburgers. It is said that beans and seed corn from Savannah have also arrived for us in Purysburg.

The 13th, April, Sunday. Commissioner Vat caused a firm and spacious guard-house to be built. We can see that it is much more suitable for holding church and school than the attic or the room in my house which have been used for this until now, so today we had our services there for the first time. We could not have stood it in my wooden house during the hot summer time, not to mention the fact that the school also prevented me from speaking with my congregation in private and from doing other necessary things. When God lets us know at which place we shall stay permanently, our dear congregation will themselves make arrangements for a church and a school.

One of them had occasion to speak about his planting and related that already he had had to re-plant Indian corn several times because nothing would grow. What had come up here and there either turned yellow and dried up or was eaten up by the birds. But this did not cause him the least bit of grief. He had proof enough that God would never leave him but had always provided as much (and often in wondrous manner) as he needed for himself and his family. If it is good for him and others, he said, God will surely arrange it so that some other place will be given them for farming; but, as God wills! Physical want is made good a thousandfold by God, for he can refresh himself from God's word to his heart's desire, both in public worship and at home. God gives him much blessing and edification from Spangenberg's works.[45] But this troubles him 1) that he is not becoming better and more pious every day even though he often resolves to, for he often falls into the slough again, etc. 2) that his children don't make much progress with God, even though he continues with admonition and punishment, etc. We gave him some instruction and comfort from the word of God and let him go.

The 14th, April. Madereiter has such swellings from both feet to his hips that he can hardly walk. With the return of the hectic cough and pressure about his heart which he had had formerly, he gave up use of our medicines for several days. But as he could see that it is not the fault of the medicines and that failure to use them only aggravates his condition, he came back to us in his weak state and asked for more. In doing so he said that the dear Lord would soon take him because he no longer was any use in this world. I asked him whether he expected to be of use in heaven. Smiling he gave the brief answer: Like the holy angels and for the praise of God, he hoped to be much more zealous there. Here it grieved him that he was indolent in praising and serving God, etc. His love for the Word of God is unusual and he attends public services even if he has to crawl to them. He considers it one of the great good deeds of God which he has seen in his life, that in His kindness and wisdom He has chosen the house of the good Moshammer for his hospital. There his heart is edified with Christian conversation, reading, and singing, while his own bodily weakness is preventing him from reading to himself. He is in truth an Israelite in whom there is no falsehood and who knows how to accept with patience and with praise of God the cross that has been imposed upon him. When visiting the sick Bacher I found him with a hymn book which the Salzburgers are accustomed to call the Sixty because of the sixty-odd hymns that are in it. He said that, lacking other good hymn books, this book had done him much service in Salzburg, although not all of the songs in it were edifying.

The 15th, April. Schoppacher seems to be quite close to death and eternity. He expressed much joy at my presence and said he would like it very much if I would talk with him about spiritual matters and pray with him. All his words and sighs bear witness that his heart is occupied with nothing but the Lord Jesus. As he has been rescued by this good Saviour from much and very great distress, he is sure that he will not be left by Him in his last need and death struggle. We strengthened him in this belief with a number of verses, especially St. John 10:27-30. Because this recalled to him some words from the strength-giving verse St. John 5:24, we told him the rest and showed that the souls who are united with Christ in faith need not fear death or the coming judgment. For them death is only a sleep and the entrance to eternal life; and, as friends and brothers of the LORD JESUS, they will not come before the judgments; all of their sins have been so completely destroyed by His blood that they are forever forgiven and forgotten forever, just as we could see no trace of the heavy fog we had a few days ago after it had once been destroyed.

This simple explanation of said verse gave him so much comfort that he raised his weak and trembling hands up high and gave thanks to the LORD JESUS with a loud and hearty prayer. He thanked Him for having had mercy upon him, the greatest of sinners, and also for having granted him the special favor (in addition to untold others during his lifetime) of letting him see his beloved Ebenezer and there letting him partake of such manifold divine comfort. Hereupon I prayed with him and at last read him the hymn; LORD JESUS CHRIST, Light of my Life, etc. Upon leaving I reminded him that he must himself keep in close touch with his good Saviour because the weakness of his body makes it impossible for him to do much listening. Even if he could not talk or pray, through the strength of the Holy Ghost he could always do what is written in Psalm 10:17: Lord, thou hast heard the desire of the humble, etc.

Adam Riedelsperger reports that for some days he had been very low in spirits because of his many ailments. He was worried that the Lord Jesus might finally grow weary of him. But finally he had remembered the words: Ye are bought with a price. Then he had thought: What one buys dearly one holds fast and keeps well. The LORD JESUS will do the same with his soul. I confirmed this verse, and the consolation derived from it, partly with

1 Peter 1:18 and partly with the parable of the head and the limbs. The head will not deliberately let a limb go for if it is torn away it hurts the head, etc. After prayer I read him the verses Romans 14:7-8, For none of us liveth to himself, etc., and showed him briefly that the faithful are the property of the LORD JESUS in life and in death. Important matters caused Commissioner Vat to make the trip to Savannah today. He will speak with Mr. Causton about steps to be taken about the war troubles and will also try to make some advantageous arrangements for the Salzburgers.

The 16th, April. This morning after five o'clock Schoppacher died quietly and happily in the wounds of his Saviour into which he had worked his way as a poor little worm, with sighs and with prayers. Although I was called, I found him dead when entering the little house. So I prayed to God with the people present and thanked Him for all the spiritual and worldly benefits that He had conferred upon this man during his entire life, thus giving an offering of thanks to the good Giver. This dead man had considered it the greatest kindness that GOD has saved him from darkness and had brought him, a despicable sinner, to full knowledge of His son through the Gospel. On his sick-and-death-bed it brought him the greatest grief and many struggles that he had not always treated the Grace received with good faith. And he used to recall the sins of his youth that he had committed partly because of his fiery and quick temper, partly because he was misled by bad examples. Such recollections always made his soul bow before God. He had an alert mind and good ability; and he also had a gift for edifying others by speaking to them about the ways of Christianity so well and impressively that I have often been surprised by it.

Last evening my dear colleague went to visit him and he also derived much edification from the visit. During the night two Salzburger men again volunteered to sit up with him in order to help him over the sleepless hours with wholesome conversation and by reading to him from Schaitberger's book,[46] in accordance with his wishes. One of them came to see me and told me with great emotion about the great good harvest he had gathered that night from the deathly sick man, for which he thanked God. His sickness was such that at the beginning his feet became tired and weak, developed some spots, and gradually swelled up. He complained of pain in all of his limbs and of pressure about the heart which made him so weak that he could not get out of bed. He believed that failure to cup was responsible for this and he had a number of dry-cups applied. But his weakness, the pressure on his heart, and the pain in his feet increased until he died.

Two other men now seem to have similar attacks, not only pain in their feet as though pins were stuck in them, but also such nausea that they almost faint. But they say that heart feels good and they have little pain in their feet and limbs as long as they stay in bed and keep warm. In others, who seem to have the same sickness as these two, bad breath disappeared after they took medicine as prescribed in Dr. Richter's treatise on scurvy.[47] As the poor sick people have to eat much salted food and other kinds are not available at any price, I have sent a letter to Mr. Causton by Commissioner Vat asking him to send us a few oxen for a fresh supply of meat. This is particularly important for the lying-in women and for those who are pregnant. May the LORD who guides the hearts of man accomplish this according to His will.

Having shown our congregation during evening prayer a number of examples of divine guidance from our travel diary, and having come to the time at which we landed in Savannah, we will now continue with our study of the Psalms of David. In the future, after our Thanksgiving and Memorial day, and if the LORD gives us life and good health, we will start where we left off at this time and bring out additional points because it is hoped that such will be useful.

The 17th, April. It gives us pleasure to know that the parents of the Salzburger children not only wish for a Christian spirit in them but that they help to further it to the best of their ability. And since kind admonitions are spared neither at home nor at school and the children see more good examples than bad, we trust that GOD will not let the work done with them in public and in private be in vain, but will turn them into plants of His praise, although we cannot yet find in them that which the word of God requires of them. They go to school, church, and prayer hour regularly and willingly; and, with God's blessing, they have acquired a rather fine understanding of certain elements of Christianity. It gives us uncommon pleasure to work with them and if we only could do so we would like to carry them in our arms and take them into the arms and the wounds of the LORD JESUS.

The 18th, April. During the daytime we are having warm and pleasant weather, but at night it continues to be so cool and fresh that the climate in which we live is hard to imagine. We have noticed this spring that thunderstorms, of which we have had several, have always been followed by cold nights. Under these circumstances we find it very necessary to urge our congregation constantly to guard themselves against becoming too hot during the day or too cold at night, because such would obviously be very damaging to their health. They tell me that they did not pay much attention to these things in their country. I have decided to impress on these people the *Consilium medicum* which was sent recently and which Mr. Zwifler has at present. I shall also see to it that it is translated into English, for many of the people in this colony who disregard the rules prescribed therein come down with dysentery and other sicknesses which cost them their lives. The postman who returned from Savannah knew nothing about the Spanish Indians' intention of raiding this colony and reported that everybody in Savannah was quite calm about the matter. God be praised for the protection granted so far. May He continue to be our shelter and shield.

The 19th, April. A young Salzburger asked for some books and help in learning the English language, which he is very eager to learn because he recognizes its usefulness in this country. A number of others have the same desire but it is not possible for them to learn this language from books, without oral instruction. Besides, under present conditions they do not have the necessary time. Frequent association with English people would be more effective, but there is little opportunity for this. We will soon start to help our schoolchildren with the learning of this necessary and useful language so that in time those adults who have the necessary ability and application can learn it from them. But for the moment the children have to learn things that are more necessary. Also, we want to spare them too much instruction because they are not yet used to the country, the food, etc., and therefore cannot be driven too hard with their studies. In addition, the largest of the children now must help their parents with their work as much as they can until the most difficult obstacles which new colonists always encounter have been overcome with God's help.

Adam Riedelsperger is still bearing the same cross and although his body is now free of pain his entire body as well as his feet are so weak and feeble that he feels very faint whenever he has to sit up. But he is still so well adjusted that he considers these difficult physical circumstances the least of his crosses. Rather, he looks upon them as a trial sent by his dear Saviour. Praise God! we have the same experience with several members of the congregation. Physical distress does not take away their courage, rather they praise God for it and leave to the care of their Father in heaven what others would look upon as misery and hard luck. Only yesterday, after prayer hour, we asked a pious woman whether she knew how to accept her cross and her manyfold trials. She answered that she knew of no cross and that sin was the greatest cross which she had to bear.

The 20th, April, Sunday. Madereiter seems to be coming closer and closer to salvation from this vale of tears, since he appears to have dropsy which has made him swell up very badly. We would like to help this dear man, just like all others who are sick, with good bodily care, but there is no opportunity for that here in Ebenezer. The best that we can have prepared for him are soups made of flour and ground up Indian corn or rice, with tea. Other things which might give strength and refreshment are not to be had at any price. He is contented with his cross and he has never been heard to complain. Instead, he praises God and consoles himself with the thought that it will serve for the best; he has enjoyed the good and he must be prepared to suffer the bad, etc. He resembles the ancient Simeon in that nothing matters to him except the LORD JESUS, his Saviour, and he longs with all his heart for peace and the journey home. The spirit of Christ and the entire image of God so radiate from this good man that you can not look at him or listen to him without deriving great edification from it. Today two additional hands were sent who are to cut boards so that, in accordance with Mr. Causton's wish, the house of my dear colleague and two additional public houses should be finished soon. The board cutter who was sent two months ago has not been able to do anything because his helper hurt his hand. Time will tell whether progress will be made from now on. We would almost prefer to see the building deferred until after the Trustees have made a decision regarding our land and have reported same to us, so that these additional expenses will not be in vain.

The 21st, April. The general condition of most people in this region is really very pitiful and it would be desirable to make arrangements not only for the care of the blind heathens but especially for the care of the blind and miserable Christians, for the godless conduct of the Christians makes the conversion of the heathens very difficult, especially because these poor people prefer to be led to the places with the greatest opportunity for misconduct. Yesterday the congregation was told that Holy Communion would be held again if the people desiring it would make their wish known at the beginning of this week, and today some of them came to see me for this purpose. Tonight Simon Reuter came to announce his intention of coming to Holy Communion, and he pleased me very much with his heartfelt and joyful spirit in Christ. After many long struggles God has helped him through and has given him such real assurance of the gracious forgiveness of all sins and of the fact that his name is registered in heaven that his body and soul are quite filled with divine joy. He thanks his heavenly Father very much for giving him an opportunity at this time to receive Holy Communion as established by Christ, along with other means of Grace.

The 22nd, April. Mr. Zwifler showed me some young roots of celery which he had found, together with a number of other good plants, at a spot situated closer to the Savannah River. He reported that this spot contained a large quantity of these good plants. They look and taste just like the celery in Germany, only their roots are very small. But they may well get larger in time. We would consider it a particularly good deed of God if such plants could be found in quantity close by, for we could use them for our refreshment in place of lettuce, which will not grow very well here. Some people report that it has done them much good to eat even one turnip, or the tops of turnips or anything else that is green.[48] As the Salzburgers cannot work during the middle of the day because of the great heat, some of both sexes have asked us to teach them to read. We had offered to do so long ago. May God let this work also redound to His honor and turn out well.

The 23rd, April. We have had no rain for a long time and our sandy soil is very dry. The Indian corn which had come up here and there seems to have dried up. May God hear our prayer and give us soon a fruitful rain. Today I have begun, in the name of God, to teach four adults to read. As soon as they have progressed enough to be able to help themselves we will do the same with the others who wish to learn. We like to do this work because we hope it will bring still more edification to the public assemblies. Those of the congregation who can read always bring their Bibles to church and they always carefully look up the verses which we select and read slowly for our explanations or for proof of the matters we discuss. And since at the beginning and at the end of every Sunday and holy day service, before and after sermons, we always read a chapter from the Bible very slowly and distinctly, the hearers derive from it the benefit of getting more practice in reading. This means a great deal to them.

God, in His great mercy, has given special blessing to some of our congregation through the 8th chapter of the 1st book on *True Christianity,* by the late Arnd. It had been recommended in last night's prayer hour in connection with the 68th Psalm and they had read some of it individually and some in a group. We have observed that much good can be accomplished if we recommend to the people for their own reading and for their individual edification parts of Arnd's *True Christianity* or some edifying hymns after having related them to certain chapters of the Bible. When two young Salzburgers visited me and asked me to give them something that would serve to awaken their hearts, I read them the hymn: Do not let us covet, etc., which turned out to be very impressive both for me and for them. The Salzburgers like singing very much and therefore good songs always please them.

The 24th, April. The great heat which we have had for several days in succession was followed tonight by a heavy rain and thunderstorm which God, in His Grace, let pass without damage. The rain did not last long. The nights have begun to be very warm and this is the time when small flies and gnats come out to give the people of this colony much discomfort, often preventing them from sleeping. Thank God that we are free of them at this place. Earlier, when we lived near the water, we have had to suffer from these pests.[49]

The 25th, April. Yesterday's thunderstorm was followed by a strong cold wind, which has been continuing all of today. Last night it was so strong that we were afraid it would blow the roofs off the houses. Some of them indeed were damaged. Rain and wind appear at times so unexpectedly and are so violent that we cannot be careful enough. Madereiter's largest swelling will not go down, and in the past few days it has spread over his entire body. He thanks God that the use of our medicines has alleviated the burning in his feet, the pressure and stabbing pain from his heart, and his difficult and painful breathing and that his entire body is free of pain. His spiritual powers continue to be great, and he uses them exclusively for the glory of his Saviour. His earlier zeal and seriousness in his love for God and Christ, the lack of which he had complained about of late, are again burning in his heart. He cannot marvel enough at the ineffable love of God for him and all the people, and he speaks about it with the greatest reverence and emotion. He considers himself unworthy of even the smallest good deed, and we must make considerable efforts to get him to accept this or that bodily refreshment. I told him that it gave me pleasure to also serve his physical needs to the best of my ability because the Lord Jesus wanted it so and would surely say: Inasmuch as ye have done it unto one of the least of these my bretheren, etc. This moved him to tears of joy, and he said: "O, I am only dirt and ashes, a poor earthworm, etc. What a great Father we have! How joyful it will be to leave this world! etc. If only I could become nothing at all, God would make something beautiful of me, etc. True, a good mother loves her children, but our heavenly Father loves us much more."

The 26th, April. We had another very cold night, which is hard to imagine at this time. Whenever cold and heat follow each other in this manner, we always find greater weakness in our patients because the dampness penetrates their little houses everywhere and they are not provided with good beds. If our dear God will let us know soon where we shall live permanently, we will fill this need also, with God's help, no matter how much effort it takes. In the last few days some of the Salzburgers have been lucky with their hunting and have brought back several deer. We are very happy for them, especially because they must eat so much salt meat. And as the sick will get their share of the game, we consider this one of God's special benefits. We have learned, however, that in this country eating of game gives some people diarrhea immediately after they eat it.

Almost ever since they came to this country, Schweighofer and his wife have had to contend with various sicknesses. At times this gets worse than at other times. At the moment both of them are very miserable, and they have three young children who are very close to their hearts. They are both upright Christians who know how to resign themselves to their cross of Christ. We would like very much to care for the two older children by taking them into our house, if only we had better opportunity for doing so. The parents and children both wish it. May God show us what to do, as we have asked Him in our prayers. We ourselves are still not without need but He, in His grace, has not let us suffer any harm from that.

The 27th, April, Sunday. Last night the air was very cold and we had frost, but today has been very warm. Some of our congregation came to Holy Communion today; and, although there were some among them who had previously lacked a proper seriousness in their Christian attitude, God seems to have bestowed some blessing on these people during the preparation and in today's celebration. Our devotion during Holy Communion service is increased by the fact that all the congregation always stay in church until the end of the service and help us sing and pray. The sick Madereiter wanted to come also but, as his weakness did not permit this and he had a great desire for it, we served him on his sickbed. This holy act caused him and others to praise God very much.

The 28th, April. Last night the Commissioner returned to us from Savannah. As he received definite news that Mr. Oglethorpe will come back to the province of Georgia in August or September, he has decided to stay with us until his arrival. He succeeded in arranging with Mr. Causton to send the Salzburgers provisions for one half year in advance so that they could be spared some of the difficult transportation and also to make sure of supplies in case of need. This is especially important now, for he learned in Savannah that little good is expected from the Spanish Indians. In accordance with our request we will also get a few oxen for fresh meat, and the oxen and cows that ran away last fall are to be sought for again. A number of hands and horses are being sent here for that purpose.

The 29th, April. As it is the wish of the Trustees that the people in our place shall be trained with weapons just as the other inhabitants of the colony are, Mr. Zwifler was today presented to them as their Constable and Mr. Ortmann and three other Salzburgers as their Tithing-men. Mr. Vat used the occasion to tell them about their duties. One man in our congregation had a physical problem which he presented to God in prayer several times and he told us with great pleasure that he could feel very definitely that God had heard him. We pointed out to him that he should become accustomed to presenting even the smallest problems of his physical existence to the Father in Heaven, for He is the Lord of the earth, the hope of the poor, etc.

The 30th, April. Last night Madereiter died quietly and happily. He died in the wounds of his Saviour in which he had hidden himself, so to speak, bare and naked as a little worm. Moshammer, in whose house he stayed during his sickness, testifies that he spent his last hours in constant and earnest prayer and that he passed from time into eternity with joy. The world always appeared to him as a murderer's den, and the knowledge of Christ together with the inestimable grace He obtained for us were so precious and dear to him that no one could hear him speak without deriving great edification. The yoke of Christ and his cross were very dear to him and he did not complain a single time about them. Instead, he talked edifyingly of their necessity and usefulness, and he praised God for them.

The last grief he revealed to anyone was that his fear that, if his pain became very much greater before death, he might commit the sin of impatience; but, as he presented this fear to his Heavenly Father, He spared him from pain and impatience until the end. He often praised God for the medicines that he received daily from our supply, as his condition required; and he told many times how he could feel their good effect in the renewed strength they gave him while at the same time eliminating all pain. He accompanied every dose with a heartfelt prayer. He greatly liked our arrangement of collecting money for the poor and needy in a special box, and therefore he gave five pounds sterling to it. His other possessions in money and clothes went to his kin, Mrs. Rotenberger. Before his death Moshammer had told him that he would surely miss him if he died because he would no longer have him with him to read and sing together. He answered briefly he believed that it would not be too long before they would be together again.

Bacher, whose scurvy has been treated by Mr. Zwifler with utmost care, is so much better that he has been able to go out. Today he told me that he used his first outing to visit the late Madereiter who used to visit him often during his sickness. As soon as he arrived the sick man asked him to read him something from Arnd's *True Christianity*. He listened to it with great devotion; and at the end he thanked him for this good deed several times and most sincerely. Nearly everyone who knew the deceased in his earlier or later years knows some good things to say about him. Yesterday and today it has been very warm and, since the soil is quite dry, everyone wishes for a soaking rain. As it was last year, spring has been hot and dry this year too. As anyone can see, this is not good for light sandy soil.

The 1st, May. Because the water in our river is very low, all of the Salzburgers have joined forces in building a bridge over it. This would have been done long ago if the high water and other matters had not prevented it. Until now we have had to make out with a foot bridge. I found one Salzburger man looking at the Bible and one of Luther's catechisms. He told me that this catechism, printed in Augsburg, contained many fine copper plates which were always captioned by a certain chapter or verse of the Bible. When he looks these up, they always give him much food for thought as well as materials explaining the truths contained in the catechism. In looking up these captions he also came across the words of Isaiah 64:4, which had been particularly edifying to him. In praise of the late Madereiter he told how the latter, shortly before his death, had praised the bliss he was soon to attain and that he had conversed most edifyingly about the 126th Psalm, which I had expounded during Holy Communion. Thus the two of us were reminded of the wonderful hymn: Poor son of man that I am, etc., and we read the last several verses.

The 2nd, May. Our nights are still very cool. This morning it was nearly as cold as it is when we have frost, but by nine o'clock it is often uncommonly hot again. The men who were to find our stock came back today without having accomplished anything. Since they found only few tracks, they are of the opinion that the animals are very far away from our place. They follow the good grass, just as our horses have been doing of which three have been brought back to us. Mine was brought back by an Indian who had been persuaded to do so by someone who knew the animal. For his reward he expected to get a few bottles of rum. When we gave him some food and some money for his troubles, he was displeased and said he had been cheated because he had troubled himself with the horse in the belief that he would get rum. He claimed to have seen our cows and oxen at a certain place. In order to persuade him to show this place to our people and to help bring the animals back, I had to promise him money in advance. He liked twelve individual half pence better than a silver shilling, particularly because the former were newly coined and shiny. I observed about this Indian what I had been told about them by others, namely, that as long as they are sober they pretend not to know any English but when they have drunk too much their tongue is loosened, so to speak. This Indian spoke to me through an interpreter although he can speak the English language fairly well.

The 3rd, May. The men returned with the Indian without having found either cattle or oxen. Meanwhile, we have promised this Indian a reward if he can find their tracks and show them to the Salzburgers. This morning the Salzburgers finished the bridge across Ebenezer Creek. They did such a fine, durable, and skillful job that we were surprised and pleased. Travelers who go on horseback from Charleston or its vicinity to Savannah, or who go there from here, will be very much pleased with this, for until now they have had to cross the river in much discomfort, especially in the wintertime when the water is high.

Today we finished our letters to London and to Germany. We intend to get everything together next Monday and send it off with the mail, unless it overtakes us tomorrow. In some of them the need of the Salzburgers has again been made clear and we hope that such letters of complaint will not be taken amiss. To be sure, the reasons for writing in several letters at some length about the condition of the soil have been given several times. But we find it necessary to add to them once again in order to avoid all suspicion and misunderstanding. 1) The Trustees and other worthy benefactors of ours would not be satisfied with us if we did not report to them in time that the Salzburgers cannot maintain themselves on the land they have at present, which means that for some time provisions have been given by them in vain and will continue to be given in vain. 2) In addition to our teaching duties we have been charged with giving the Salzburgers help and advice in worldly matters and to see to it that everything is maintained in good order. Thus the love we owe them on both counts requires us to tell the proper authorities about the bad condition of their land, as we have done earlier in more detailed fashion. If God does not give His blessings to our representations we will still have done what we could. This maintains and strengthens their trust in us, which means a great deal to us in carrying out the duties of our office. 3) It is undeniable that our benefactors' concern and love for the well-being of the Salzburgers are uncommonly great. As there is no doubt that they are of the opinion that the people have been settled on some very rich land, which impression was confirmed by our first letters from Savannah and also by other means, they will doubtless be glad to learn the truth about the real condition of this region, etc. At this time I will not mention other reasons which have been given already. This much is certain. If God should so arrange it that these people are sent to some other and more fertile region, our praise for God and the joy we would feel over it could certainly not be put into words.

The 4th, May, Sunday. When visiting some children I found a pious mother looking at the numbers in a book which she wanted to learn very much. She said it grieved her no little bit that she was not able, like other people, to look up in the Bible the verses which are read and quoted during services, and she did not propose to rest until she could do the same because it was such a useful and salutary thing to know. She praised God for having let her children progress as much as they have, but she also expressed concern over their light-mindedness, etc. A sick man also was occupied with looking up and reading the verses which his wife had brought home to him. Man and wife sat together and read for their edification as best they could. Truly, the Word of God is sweeter than honey to many of us and worth more than many thousand pieces of gold and silver. This they not only express orally but also prove it with their deeds, thus putting great joy into our heart.

The 6th, May. It had been our intention to send our letters and diaries by mail to Charleston and from there on to England. But it so happened that two fine gentlemen and planters from Carolina came to see us in order to inspect this region; and one of them offered to deliver the letters safely at the right place, since he intended to leave on the next ship for London on his way to Geneva. His name is Monsieur Savy. He also promised to make some representations in London regarding the conditions of our soil and the circumstances of the Salzburgers. He had no doubt that, once the Trustees had reports of our location, they would not leave the good people in this place, for their intention was none other than to do the best they could for all colonists and, consequently, for the Salzburgers. This man has lived among the Indians for nearly three years several hundred miles further up the Savannah river. When he learned that we had a great desire to learn the Indian language for the benefit of these miserable people, he said that it was a very poor language, that often they had to use the same word to express ten different things, and he gave several examples. He reported that the Indians themselves showed their least talent in the matter of grasping things that require a little reflection and did not make the least effort in such matters. He learned one thing that gave him cause for thought. When one of them dies, an especially designated man must prepare the dead for burial and must tell those present about his past life as well as about his future fate. If he has lived a good life he will come to a happy place where pleasures are not lacking: but if he has lived a disorderly life he will come to a great, swampy place full of thorns and other disagreeable things, where he will be constantly subjected to inconveniences.

His greatest misery here will be that he will be able to see a beautiful and joyful region not far away but will never be able to reach it.

Through God's blessing Bacher has been freed of scurvy to such a degree that he could come to church for the first time last Sunday; but his feet and entire body are still lacking strength. His hearing had been impaired, but today he reported joyfully that during the sermon it seemed as if something in his ears had burst and that from then on he could understand everything much better. He considered this a great blessing of God, and he and I praise the Father in Heaven with prayer for all the grace he had received so far. Adam Riedelsperger also is nearly well again and he, likewise, needs only the strength necessary to work. Whenever we visit him or said Bacher we find their minds filled with edifying verses and thoughts, and this makes it very easy to get good material for a spirited conversation. Specifically, we often hear from them that they understand very well the necessity for killing the Old Adam and for being born anew if we want Christ with all of His grace to be of use to us, and they know that the Cross is a very salutary means toward this end.

The 7th, May. Mr. Causton has sent a large supply of provisions to our landing place, one German mile[50] from here. Our people are now bringing them up by land, because it cannot be done on our river which is nearly dry in spots. God has so arranged it that our horses, which had been straying about the woods all winter, were returned to us a few days ago. Now we can use them very well for the transportation of the provisions.

The 8th, May. For some time we not only have had no rain but the days have been so hot that it does not feel like the same time last year when we did have frequent rains. Whatever was planted earlier has dried up. The new Salzburgers cannot plant their corn and beans, for which they have prepared a large field, since all of the seed would burn in the hot sand and would not come up.

The 9th, May. Mr. Causton came to see us this afternoon. He brought with him Captain Thompson, the one who took the last Salzburgers from Rotterdam to London, as well as two inhabitants of Savannah who will soon go to London, in order to show them our land. This time again we did not refrain from making representations about the circumstances of the Salzburgers and about the poor land they have, drawing partly on our experience and partly on the expressions of some highly regarded and intelligent Englishmen. We hope that Captain Thompson will report what he found here, for we consider him an impartial man who likes the Salzburgers, according to their own reports.

The transportation of our provisions, which Mr. Causton has sent by Englishmen only as far as our landing, causes so much expense that it makes us wonder. In addition, our poor people have many hard days bringing them up the rest of the way and we can say of them, with particularly good reason, that they must get their food by the sweat of their brow (for in this great heat they daily carry some of it up on their backs and bring some up in a small wagon). If we were nearer the river much of the great expense and many of the hardships would be unnecessary. The best thing we can say about our land is that it makes good pasture and is very pretty.

The 10th, May. This morning the persons above mentioned went back to Savannah via Abercorn, for which purpose we gave them our three horses. Mr. Causton delivered to me a letter which he had recently received from England. It was written by Secretary Newman and it pleased us very much because it gave testimony of his and the Society's love for us and also because it mentioned that our letters of December 12th, 1734, as well as our diary, had been received in good order. It is hoped that our worthy benefactors will get a true picture of our situation from them.

The 11th, May, Sunday. Thank God! Sickness has almost disappeared from among the Salzburgers so that all can now go out again and can attend public worship, although they are not yet ready to work. There is no lack of various weaknesses, but it is hoped that these will pass soon. May our dear God continue to do with us as He pleases. We must always strengthen and refresh each other with the thought that as long as we give our hearts over to our heavenly Father He will always let us look with pleasure upon His ways and His guidance. Proverbs 23:26. He is the Father, and consequently He cannot mean any harm when imposing various sicknesses or other distress. Today and in last night's prayer hour God's fatherly heart showed us some Gospel verses which gave particular strength to all of us, such as Jeremiah 31:9 and 20 (comp. Ezekiel 16:5 ff.) and Isaiah 46:3-4.

For some time I have used part of Saturday night's prayer hour to hold a short question and answer period with the children, over matters which particularly impressed them during the week. But I am using most of it to prepare everyone for the following Sunday. Toward this end the children recite the verse they have been taught at school. This is expounded at the beginning, and then the congregation is given the main content of the sermon that is to be delivered, together with an application of same. This is profitable in various ways. Because the entire congregation can derive no little edification during prayer hours and on Sundays from the children, we teach them for the most part ourselves and get them used to our method of teaching. In this we also follow the command of the Highest Shepherd which says that we must tend not only His sheep but also His lambs.

The 12th, May. God has heard our prayer and has sent us a fruitful rain, which came yesterday and last night. Our land has been needing this for a long time. Ordinarily the rains are accompanied by thunder, and when this stops the rain stops also. After a rain it is usually much more agreeable and pleasant than before. The last group of Salzburgers started today at Mr. Causton's command to fence in a certain piece of land, in which the cattle that are to be sent to them in the near future are to be confined until they have become used to our place. Afterwards they intend to use this place for the planting of rice, for which only wet ground such as this is said to be suitable. The good people spare no efforts in doing their work and in complying with the wishes of their worthy benefactors. May God reward their labors with worldly blessing as well.

The 13th, May. Toward evening I visited with some of the Salzburgers in the gardens which they have started for themselves here and there along the river. The good people, men as well as women, work hard at watering, weeding, etc., so that they may get a few garden vegetables. And when, for instance, they discover just one bean or pea, their joy over it is very obvious. They have learned that everything grows well in places where they have put manure or woodashes. Where they have neither they can water and do what they may, but nothing will grow.

The 14th, May. The new Salzburgers returned with the boat from Purysburg, where they had gone three days ago to get the syrup Mr. Causton had sent there for them. They related not only that the fast running water had given much trouble but also that God had saved them from an apparent mishap. God be praised for that. There are many trees and old logs in the rivers, and the swift current can easily carry them onto these if they are not very careful. The danger of this is much greater when the boat is heavily loaded, as was the case on this trip.

The 15th, May. This morning a Christian man from Purysburg came to see us with his two sons. He came, partly to attend
our services on this day of Ascension, and partly to speak to us
about a letter we had written to him. He and others in Purysburg are very anxious to continue taking advantage of our office
and they will do their best, with God's help, to cease all offenses
and to grace the teachings of Christ with a pious conduct. If our
people are moved to a better region he would like very much
to come to live with us, with his strong family, so that he can
send his children to school and thus take proper care of their
souls. He brought us a large quantity of fish which his two sons
had caught in the Savannah river with little trouble and in a
very short time. These were distributed among some of the Salzburgers. To be sure, there are a few fish in our river also, such
as eels and another kind with large heads and without scales.[51]
But there must not be quite so many for it takes the people a
long time to catch a few of them. There are very many alligators
(a kind of crocodile) here which are very harmful to the fish.
Our river rises (as we have been told recently) not far from our
place, in a certain swampy region where the rainwater collects.
Thus it becomes very small when we have no rain for a long
period, so small that the water hardly moves.

The 16th, May. Among the last group of Salzburgers there are
a few very skilfull men who are used for various necessary jobs
and useful matters. Especially two of them, Rotenberger and
Nicolaus Riedelsperger, can make nearly everything they see if
only they can get the necessary tools. Thus they are employed
by us in various cases. The latter is especially good at handling
animals and is very useful to us for that reason. If we had a
shoemaker and a blacksmith we would be supplied with the most
necessary artisans, although we can still spare the blacksmith because there is an Englishman in Abercorn who follows this trade
and who serves us well. It is said that this man would like to move
to us for the sake of his children, whom he wants to send to school,
if we are transferred to a different location. One man in our
neighborhood wanted to dig a cellar but soon came upon a beautiful spring which he liked much better than a cellar. It is easy
to find water at our place, although not all of it is clear and pure
enough so that it can be used for drinking and cooking. This
makes it hard to dig cellars which, in many instances, are most
necessary during the hot summer days.

The 17th, May. One great inconvenience in this country is

that paper money is used, of which the smallest is 5 shillings, or, in English money, 8 pence. English copper coins, called half-pence, which could be used for small change, are very rare; and in Carolina they are not accepted at all. The Salzburgers are in a bad position in regard to this paper money because most of them cannot read the printing on these pieces of paper and can-not distinguish one piece from the other. They usually suffer loss when they spend or change any of it, as happened in the last few days in Purysburg.

We are always happy when our Father in Heaven lets us see another Sunday. Not only does it give the people a chance to rest their bodies from the strains of the week, but it also gives them more opportunity than other days to refresh their souls more fully with the Gospel of Christ, for which most of them have a great desire. Praise God! until now our Sundays have been true days of refreshment and joy. One of the new Salzburgers told us that in Germany his master would not even let him rest on Sunday but made him do things that could have been left or have been done on some other day.

The 18th, May, Sunday. Today we received the news that Roth, who some time ago had to leave our place and move somewhere else, had died of a hot fever.[52] All those who knew the late Made-reiter continue to think of him with fondness, because of his edifying talk and his true godly spirit, and they often talk about him in our presence with genuine pleasure. Among other things, one man told us that he had complained to him (Madereiter) about the weakness of his body which made him a burden to others and kept him from working. Hereupon he had consoled him with these words: he should let Him provide who cares for the children in the womb and then everything will be all right, etc. These words had given him much comfort. We find that most people are not troubled much about their physical condi-tion because God gives them in such plenty that which is better, namely, His word. What unhappy people we would be (some of them say), if our bodies were well but our souls were not taken care of. In Salzburg we suffered no physical wants, but did not get the Word of God. Now God has granted our wish and has given it to us. What more can we want? etc.

The 19th, May. We have received definite news that the Governor of Carolina, Robert Johnston, recently died in Charles-ton. He had been highly esteemed by everyone because of his many admirable qualities, and this province of Georgia too has

lost in him a great patron. We consider it one of God's severe
chastisements that we have had no rain for so long. We suspect
that this will bring a great crop failure and famine. LORD, here
we are. Do as Thou wilt in this matter too.

The 20th, May. Quite unexpectedly God sent us today a drench-
ing and fruitful rain which pleased all of us very much and gavé
us new reasons for praising God. True, a thunderstorm also could
be heard, but it did not last long. We had stopped the reading
lesson for the bigger children on the condition that they would
practice at home. But since they are not doing this and some
of them are getting worse in their reading, we have found it
necessary to use one hour daily for it so that they have to remain
in school for five hours every day. They come to school regularly
and willingly because we do our best to make everything easy
for them and we apply discipline in a fatherly way.

The 21st, May. It had been my intention to use today's period
after the noon meal to explain to the entire congregation certain
points pertaining to our physical circumstances. Having been
prevented from doing so, partly by the rainy weather and partly
by other duties, I intend to accomplish this tomorrow. It is very
necessary and useful on occasion for us not only to strengthen
their spirits with the Word of God but also to call them together
sometimes to talk about other matters which they cannot understand by themselves and thus to help them in their weakness.
Examples of God's chosen people from the Old and the New
Testament, in addition to the Psalms of David which we continue
to study in our daily prayer hours, are giving us much blessing.
Frequently certain conditions which others might not notice but
which resemble ours very much serve to provide a good lesson,
comfort, and admonition for these dear people.

An Indian came to see us with an Englishman and reported
that he knew where to find two of our cows. He offered to bring
them to us if we would give him one pound in paper money
per head. Rather than to miss them or lose them completely,
we promised him the money, for six of our cows and four oxen
are straying about. The Englishman was on such intimate terms
with the Indian that I was surprised. He intends to associate
even more closely with these heathen people by marrying an Indian woman. Just recently a gardener in Savannah has done the
same thing.

Today we learned that we have amongst us a blacksmith, a
locksmith, and a cabinetmaker, all of whom lack nothing but

tools to be able to serve us. There is also one who could make shoes if only he had the equipment. Nicolaus Riedelsperger knows how to tan skins for shoeleather and has already given some proof of that. Likewise, Rotenberger understands the cooper's trade and has already helped us greatly with his work. Perhaps God will so arrange it that the necessary tools will be sent to us from England or Germany with one of the transports or by some other means. This would be of great help to all of us. The people also wish very much to obtain some wood-axes of the kind that they have used so profitably in Germany. Those available here are not very good and do not last long.

The 22nd, May. As we suspect that Captain Thomson, who is still anchored in Savannah with his ship, will go to London soon, we shall send him our letters and diaries. The man we mentioned on the 6th of May, to whom we recently gave a big package of letters and a large section of the diary, will go with the captain. In order to put these things safely into the captain's hands, my dear colleague will go to Savannah himself with a few Salzburgers, for which purpose the boat from Abercorn will be lent us. We have been told that some very poor Salzburgers have no shoes, and this occasion will be used to bring them some. Shoes cost a great deal of money in this country and they last only a short time. This increases our desire to have our own shoemaker, or at least the necessary tools for one. When we told an elderly man that this provision of shoes should make him recognize divine providence, he said: "Praise God and thanks that we have a rich GOD who looks after the poor." This last point was probably particularly impressive to him in last night's prayer hour in which we treated the 82nd Psalm.

The 23rd, May. Yesterday our letters and the last part of the diary, from the 6th to the 22nd of May, were handed over to Captain Thomson. May God soon let us have the pleasure of a reply from the Trustees and the very praiseworthy Society, for we have full confidence that our worthy benefactors will grant our humble and sincere request to transfer the Salzburgers to a more convenient and fertile region. Mr. Quincy, the pastor in Savannah, has sent me a letter assuring me that they will, for he well knows the good will of our worthy benefactors in London.

The 24th, May. Two of the cows that ran away last fall were brought back today with great difficulty. We must wait and see whether the Indian we mentioned recently will keep his promise to find and bring us the rest of the cows and oxen. Some of the people now have milk-giving cows, for which they cannot thank God enough. And some of them have begun to make fresh butter, which is very rare in this colony and especially amongst us. During today's preparation for holy Pentecost we showed our congregation God's salutary purposes in letting us celebrate holy Pentecost in peace and in good health, namely, 1) that we must recognize it as a great benefit which we enjoy over many people in America, and that we must show our gratitude by accepting in good faith the dear Grace of God that is being offered to us, and by leading a godly life. 2) That the Lord Jesus is ready and willing to give to each and everyone the treasure of His Grace and the Holy Ghost if they will only follow His instructions. On the last point we gave a number of special exhortations. And since we find some things in many of the people of the congregation that are not in accordance with Christianity, we spoke to them about the Grace God has given, seriously and from our heart and in accordance with the laws of the Gospel. Some of them, we find, live in a state that is outwardly quite in order; for they do their share, cling to the Word of God, and have their pleasure in it, etc., but they do not yet know the true essence of Christianity and they put more stress on the execution of outward duties than they would if they recognized and tasted the Grace of Christ in an evangelical spirit. For this reason in nearly all sermons and during all prayer hours we praise Christ and the treasures of His salvation and show them how the duties of Christianity flow from this spring easily and in a manner pleasing to God.

The 26th, May, Monday. One of the Salzburgers asked us for some ink in order to write down the verses which God blessed for him particularly during the preaching of His word, so that he could remember them longer. He also asked us to underline for him a few strength-giving verses in red ink, such as we usually do for the schoolchildren. We can see that they appreciate it very much when, in addition to letting them look up the verses during the sermon, we give them such Biblical verses to take home after the service that they have, so to speak, the juice and the core of the matters discussed. Experience constantly strengthens our conviction that simple private association of a teacher with his listeners is one of the noblest parts of the office of pastor and that much good can be accomplished with it. But good teachers are not well off in this respect if they have too large a congregation and also have so many other duties that they must give up almost altogether their private associations with the young and the old of their congregation. The good shepherd, meanwhile, is obligated to care not only for the entire flock, but also for each sheep, and in particular each lamb, as much as possible.

Our heartfelt praise be to God for letting us live through this Festival of Pentecost not only in outward calm but also with much edification for our hearts. In some persons our Heavenly Father has let us see distinctly the blessing which He has given to the preaching of the magnificent Gospel of Christ. It also applies to us to a certain extent what is written in Isaiah 41:17-18. Much was contributed to furthering my own Christian spirit by the edifying preface in front of the prayerbook that was printed for use in the German Chapel in London and which was probably written by the late Boehme.[53] And my dear colleague derived much refreshment from the late Dr. Antonius' household conversations about salvation.[54] We read edifying tracts as much as time permits in order to awaken our hearts, and we let the congregation participate in this.

The 27th, May. Some of the people are still due some money from Salzburg and they asked us to report this at the proper place and to help them collect same.[55] Commissioner Vat will report the matter in a letter to the praiseworthy Society, especially since he had received orders in London to get information about the property the Salzburgers had left behind. The weather at this time is very pleasant, although rather dry. During the day the heat is moderate because it is tempered by cool breezes, but the nights are not so dreadfully warm as they are in Germany at times, and also occasionally in this country. The pleasant coolness gives the people refreshing sleep and the few garden plants which seem to dry up during the day are refreshed by the lovely cool dew.

The 28th, May. Mr. Causton has sent several bushels of rice for planting, with the earnest desire that the Salzburgers should clear some swampy and wet places of trees, bushes, and roots, and try this seed. The people intend to be obedient and start with this tomorrow, now that they have finished their planting of corn and beans. Since nothing has been accomplished by the Indian who recently took over the job of finding our cattle and oxen, two of our people who know how to handle animals have ridden into the forest to spend several days and nights in intensive search. Many of them know the forest so well by now that they can ride around in it without running any risk of getting lost.

It is much safer on horseback than on foot, for the horses know how to find their way back to Ebenezer if they are just given free rein. In this country we need not fear wild and dangerous animals. True, we have bears and wolves, but they are so cowardly that they do not even harm the cows and calves. What we have been told earlier about terrible tigers is a fable, for none are said to be in this colony.[56] Nor is it true, as has once been said, that one of our horses has been devoured by wolves.

The 29th, May. The Lutheran people of Purysburg have again requested that one of us come to them in order to celebrate Holy Communion; and we have determined to do so next week, if nothing interferes. Just recently we explained to these people, orally and in writing, that we are more than eager to serve them with our office but that we wish to have a private chamber or room there in which we can speak with each of them individually and inquire about the condition of his soul. This has been lacking completely until now and we have had to let them all come to Holy Communion, without distinction, after showing them during the preparatory lessons the order of penance and of faith, and after warning them with all our heart against the misuse of this important sacrament. The daily prayer hours and conferences which are being held as circumstances require contribute much to the maintenance of outward order. God be praised for this, and may He grant that no hindrance will be created to His kingdom amongst us in any way and that His holy name will not be used shamefully and blasphemously.

The 30th, May. As we suppose that Captain Thomson, who was recently handed our letters, is still in Savannah, we have decided to send him with today's post Mr. Vat's letter to the praiseworthy Society[57] as well as one to the Rev. Senior Urlsperger, in which are reported the sums of money that some of the Salzburgers can claim in Salzburg. Also, some of the people would have written to their kin in Germany if they had not been overtaken by the post. After this letter had been dispatched, some more Salzburgers came to me to report that they too had claims for money in Salzburg, about which we shall report at the next opportunity. The good people need whatever is due them very much, especially because everything they need in the way of clothes and food is very expensive in this country. For example, for a pair of shoes they must pay 5, 6, even 7 shillings sterling, and they are poorly shod at that. It is the same with other things.

One of us had sent a fifteen-pound note to Charleston for the purpose of buying some things there; but the postman brought it back with the news that the note had been declared invalid in Carolina because it had been made by a counterfeiter in Savannah. This report was confirmed by a man who brought us provisions from Savannah. I still have five of such fifteen pound notes which Monsieur Montaigut gave me for the bill of exchange that the very praiseworthy Society had sent me for my salary. We will soon know whether this merchant will take them back.[58]

The 31st, May. The two men who had been sent after the cows and oxen have returned without having accomplished anything. Occasionally Satan will plant the weeds of discord, but our dear Lord hears our prayers and does not let such evil gather strength, as we have experienced on this very day. May He teach us by His example to be patient and understanding, and may He give us wisdom for all occasions.

The 1st, June, Sunday. It appears that some fruits of our labors are beginning to show on some of those children who heretofore gave evidence only in outward obedience, faithful attendance in church and school, etc. May our heavenly Father pour His spirit over them, in accordance with His promise, so that we here in Ebenezer will also grow like grass, like the willows along water courses, etc.

The 2nd, June. Some important circumstances have compelled my dear colleague, Mr. Boltzius, to go to Savannah today. As soon as his affairs have been settled, he intends to go to Purysburg, where he will remain until next Sunday because the Lutherans there wish to go to Holy Communion again. May the LORD be with him and arm him with the strength of the Holy Ghost so that he can proclaim there, with much blessing, the wonderful things that are preached in the City of God, in order that the name of our JESUS may be glorified more and more in Purysburg. We wish that the poor heathens in our country could hear what is written in Psalm 87:3, and that it could be fulfilled in them what David knew long in advance, namely, that at the time of the New Testament many heathens would be brought to our Saviour.

The 3rd, June. Our Father in Heaven has refreshed our dry land today with a fruitful rain, after which everything looked much greener and more beautiful than before. May He be praised for it and may He continue to care for our needs in a kind and fatherly manner. For some time one of our schoolchildren has given good indications of wanting to give itself over to the Lord

Jesus; and after our dear God confined it to the sickbed, even more good was accomplished with it. The LORD be praised, and may He help this and the rest of the children in the future.

The 4th, June. Our Salzburgers are well satisfied with the guidance of God. In all situations they have the consolation of knowing that they did not come to Georgia on their own but that our dear God has sent them here. The parents are particularly pleased that their children are in a place where they are urged and admonished to everything that is good and that they live in the wilderness where they cannot be led astray by bad examples of other children; this, they say, is not the case in Germany, particularly in the large cities. There one child learns bad things from another, and what one cannot do another can. May the LORD stem all offenses in Germany and grant that the image of JESUS CHRIST be transfigured more and more even in old people in order that the young ones will be edified thereby and urged to endeavor to reflect the clarity of their Saviour even in themselves and that they may be transfigured into the same image from one clarity to the next.

The 5th, June. Very early this morning Mr. Bryan, a rich planter from Carolina, came and brought the thirty-five cows and thirty-five calves which the very praiseworthy Society *de promov. Christi Cognit.*[59] had destined as a present for the Salzburgers. This is a very great and considerable present, which caused the Salzburgers to express much joy and praise of God. Now nearly everyone is anxious to build a stall in which to put the cow he expects to get by drawing lots, so that he can give it the best of care and get it completely used to himself. So far it has been our experience that stock is of the greatest use when it is put up in barns, as is done in Germany. At the beginning the animals are wild but they get tame very quickly so that soon they will go into the stable by themselves, especially when they are given some salt, for they are very much attracted by it and it entices them to come back. The LORD be praised for this benefit, and may He strengthen our faith through it and teach us to see more and more that He means to do well for us, and that He will not leave us in any difficult situations that might come up in the future. The Salzburgers who had taken Mr. Boltzius to Savannah returned today from Purysburg and brought me a letter from my dear colleague.

The 6th, June. The beautiful rainy weather has once again been followed by a heat wave so great that the soil has dried out so quickly as to make it impossible to see where the beautiful rain has fallen. During the night it is usually cool, so much so that one must be careful not to damage one's health. The Salzburgers bring up their children so that they will become used to the heat and the cold while they are still young by dressing them lightly both when it is warm and when it is cool.

The 7th, June. The very great heat was followed this afternoon by a violent thunderstorm. The wind which accompanied it was so violent that the rain penetrated nearly everything and nearly all of the garden vegetables were beaten to the ground. In a situation like this we are very badly off in our poorly constructed houses, for the rain goes through them and one can hardly keep anything dry inside. Even my dear colleague's house, which is better built than any of them, is not so well constructed that the rain cannot come through on many occasions. However, since our Father in Heaven does all of these things, they are done for the best; and He will continue to help in the future as He has done in the past, and will be with us always. May He be praised forever and in eternity, amen. In the evening we had another thunderstorm during which we were startled by a report so loud that it seemed a cannon had been shot in our place.

The 8th, June. Yesterday's storm, especially the very loud thunderclap, brought a great awakening among young and old. One of the Salzburgers said that it made him feel very good to be so awakened by God and he wished that this would happen more often.

The 9th, June. This forenoon, Praise God! I, Boltzius, came back to Ebenezer via Abercorn. In Savannah I presented a Jew, who seemed to have a good attitude, a tract in the Jewish-German language.[60] I will learn later how it has been accepted. Mr. Causton had received a number of letters from London; and, among other things, he received the good news that the Trustees had received from Parliament the sum of twenty-six thousand pounds sterling to be used for the best interest of this colony. A number of citadels and forts are to be built throughout the colony, each to be garrisoned with fifty soldiers, so that Georgia will be, so to speak, the outer wall and protection of other English plantations.

As soon as I had taken care of my affairs I went back to Purysburg. The people there were very much pleased to have one of us with them once again so that they could go to Holy Communion. As I had requested that I be given a better opportunity to speak with the people in private than I had had on previous occasions, a chamber was prepared for me in which I could be alone and to which I could have the communicants come individually. I christened one child that was fairly old already. The local pastor has been away from home for some months, and since several persons wanted to be married, and since they had written permission from Mr. Pury, I consented to marry three couples. A man told me that during their Sunday assemblies they are making considerable use of the short sermons of the late Professor Francke which we had lent them.[61] They benefited from them, he said, because they were based on the right foundation.

During the hours of preparation I announced that those who wished to go to Holy Communion had to announce their intention to me so that I could speak with them about the Word of God and lead them to the right path with love and gentleness. I was very much grieved to see that the children in this place are growing up wild and without instruction or discipline. Some of the parents again revealed to me their sorrow and told how much they wish to send them to Ebenezer for some time, but they lack the means of supporting them there. It would be a particularly great deed of love if someone would let himself be awakened by God to contribute some of his abundance toward the schooling of poor children, for it is hoped that the ignorant in this country could be helped in this way and that perhaps even the children of the heathens could be given an opportunity to learn about Christ.

The 10th, June. It had been our intention to have Holy Communion next Sunday, and some of the members of the congregation have already announced their intention of coming. But we found it necessary to postpone it for a week because their communal labors as well as their individual chores do not leave the people enough time for preparation. They like us to arrange matters to suit their convenience because they do not like to participate in this holy act as though it were an ordinary occasion. This month the heat has become so great that those who have to work during the day can hardly bear it. True, the people carry on their communal labors only in the morning, and from four in the afternoon until evening. But since they also want to work for themselves and do everything that is useful and necessary, they do this during the time of the most intense heat. We have always advised them against this but we have not been completely successful.

The 11th, June. Mr. Bryan, who recently brought us the cattle, returned today to our place from Savannah. He wanted to collect the money for some cows he had brought by special order and wanted to know whether he could serve the Salzburgers, whom he loves, with some additional cows. As the people are used to handling cows, and since they can use them in many ways in this wilderness, thirteen head and as many calves were ordered from him. He will let them have these for cash, and several men will have to go with him in order to get them. Milk and butter are very expensive in this country, especially here, because we are so far away from other people. Besides, the poor sandy soil increases our need for livestock.

The 12th, June. The board cutter who recently left his work came back to us today, with his helpers, in order to continue his work. And since he brought six helpers with him it is hoped that he will not be a burden to the Salzburgers by expecting them to give him additional help. At present we have with us two Indians who caused a great deal of trouble in Abercorn recently. Nothing is to be feared as long as they are sober, and they behave well amongst us and enjoy the best of treatment. We have been told that the board-cutter who arrived recently promised one of the Indians some strong drink, called rum, in return for his services. But I have sent word to him to be careful about doing anything contrary to the orders of the Trustees who have banned this strong drink in order to prevent mischief among the Christians and heathens.

The 13th, June. Those Salzburgers who had gone to Pallacho-colas after our cows returned today. They have many good things to say about the friendliness of Mr. Bryan, and they brought with them fifteen cows and as many calves.

The 14th, June. We are anxiously waiting for the man who has orders from Mr. Causton to bring fourteen fat steers to our place. They are to be slaughtered because it cannot be healthy to eat saltmeat in this very hot weather. Praise God! All of the members of the congregation are well off at present, except that now and then one or the other is overcome by a spell of weakness which passes soon.

The 15th, June, Sunday. For some days and especially today the heat has been so great that we were subjected to great discomfort even during our public worship, notwithstanding the fact that we assembled in the guardhouse which is built of strong timbers and which, previously, had not been penetrated by the heat.

Last year it was hot, to be sure, but not as burning and stinging as it is now. Besides, we then had more rains and thunderstorms. A young Salzburger complained very much about the naughtiness and frivolity of his heart and said that he continued to be amazed at the great love and kindness of God, who not only convinced him very quickly of his wrongdoing and gave him heartfelt sadness but also answered his prayer and cleansed him of such evil with the Blood of Christ so that he could distinctly feel its recreative powers. He said that now he was quite different from the way he used to be, when sin did not mean anything to him and often-times he did not know that this or that act was sinful, etc. He was glad that he soon would be able to read and he hoped that this would help him with the furtherance of his Christian attitude.

The 16th, June. Last evening Ruprecht Steiner's wife brought a young daughter into this world who was christened today and was named Agatha. God be praised for having heard our prayer in His Grace and for having eliminated the sad conditions which befell pregnant women in previous times. The child is healthy but the mother is very weak. Since there are two more pregnant women who have had and still have various attacks, we have asked Commissioner Vat to have the steer slaughtered which Mr. Bryan gave to the last Salzburgers, so that healthful soups could be prepared for these persons. This is especially important be-cause we cannot get anything but salted meat at our place. Dur-ing the last few days, to His glory and our joy, our dear God has given obvious blessing to the medicine we administered to a number of persons who had unexpected, and in some cases dan-gerous, attacks.

The 17th, June. Last evening a few Indians arrived here, and today they traveled on to Savannah. Quite a number of them are still on their way, all of whom are going to Savannah to receive some presents and to renew their treaty of peace with the English nation. Yesterday and today we have had a soaking rain, which did not last long, yet the great heat abated afterwards. Some of the people who have announced their intention of coming to Holy Communion give me much pleasure with their sincere be-haviour and their edifying talk. Two married people, who until recently had to bear heavy crosses, knew how to get so much com-fort from the Word of God and from the examples of the be-lievers in the Old and the New Testament that I was surprised.

An upright young man who has always tried to dig deep into the spirit of Christianity registered for Holy Communion and, when doing so, heard the verse from next Sunday's Gospel: He accepts the sinners and eats with them. He was overjoyed to know that the great LORD would be so friendly to him and would eat and drink with him. He believed that partaking of the very holy Sacrament this time would strengthen and refresh him as much as it did last time and that he only had to make sure he would come even as a poor sinner. The above-mentioned words were so very impressive to him because he had heard them for the first time on our sea-voyage from a pious Salzburger; and he had not known before then that they are written in the Bible. Ever since then they have been particularly dear to him.

The 18th, June. The people have been busy with the distribution of the cows, and they are overjoyed with the blessings which God has given them through their worthy benefactors. In other parts it is not the custom in this country to keep livestock in stalls. But the first Salzburgers whose cows have returned from the forest have begun to build stalls. They find that this is very good for the animals, which return on their own accord during the heat of the day and also at night. After the first animals, which had been brought up on marsh grass, became used to our grass they gained weight so well that everyone is pleased. People who know about these things say for our region that we have the best pastures here. Mr. Causton has furnished the Salzburgers with various tools necessary to make hay so that the animals will not be allowed to run away again in the winter.

Musgrove,[62] the interpreter who went to London with the Indians the last time, died during the last few days. This is a great loss to this colony. Today the people finally finished transporting our provisions, and thus God lets us overcome one burdensome task after another. Mr. Oglethorpe cared for us in a very fatherly manner when he furnished us with a few horses. Last winter there was no work for them, but now that they have become stronger we can use them very well.

The 19th, June. Some of those who have announced their intention of coming to Holy Communion are so bent and cast down by their sins that we have to lift up their spirits through the Gospel. Among others, the following verses were blessed for them: Isaiah 30:18; Jeremiah 33:8-9; and St. Luke 15:2, and 14; 17. During yesterday's preparation hour we recommended the 9th chapter of the 2nd book of Johannes Arnd's *True Christianity;* and, as many have told us, this proved to be of great benefit. We decided this time to base our preparation on the lesson about penance, as it is presented in question and answer form by the late Maederjan, pastor of Thommendorf, in his booklet *Instructions for Salvation*. It was reported to me recently that this faithful servant of God has already entered the eternal peace of his LORD. Because his example and the blessed conduct of his office have made a deep impression on me, I would be very happy to learn the details of his departure from this vale of tears.

The 20th, June. This afternoon we had scattered showers and a few thunderstorms which passed quickly, after which the air became very cool and pleasant. A former servant to some master is now learning to cut boards. He seems to be strong enough for it. He made an agreement with the board-cutter whom Mr. Causton had sent us, according to which he will learn from him and receive his food and weekly pay of five shillings sterling. To be sure, this work is very difficult and hard, especially in the summer, but it brings more money than anything else because many boards are needed in this new colony and high prices are paid for them because there are so few workers. Some time ago a certain skillful man started a sawmill in this colony and spent a great deal of money on it. But he ruined himself completely with it since it can be used only at certain hours during the day because of the high and low tides. It appears that the rivers here cannot be used for either grist mills or saw mills.

The 21st, June. The Salzburgers have a great desire to read Schaitberger's book,[63] and they would be very much pleased if a few copies of it could be sent here. In the last shipment there were only two, and we have kept them to be lent out only. But since many of them have a great desire to own a copy, it has been decided that those who asked for some at Augsburg and have been promised to get them shall draw lots for these. We also give hope to those who still have no hymn book, and we do not doubt that God will awaken someone who will help us get a number of copies of the first part of the *Halle Hymn Book*.[64] This book has contributed much already to the praise of God and to the edification of our hearts.

The 22nd, June, Sunday. Today fifty-seven persons came to Holy Communion. May God bless this holy act in all of them, for Christ's sake. Some people from Purysburg came to us with the request that I marry a young single woman to a widower whose wife had recently died at sea. They had been sent here by the pastor of Purysburg himself because he could not and would not marry them in the German language. I had known these people before and, because they could give proof that no important objections were present, the ceremony was held after the noon services. I showed them briefly from the Word of God the things that should be the object of our chief worry and effort during our short and fragile life, namely, that we should come to the true knowledge of Christ in the right manner, and through Him become saved and glorified. I then talked especially about the state of holy matrimony among the children of God and reminded them that the devil, who wishes nothing good for people and begrudges them their salvation in Christ, makes constant attempts to keep them from it in all sorts of ways and, among other things, even uses the institution of marriage for this purpose whenever people are not alert or fail to pray, etc. May God give those present a good reaction to this.

The 23, June. There are three boys in the congregation who will soon go to Holy Communion for the first time. For this reason I have them come to me daily for private lessons. As the late Maederjan's little book entitled *Instruction for Salvation*[65] gave much edification in last week's preparation hours, I am using it for a basis now and intend to use its method to teach the articles of faith to the children as well as to some adults who are attending these lessons. In order that everything may be remembered more easily, and so that the entire congregation may benefit from this, I intend to repeat in the evening prayer hour, in the form of questions and answers, the main content of everything that has been taken up in the hour of preparation. The dear people like Sunday's review lesson very much and, as they have told us with praise of God, they have derived many blessings from it. I have no doubt that they will like the methods I intend to apply and that, through God's grace, they will derive blessings from them too.

The 24th, June. Last evening three men from Purysburg arrived at our place after having been lost for two days while suffering indescribable thirst. During the dark night, after they had come close to our river, they still did not know where they were. But when they heard us sing during evening prayer, they were put on the right path by the sound of it. We have tried, with God's grace, to use our time for the edification of all. Today we have had such hot weather that it was almost unbearable. Toward evening a thunderstorm arose which lasted into the night, but the rain stopped after a few hours.

The 25th, June. As the newly established preparation lessons have given me additional work, and as I am not feeling very strong physically, probably because of the very great heat, I have been forced to discontinue my work with the children in school for the time being. All of the bigger children are attending the preparation so that they can repeat the divine truths in the evenings for the edification of the entire congregation. Thus the hour of questions and answers which my dear colleague holds with them is enough for them. I must hold said lessons in the middle of the day at about two o'clock, for the sake of some grown people who cannot work at this time because of the intense heat. The three men from Purysburg were very much pleased with the children and their answers during the period of catechization. They were pleased with the entire congregation as well, and we ourselves received no little edification from their discourse and from their own great desire to be edified themselves. One of them has decided to take care of the poor children in Purysburg and to instruct them in the Word of God, in reading, writing, etc. He is well qualified for that. May God guide the spirit of the people to him.

The 28th, June. As the quarterly provisions are due the first Salzburgers tomorrow, Mr. Vat started today with the distribution of some things. We have God to thank for the fact that we now have victuals here for more than a quarter of a year, otherwise the poor people would have to work on their transportation in this great heat until they get sick or deathly ill. As time goes by, things get much easier for them; and, although we now have more comfort in many ways than we had a year ago, we hope that God, in His fatherly care, will remove the difficulties we are still facing and will at last make us so worthy of His blessings so that we can leave to others the benefits coming from the storehouses.

The 30th, June, Monday. Mrs. Schweighofer became so dangerously ill that her death was expected at any moment, but God blessed one of our life-powders very obviously to His glory and to our joy. Her heart has always been right with the LORD, and even now she has nothing but praise for the kindness and love of GOD which she has seen in such plenty in her days. Our conversation recalled to me the hymn: O, Let us not covet, etc. She not only listened with the greatest attention when I read it but asked for the beginning of it when I visited her again, so that she could make use of it in the future. She thanks GOD just as much for the many crosses she has had to bear from the beginning of the sea-voyage until now as she thanks Him for all other good deeds.

The 1st of July. The great drought of this summer continues. Now and then we hear thunder in the distance and in the evenings we see strong sheet-lightning toward the north, but we seldom get thunder and rain. Now the great heat of the day is often tempered by cool winds and the nights are very pleasant.

The 2nd, July. Last night Bichler's wife brought a young daughter into this world. It has been said that God showed much mercy on this occasion. Our people have great confidence in the medicines that were sent us from Halle, and God is often praised for this. May He, the truly Merciful, give rich reward for this benefit; and may He refresh the worthy benefactors whom we have to thank for these medicines which have helped Bichler's wife so much, just as they have done much good for us and others.

The 4th, July. Today we have had a soaking and fruitful rain which surpasses any we have had this year. During and after the rain it is usually so cool and pleasant that one could wish nothing better.

The 6th, July. The twenty fat steers which had been assigned to us by the Trustees for fresh meat arrived last night. The Englishman who brought them, Mackpherson by name, is a captain from Fort Ogeechee. Upon my questioning he assured us that fear of the Spanish Indians was unfounded. In the first place, they had not heard anything about the supposed starting of hostilities. Besides, he stated, they could not harm us in this colony without the consent and permission of the Creek Indians who were friends of the English and who had been in Savannah a few weeks ago to seal their friendship and to receive a number of presents. They do not stand up on the battlefield because they love their lives too much. But they consider it a great and heroic deed when they succeed in shooting people down when in hiding and unseen. The more quietly and secretly they can do this the more their deed is acclaimed. It is said that on occasion they tell their comrades of such deeds, to the accompaniment of great applause.

I wanted to become better acquainted with an old man in his service who understands the Indian language and I asked him to leave him with me for a few months so that he could help me learn it. He answered that this man did not know all of the language, but only as much as he had learned by associating with the Indians. His knowledge consisted of being able to understand and answer questions in matters that pertain to eating, drinking, and trading, such as come up from day to day. Thus he could not be of much use to me. He said I would do best to get Mrs.

Musgrove for this instruction, since she had a special talent for expressing Indian terms in English, a talent not even possessed by her recently dead husband. May the LORD let us command to His blessing this matter which is entangled in so many difficulties. It would be hard for me to leave my congregation for a while for the sake of learning this language.

The 7th, July. The rain that started last Friday lasted until today and has done the soil a very great deal of good. The people of Carolina say that if the rain had stayed away much longer the corn and rice crops would have been ruined.[66] Veit Langfelder and Mrs. Schoppacher, whose husband died here three months ago, announced to me that they wished to enter the state of holy matrimony and they requested that their banns be published for the first time next Sunday. The class in which several children are being prepared for Holy Communion has been held until now after the noon meal for the sake of some adults; but the weak condition of my body is forcing me to change it to some time during the morning. The matters explained and pointed out to the children are repeated in question and answer form during evening prayers. This has already been very useful to a number of the young and old.

The 8th, July. Water melons in this country grow so big and are of such delicious and pleasant flavor that we must marvel at them. Some of them have black and some have brown seeds inside. The latter are preferable to the first because of their pleasant flavor. They are red inside and full of seeds. They are not unhealthy, and one's body suffers no ill effects even after eating a great portion. It is hard to tell when they are ripe, consequently many were opened by us before they were ripe. But even these can be eaten like cucumber salad, with vinegar, pepper, butter, and oil. The cucumbers in this country also appear to us tastier and healthier than in Germany. Some people eat them quite raw, like apples. In addition, there is in this country a kind of small, white gourd which is called squash. These are picked young and while they are still white, and are cooked whole, with the skin, and then mashed between two boards. When prepared with butter, salt, and pepper they have a flavor similar to that of white cabbage. These squash and melons do better in our gardens than anything else.

The 9th, July. Indians came to us from Savannah, where they had gone to receive presents. Tomorrow they will travel on toward the mountains, where they live. Six of them came to my room and all of these not only made a good outward appearance but they also showed themselves to be very friendly and orderly. Whenever I see such poor heathens at our place my desire for learning their language is renewed and I wish to have an opportunity for doing so. But, whoever knows anything about our situation and duties can see very well that we are prevented from doing so by almost insurmountable difficulties. Anyone wanting to do something with these heathens must have a profession the duties of which do not prevent him from learning their language and from associating with them frequently.

I have been told that these Indians who live further up the mountains not only work and lead an orderly life but that they also refrain from the disorderly conduct so common with others that live in this colony. It is said also that they have requested of the late Governor of Carolina that no strong drink which might make them drunk should be brought to them and traded to them. It would be more possible to accomplish something with these people if a man's heart were filled with love for Jesus and for the soul of men and if he knew their language. If only he would receive some instruction from someone in this colony he could easily be given opportunity by Mr. Causton or by Mr. Oglethorpe, who is expected soon, to be well received at their place, especially since they now have very good relations with the English. Today we again had a fertile rain. Since the rain water fell, it has been as cool both night and day as it usually is in Germany in rainy and stormy weather.

The 10th, July. The wet and cool weather we are having at present has caused some sickness here and there among the congregation. We are constantly solicited for our medicines, which we can not refuse to our people through our love for their health and life. Praise God! it has been our experience that, whenever the symptoms are properly recognized and the medicines applied accordingly, their effect has always shown itself very soon, to the surprise of the patient and others. In blood-letting, cupping, and surgery Mr. Zwifler serves the people as best he can and gradually gets more and more practice in his medicine. He also shows great diligence and loyalty in our supply house in preserving and distributing the provisions, as well as in other matters pertaining to our external order.

The 11th, July. Mr. Gronau and Mr. Vat intended to be back in Ebenezer on Tuesday, and for this reason we had sent two horses to Abercorn for them. Because we heard that they had no opportunity to travel from Savannah to Abercorn, a few Salzburgers went there by boat to get them, but so far none of them have come back and we do not know the reason for this. It is very difficult to travel to Savannah. To go there from here by water we must take many detours and, in addition, must trouble other people to act as guides. By land we cannot get any further than Musgrove's cowpen, and from there we must continue to Savannah by boat. After a rain the road to the said cowpen is impassable because of the mudholes and swamps which fill up with water very quickly. If the Salzburgers were to remain here we would soon make arrangements for the improvement of the road. But it is amazing that the Englishmen have not long since taken any measures to improve this path, since the post and other travellers from Charleston must pass this way with discomfort and danger.

The 12th, July. Again this afternoon quite a number of Indians passed through our place carrying the presents which they had received in Savannah. Now and then they have asked for and received meat and beans at our place because they had no provisions with them. Some of them do not mind asking the people for anything they may see. Even in my room an Indian was attracted by a number of things.

The 13th, July. Toward evening my dear colleague came back to our place in good health; but Commissioner Vat will not come until tomorrow, and consequently a few Salzburgers have gone to Savannah to get him. Captain Thompson was still in Savannah, so the continuation of our diary from 23 May to 4 July could be given to him.

The 14th, July. Because shoes are very expensive here, the Salzburgers have started making wooden shoes which they fasten with a small leather strap across the foot. The ones I have seen were light and well chiseled out. It is said that you can stand and walk in them very well once you are used to them. Some people here are badly lacking shirts, and linen for them here is exceptionally expensive. The sweat that people shed both day and night damages them greatly.

The 15th, July. Although the weather is usually at its hottest from this month until the beginning of the next, we have had until now pleasant and temperate weather by day and by night. We are also becoming more and more used to the land, and many things that were difficult for us in earlier times are bearable now. Wherever the soil is good and fertile the workers cannot ask for better land than that here in Georgia, especially because in their work they have many advantages over the people in Germany. Once the trees and roots have been cleared out, they can turn the soil very easily because it is soft and pliable. In addition, they can work on it all winter because they are not prevented from doing so by either severe cold or snow. All winter long there is enough light for work until nearly six o'clock. Raising animals does not give them half as much trouble as it does in Germany, for the cattle can go out into the grass or cane winter and summer. They like to eat the cane best of all. And those cows that do not give any milk are allowed to wander in the forest until they get calves, and then they are brought in and joined with the rest that are driven out to pasture and watched by a cowherd. All this is in addition to other advantages they enjoy in regard to freedom of religion, civil liberties and rights, etc., which we are not mentioning. Last night as well as this afternoon we had strong, sudden showers and thunderstorms; but, through God's grace, no damage was done. We now have the most fruitful weather anyone could wish, and in the places where a little manure has been put down the corn, beans, and pumpkins are growing very well.

The 17th, July. After having been sickly nearly all the time since birth, Ruprecht Steiner's child died this morning. Of late it had had severe diarrhea with many aches and pain. A few small doses of life-powder and powder for acidity alleviated the latter, but it was not God's pleasure to bless these medicines to the point of bringing the child back to complete health. Both parents are truly pious people and they gladly delivered this their small child to the LORD JESUS with prayer and tears. Early this morning I found the father kneeling and praying by the bed of the sick child. Last night preparations were made to slaughter one of the oxen that were sent [which Captain MacPherson brought] to us recently. Mr. Causton has given orders to select six of the twenty for the purpose of training them for work and for pulling loads.

The 18th, July. In the afternoon we had a very heavy rain and thunderstorm which covered everything with water and flooded half of our garden. Some of our people are away on a journey and they have probably had to suffer much from it. Meanwhile, it is cool and pleasant by day and by night, which is good for the work during the day and good for rest at night. We hear that a Swiss who serves as a laborer in Savannah has asked Mr. Causton for permission to move to us at Ebenezer because of his children as soon as he has been freed from his service. We are, to be sure, happy to have more children in our school and to be able to work with hope on the grown people who are not Salzburgers. However, because it has turned out so badly and such people have caused us and the Salzburgers much annoyance, we are a bit fearful of it. When the occasion arises I shall reveal my worried thoughts to Mr. Causton. The people who came with the last Salzburgers all behave themselves well and show great diligence in using the means of salvation.

The 19th, July. Two Salzburgers have gathered a great quantity of peaches in a region not far from here. They are free and can be picked by anybody. The trees were planted by Indians who lived there some time ago and they have multiplied from year to year. They grow and bear fruit very quickly in this country. They also brought some grapes which looked and tasted like the ones in Germany. Besides these there is a kind of grape here the fruits of which are as large as a medium size button, and they grow far apart. Said region is said to contain a large quantity of the former. Although we had no rain today we had, toward evening, a very unexpected and violent thunderstorm which, however, (Thanks be to GOD) passed by quickly and without damage. Last night we again had a strong rain and thunderstorm.

Of the three boys who are to be prepared now for Holy Communion, Rieser's boy is the best and, to judge by appearances, gives us the greatest hope. Things still seem very bad with regard to R. and Q. even though, according to the Grace that God gives, we do the best we can both publicly and privately to lead these souls to the Lord God in truth. To all appearances they like to come to school, to the prayer hours, and also to me so that I may admonish them and pray with them. They promise much, also weep a bit, and increase in their knowledge of divine Truth; yet we do not yet see a true hate of sin and genuine love for the Lord Jesus. If it costs so much in the midst of Christendom to bring people to a true conversion and mortification of the world and of sin, how much work must it cost among the heathens? Yet to the glory of God we must acknowledge that He has among us His Kingdom which, for the comfort and strengthening of our hearts, has revealed itself most dearly in many members of our congregation through their words and deeds. Formerly we have imparted more details of this in our diary, but now we are hesitant to continue doing so because it might be imputed to us that we wished to praise ourselves and our congregation above all others.

The 22nd, July. The board-cutter who has been with us for some time with his helpers has finished a supply of boards so large that my dear colleague's house as well as the two public houses ordered by Mr. Oglethorpe can nearly be finished with them. This man has now gone to Savannah and he will probably bring back instructions from Mr. Causton as to whether or not we should proceed with construction. Since the construction has been delayed for so long we would almost rather see it delayed further, until Mr. Oglethorpe himself gets here. Everyone expects him to give the Salzburgers permission to move to a more fertile region, in which case the money spent on these houses would have been spent in vain.[67]

The 23rd, July. For the sake of our congregation we wish very much to get letters from London and Germany so that they will know whether they are to stay here or whether they will move to some other place. Their desire to work is very great, especially to work in their own fields. The communal labors which the last Salzburgers have performed in the field have been in vain, a fact that must be attributed to the lack of rain over such a long period. Some of the first Salzburgers hope to harvest some corn and some beans, for some of them have good tracts of land situated near the river where they have tried to improve the sandy soil with manure.[68] Perhaps some letters arrived for us with the two ships which are said to have just brought a large number of people from the Palatinate to this colony.

The 25, July. One of our men brought a large quantity of grapes from the forest, the berries of which were of unusual size and grew close together in bunches as they do in Germany. Last summer we did not see any like this. They are of such strong flavor that your head can feel their potency very quickly. Also, they have thinner skins than those we found last year. It is believed that they would grow to be even bigger and sweeter if they were properly cultivated and left on the vines longer. They do not last long in the woods because of the birds. Come fall, we will perhaps have an opportunity to plant some of them in our gardens.

The 26th, July. Today a number of foreign Indians again came to our place. They were much bolder than those who were here earlier. There was one among them who had received food and drink from us on another occasion, and he demanded the same for himself and the others. Eventually all of them came into my house and they were not at all polite about it. When they come to visit the first time they are usually very timid as long as they are sober; but if they come back several times they get quite bold in their talks with each other and in the demands they make. On several occasions they have demanded that I give them small medicine bottles, in which they want to keep the grease they use to oil their guns.

The 27th, July. This Sunday has been a very remarkable day for me on which I have had much reason to praise God. In yesterday evening's prayer hour God gave special blessing to some people I know, through the Gospel about the vindication of a repentant sinner. He also bestowed His blessing upon children as well as adults during the presentations of His word, both in the morning and in the afternoon. The children came to see me in my quarters and some of them were moved to tears when I talked to them in simple fashion about the verses from Mark 10: 14, 15, 16, which tell of the uncommon friendliness the LORD JESUS has for children, and when I told them and read to them examples of children who loved the Lord Jesus with all their hearts. Also, God has bestowed upon me such great benefits and grace that I consider myself obliged to praise Him as long as I live. The name of the LORD JESUS be praised from now until eternity.

The 28th, July. Veit Landfelder and the widow of the late Schoppacher were married today in the presence of the congregation. It is still so cool and pleasant, especially at night, that one cannot wish it any better. Two of the Indians that were here recently came to see me this morning and brought some venison. Doubtless this was to be in return for what they enjoyed at my house not long ago.

The 30th, July. My dear colleague and Mr. Vat returned home last night.[69]

The 31st of July and the 1st of August. On these two days in Savannah I again enjoyed much love and kindness from Mr. Causton. It is a pleasure to him to serve us and the Salzburgers with good deeds, for in doing so he is acting, as he admits, according to the Trustees' intention. GOD be praised for all of His kindness. A ship arrived in Savannah which brought a number of Swiss men and women who are to be servants for the inhabitants of the city. By this same ship we not only received a large number of enjoyable letters and good news from England and Germany, but also half our salary and a present of good Madeira wine. How happy we are to know that the complaints we sent to the proper places, about our poor soil as well as other matters, have not done any harm but, with God's blessings, may well do some good for our congregation. In the next few days we intend to share with our congregation the happiness we received from this good news by reading them the content of the letters as we have done in the past.

The 2nd, Aug. With God's help, we returned to Ebenezer this morning, going via Abercorn. Our boat will follow to bring up some provisions by water. While still in Abercorn, I received the sad news that two pious women of the congregation, Mrs. Schweighofer and Mrs. Eischberger, had been lost in the woods. Back in Ebenezer I learned that it was true but that they had been found after they had to spend a night in the woods. But one of the men, Resch by name, who was sent after them must have become lost as well, for he has failed to return since yesterday. Some of the Salzburgers offered to go after this lost sheep too and to continue signaling throughout the night with fire and shooting. I was delighted at this love and promised them some biscuits from our storehouse, because they can take this with them best of all and because they prefer bread, which is rare here, to all other food.

The 3rd, Aug. The eight Salzburgers who went after the lost Resch last night returned this morning, but they were unable to find him, even though they made every effort to do so. I was particularly pleased to hear that they had cut down many dead trees and placed them around a tree that was still standing and had then fired these with materials that burn easily, so that the light of the fire shone through the woods and could be seen from far away. At the same time they marked the trees from this fire all the way to our place so that he might find his way home if he were to make his way to the glowing coals and smoke. Today others came to announce that they wanted to go into the forest and try this method at some other place. Perhaps God will be pleased by this labor of love and will hear our prayer and grant our wish.

The wife of this lost man is very depressed. She would not be satisfied and wished to look for her husband herself when he could not be found by the Salzburgers. But I had her come to me and spoke with her in most simple fashion, in accordance with her situation and her present state of mind. Thank God! this was not without effect. The text which I had used for their marriage ceremony, on Monday after the 2nd Sunday after Epiphany, served me particularly well for this. It was the Gospel of that day, John 2: 1-2; and, to my great joy, this otherwise simple woman remembered several outstanding matters which had been edifying to her, and she gave me a splendid opportunity to apply this to her present situation.

It seems to me to be very useful for a teacher to keep in mind for every member of the congregation those verses, things, and circumstances which have been useful and blessed for the congregation as a whole or for individual members. When these are recalled to them they do them no small service in times of need. At times, during private conversations, the people tell me of remarkable proofs of divine guidance which they have experienced themselves. In times of trials and tribulations they often fail to remember them, but when reminded of them they derive much comfort for their hearts. For this reason I decided some time ago to keep a special book for this purpose. Each page will have as its title one of the names and under it I will record special matters and circumstances that I have noticed here and there. In a congregation that is not too large, such as ours, this can be done very well.

Mrs. Schweighofer is suffering no little grief and pangs of conscience over the fact that Resch has been lost and has not come back so far.[70] She feels that she is responsible for his present misery because he got lost when going with the other men to find her and the other Salzburger woman. During my visit with her she shed many tears. Although she praised God for having brought her back to her small children, she is very depressed and stricken with grief over the mishap that has now befallen Resch. I attempted to talk her out of the idea that she was responsible for his going astray by using simple and easily understood reasoning and argument. But her sensitive conscience was not satisfied with this, although another pious man supported my words with additional arguments. Since she was sure that she had committed a grave sin I advised her that this sin too must be presented to our most friendly Saviour, especially since she knew His great love for mankind from her own experience, also because she knew that it is as easy for Him to forgive all sins as one, and one as all, and that His heart, overflowing with kindness, does not lack the willingness for this. I also made use of the verse Zechariah 13: I because God had not let it be without blessing when I used it a few days ago during the application of the doctrine of justification. May we learn soon whatever blessing the LORD may wish to bestow upon this. We also gave her some bodily refreshment, particularly because her sick body needs it very much.

Before I left she told me that she had had no idea of ever seeing Ebenezer again, but that her heart had been right with God and happy, and when she became tired she gladly would have sat down to await death. But Mrs. Eischberger had urged her to keep on walking. This afternoon eight men again went into the woods to look for the lost Resch. May God accompany them with His angels and let them achieve the purpose of their efforts as all of us wish with all our hearts. They have so arranged matters among themselves that none of them can get lost. I also have sent my boys to Abercorn on horseback to have the cannons there shot off today and tomorrow. So far, we have not been supplied with any.

The 4th, Aug.[71] Last evening, after the review lesson, Mrs. Schweighofer came to me again and said that God had blessed what we had told her about the nature of her situation and had given peace and contentment to her heart. She also said that much had been contributed to this by the two verses Isaiah 32: 17-18 and Song of Solomon 2: 13-14, whose most evangelical content had been explained to the timid souls during the review lesson. Her present complaint was that she was still being prevented from being properly serious with her Christianity and that her shortcomings were so many that one should not be surprised if GOD became tired of showing mercy. But her spirit was encouraged to praise God even more when I told her my daily exercises, how sin and Satan gave me much trouble every day, how I refused to be discouraged, but, as a miserable worm that is truly penitent, crawled deeper and deeper into the holes and crevices of the wounds of Christ, and that this was the daily exercise of the most pious people in the Bible, whose shortcomings have been recorded for us. When dealing with such souls that are very depressed by the recognition of their miserable sins, I have often thought that it shows particularly great wisdom and friendliness on God's part to have had recorded for us in His word the faults and weaknesses and even greater offenses of His dearest children.

During the noon hour I had the congregation gather in order to acquaint them with some of the news I had received in the letters from London and Germany. The Rev. Senior Urlsperger's letter gave me a good opportunity to warn them against underestimating the Grace of the Gospel or being indifferent toward the Grace already received, and to show them how many spiritual and physical advantages they have over many people in Germany and America because of the trials they have had and those they may expect in the future, all of which they easily understood. And

since we also told them that the Heavenly Father had not ceased
to inspire Christian friends to serve our best interests, spiritual
and worldly, and to care for the needy, they could not be otherwise than highly pleased.

[The 6th, Aug. Geschwandel informed me of his intention to
marry a woman in N. In reply I told him what marriage is in general, and how necessary prayer, struggle, and caution are. These
he would have to observe in his case, if his marriage were to turn
out happily. In regard to this woman he should well remember
that it is no minor matter to be burdened with a wife of such a
kind who has not even been converted. It would probably then occur to him what he lost in his late wife; and this would just increase his present troubles should his plans not turn out well. In
addition I could conclude from many things that the benefactors
in England and Germany would not like it if all sorts of people
joined the Salzburgers, as he himself could find out from the last
arrivals. Perhaps God will ordain that some unmarried women
will come in the next expected transport, because our friends in
Germany know our troubles and are greatly concerned, as I see
from Senior Urlsperger's letters. Finally I prayed with him and
observed that he was satisfied with my advice and representations.
For some time this Geschwandel has again indicated much goodness and has also so conducted himself that we can be content
with him. Schweiger too is involved with a single woman in Purysburg, in whose case there is less difficulty and who might suit him
very well. And yet we have admonished him, like the former, to
much Christian caution and prayer.]

The 5th [6th], Aug. Despite the intensive search that the Salzburgers carried on during the last few days it was impossible to
find the lost Resch. Although he had had poor Christian instruction[72] he had a heart full of love for the Lord Jesus and the
Word of God and he never knew how to give enough thankful
praise for the rich preaching of the Gospel at our place. Because of
this dear and good benefit, physical wants meant nothing to him
and I never heard him complain about matters of the body. Others
say in praise of him that he was satisfied with everything, thanked
God for even the smallest good deed, and worked with all his
strength on his worldly duties. His wife, who is also a very simple
and good disciple of the Lord Jesus, has much to tell that is truth-
full about his righteous attitude. In her present trying situation it
gives her the greatest comfort to know and to hope that she will
find her late husband again in eternity. [73]

The 6th [7th], Aug. As our money and other things which we received with the last ship from London could not be delivered to Savannah when I was there, my dear colleague and a few Salzburgers had to go there again this morning. And since it is the judgment of the magistrate that Mr. Montaigut should agree to take back the counterfeit money bills, we hope to be relieved for some time from having to make this trip again.

The 7th [8th], Aug. For some time Mrs. R.[74] has been waiting for us to admit her to Holy Communion; but we have not been able to hurry this because she has not had enough instruction in the Evangelical religion. [As long as she has been with us she has improved in many ways so that those who knew her previously are amazed at how diligently she listens to the Word of God and how she gives evidence of grasping the power of the Word in her heart in good actions, and how she and her husband practice the means of salvation at home.] She comes regularly to listen to the Word of God. We cannot help her too well with her preparation for Holy Communion because she has not learned to understand the German language well enough and it is even more difficult for her to express in German words what she does hear and understand. We have urged her husband to do the best he can with her. He has promised to do so and has repeated his promise.

R. himself is often very much moved by the sermons and during prayer hour and we hear that he considers himself and others lucky for having left Germany and having gone into solitude at Ebenezer. He says himself that his wife considers it one of the greatest benefits to have been given the opportunity to live with us.] Although we have greatly opposed this R.'s plan to bring his present wife here from Purysburg and have made the matter very difficult for him, our actions have nevertheless turned neither him nor his wife against me or my office. Rather they both show a right genuine love, confidence, and obedience toward me, which encourages me, . . .] These two people encourage me to continue to carry out my office, in JESUS' name, with love and devotion, so that neither love nor the justice of GOD shall be neglected. I know of no instance in the congregation in which seriousness and sharpness, if required by direst need, have done any damage, although they may have appeared to do so in the beginning. In this also God does very much more than we ask for or can understand.

[The 8th [9th], Aug. In the case of the three children who are to be admitted to Holy Communion for the first time, we are making all possible efforts in the school and privately to bend their poor frivolous hearts to a true surrender to Christ.] The children who are to go to Holy Communion for the first time are giving us much pleasure because they gladly come to us to get good advice, to learn verses, to say many good things, and to pray with us. We hope that JESUS, the lover of life, will also tear these tender souls [from all frivolity and disorder and draw them] into His community.

The 9th [10th], Aug. This afternoon my esteemed colleague and the four Salzburgers returned home from Savannah. By day and by night they have had to suffer a great deal from the rain that we have had for several days. In addition, the things they had in the boat could have been lost through a great misfortune if God had not come to their aid through some good people. We hope that we will be relieved of this arduous trip for some time because Mr. Montaigut has given good money for the counterfeit bills and we also have with us all of the things that were sent from London. The very praiseworthy Society has given new proof of their particular fondness for us by sending us twelve dozen quarts of good Madeira wine, of which we shall and will let the sick members of the congregation have some. May God give gracious and rich rewards for this and for all of the other good deeds done for us and for the Salzburgers.

The 10th [11th], Aug. A married woman came to church with her infant child and we have done the following for the first time. On the Sunday on which this occurs it is announced briefly to the congregation, and the members are asked to remain after the morning service in order to pray together for mother and child. The mother comes to the altar with her newborn child, and the pastor gives her in four points that which is applicable to her situation: 1) the particular spiritual and bodily benefits which she and her child have received from the fatherly hand of GOD; 2) that GOD asks nothing for this in return except heartfelt gratitude in word and deed; 3) the duties of a good mother toward her child; 4) that she needs for the execution of such duties the serious use of the Means of Salvation, especially prayer. Upon this a public prayer is offered for them and the benediction is pronounced over mother and child.

The 11th [12th], Aug. Mr. Causton has sent twenty pigs for the last Salzburgers. He intends to send more of them, also fowl, so that each family will have a small start in animal husbandry. [Our dear benefactors could hardly do more for the Salzburgers than they are doing.] They supply good provisions whenever it is possible, and Mr. Causton is always ready and eager to help in any way he can. And the transportation of provisions which formerly caused such great difficulty has seen a remarkable change since we made some representations about it to Mr. Oglethorpe. We often hear the dear people talk thankfully and edifyingly about the many good things which GOD has sent them through these worthy benefactors. For our part, we do not fail to remind them of these, in public and in private, and to urge them on to thankfulness and to intercession. One thing we have wished for a long time, namely, that the fields and building lots should be surveyed for the people so that they will no longer be prevented from doing the field work on which their heart is set. We wish this all the more because it now appears that Mr. Causton has made it fairly certain we will have to remain in this place.

The 12th [13th], Aug. Some time ago I asked the entire congregation to report impartially to me or my dear colleague anything that we should know about matters that they may have noticed in one or the other member of the congregation because we wanted to come to the aid of such a member at the start and help him in matters spiritual or physical, depending on his circumstances, and at the same time try to prevent further troubles. So far this request has not been in vain and God has not denied His blessing to the duties we performed for those who did not want to tell us themselves about distressing spiritual or physical circumstances which had befallen them.

[This afternoon a man came to me and reported that a Salzburger couple had had a misunderstanding and altercation because of their children and that he had been asked by the woman herself to tell me about it when the opportunity presented itself, since she could not do it herself because of bashfulness. When I passed their house after visiting the sick, she called me in and sorrowfully told me what had happened, but that God had soon been so gracious as to reconcile them right cordially. The man then joined us and regretted his anger and hastiness and said that he would let this occurrence serve him to his greater caution, vigilance, and prayer. I told them that even the heathens had advised angry people to say the ABC's before speaking a word in anger, and this pleased him very well in its application to us Christians. After punishing the oldest child, who had been to blame for this misunderstanding, the mother had driven her out of the house and forbidden her to return because she would not yet reform despite all hearty admonitions. However, her motherly heart had been greatly moved to compassion and pity when this girl sorrowfully asked with many tears and petitions whether the mother might not take her back if she became devout again, for which purpose she would pray diligently to our Lord.]

The very praiseworthy Society and the court chaplain Mr. Ziegenhagen did us a great favor when they transmitted our salary and the benefactions received from Germany in English copper coins. We will be able to serve the members of our congregation with these because they can not make out very well in purchasing necessities with the paper money in use here, since most of them do not know it and suffer frequent losses as a consequence.

The 13th [14th], Aug. Mrs. Resch is still very much grieved about her husband who was lost in the woods, and she requested today that some more people be sent into the forest to look for him. Her wish was granted in order to give her the assurance and comfort of knowing that we want to do everything in our power and to leave nothing undone that might bring him back, although this brings the constant worry that the search may increase our grief by causing someone else to get lost. The recent rainy weather has been followed by very hot days which exceed anything we have had this summer. But most of the people are used to this already and they use the hours of the morning and of the evening for their work. It is not as hot as people may think or as we have been told it would be. On the contrary, the heat can be stood very well. And during the night, as well as mornings and evenings, it is that much more lovely and pleasant.

The 14th [15th], Aug. Bartholomaeus Zent, who is not a Salzburger, announced his intention today to take Holy Communion. What he told me about his experience with that part of the Gospel he had heard so far proved to be very edifying to me. [Among other things he confessed that he had previously had to fight with many doubts but that recently the light of the Gospel had shown so brightly into his heart and that he had felt its strength so strongly that he was unable to thank God enough for His Grace in letting him come to Ebenezer.] Now he wishes nothing more than that his brother, who is still in Switzerland, might follow him over here; and he is sure that he would come if he could learn about the good things he can enjoy here, both spiritually and physically. He wants to send him a letter through us in the near future.

We learn of such joy in the Gospel and such happy feelings

about their physical existence from most of the people in the congregation. And even if previously they enjoyed better advantages in respect to physical care, they consider these to be very small in relation to other advantages they are now enjoying. I cannot express with words the joy and jubilation that is awakened in our hearts, when we learn such edifying facts about the members of the congregation. Nor can we express how happy we are to continue our office for old and young with increasing seriousness and purity of purpose, through the Grace of God.

The 16th [17th], Aug. During the noon hour I again had the congregation called together to read them some additional letters from London and Germany, together with an application, because I had not been able to finish them the other time. The content of the letter which Mr. Vernon had written to us was edifying and very important, and I used it for the special benefit of the congregation. In our present situation it is particularly heartening to all of us that God has awakened so many upright and prominent people in England and Germany who not only wish us well but also pray for us and care for us to the best of their ability. The letters we received, and also the presents, have given reliable proof of this; and we have made all of this known to the members of the congregation so that they will praise God and trust in His fatherly care.

In physical as well as spiritual matters, especially as regards the conduct of our office, the two of us benefit from the love of God to such an extent that we cannot marvel enough about it or praise HIM sufficiently for it. And since part of our thanks for all these blessings is due to so many worthy benefactors, friends, and pious Christians and their intercession for us, we ask that the LORD will richly reward them for these good deeds, which mean more to us than gold and silver, and repay them here and in eternity. On this occasion I also talked with the Salzburgers about some worldly matters which should be accomplished with communal labor next week, and for this I found them all quite ready. [The Commissioner now entrusts me more than previously with the management of external affairs. We live together in love and friendship.]

Through God's grace we are not embarrassed by even the smallest matters that occur in the community, and these dear people seek refuge with us with all of their problems, asking our advice and, whenever possible, taking advantage of our assistance in a manner that is very fine and pleasing to us. Depending on the nature of various circumstances, the name of God can be honored or abused even in small matters. May GOD continue to help us and may He never let us be without His divine light.

Toward evening, after the great heat had let up somewhat, we met with those who intended to go to Holy Communion in order to have penance and confession with them in the same manner in which we had them on previous occasions. At the beginning I reviewed part of what had been said last week about the regular Gospel, namely that the Jews' greatest sins have been 1) missing the invaluable period of grace, 2) being contemptuous of the grace offered to them in Christ; with this I led up to the remarkable words in Psalm 95:7-11 and discussed them for their instruction, warning, and comfort.

[The three boys who have been especially prepared up to now for Holy Communion are, to be sure, not as we might wish them; yet our dear Lord has granted some blessing to the private instruction and prayers that we have often had with them. Consequently, not only have they made a firm resolution to dedicate themselves honestly to the Lord and to use the means of salvation diligently for this purpose but also we can not deny them all goodness and change of heart, even if more is necessary for a complete breakthrough. We have also had their parents with us recently and emphatically reminded them of their duty toward these children; and on this occasion we also gave them many emphatic admonitions that they might not otherwise have accepted so well. Ott pleases me best of these three boys, and he also is well recommended by the Salzburgers who live around him and who are heartily happy about his change and therefore show him as much steadfast love as they can.] Unless he has tried it and experienced it himself, no one can really understand the benefits derived from private conversation and individual contact between a teacher and his listeners both old and young. As long as one does not get to know the individual characteristics of each but instead assumes this or that, so long his preaching and work might as well be to the wind, for the teaching cannot be adjusted for the benefit of those listeners who need it the most and are often waiting to hear something that will suit the condition of their souls.

In addition, one can avoid many wrong applications and set straight with a few words those timid souls who never regard the Gospel as applying to them. Of course, this method is embarrassing and almost unbearable for impudent people, but even for them it is not without value. At least (so they say) they are on guard against excesses, as much as is humanly possible for them, so that they will not be called to the pastor's house. And since we also take every opportunity to publicly denounce known cases of misconduct and, motivated by seriousness and heartfelt compassion, to present its ugliness publicly in our sermons, we can say that the two are bridle and bit, so to speak, for wayward people.

Master Kiefer, a good man from Purysburg, joined us with his family in order to have Holy Communion with the congregation. He hopes to derive much edification from being here. He is very anxious for Mr. Oglethorpe's arrival, for he hopes to get permission from him to live with the Salzburgers (where he is to be assigned some of the better land) for the sake of his and his family's spiritual well being. Mr. Oglethorpe is very fond of him because of his honesty and industry.[75]

The 17th [18th], Aug. Before beginning our morning service I announced to the congregation that three children were to be admitted to the Table of the Lord for the first time, but that first their knowledge of the Lutheran religion would be examined in public and their bond of baptism would be confirmed. After the hymn Come Holy Ghost had been sung, these three children stepped forward and were examined on the strength-giving verse John 3:16. In accordance with the direction given in this verse, the entire examination dealt with four areas, 1) the Originator, 2) the Acquirer of Salvation, 3) the Order and Means, and finally 4) Salvation itself, which can be achieved by people through God's order. God gave His blessing so that these children gave good answers to everything, proved their points with Gospel verses, compared and confirmed the matters discussed with the main parts of the catechism, and answered everything concerning theoretical and practical articles of the Christian doctrine in such a way that no human being could have spent this hour without edification and pleasure. This is reported only for the praise of God, who liveth among us.

At the end of the examination we made a special application for them and showed by means of questions and answers the love and kindness God had bestowed upon them during the recent preparation and especially during their infancy, when He washed away their sins with holy baptism, accepted them as His children, and formed a bond with them. And now that their bond of baptism was to be confirmed, we told them and others what the meaning of this baptismal bond should be, what the divine Trinity had promised them and what they, in turn, had promised their dear God.[76] We showed what a terrible sin it would be to break this bond with wanton sin and what it would take to renew it. Hereupon we all stood up and the children answered with a loud YES a number of questions regarding the renewal of their bond of baptism, belief in the triune God and how to show this with Godfearing conduct. At last they knelt down and I read a prepared prayer over them. Then I had them say the Lord's Prayer aloud and gave each of them the benediction with my hands laid upon him. This ceremony brought tears of joy to the parents of these and other children, and the rest of the people also were edified no little. God be praised for His unspeakably great Grace.

Toward evening I heard a married woman say that she had begged God to let her live long enough so that she could see her child go to Holy Communion for the first time. She would consider this a very great good deed of GOD. During the afternoon service we had a very violent rain and thunderstorm which lasted until evening. This prevented us from repeating the sermon we had delivered in the morning. Meanwhile, three boys and several other children came to my room to get some words of advice and to sing and pray with me. This I did, as much as my strength permitted. The LORD is the strength of my life.

The 18th [19th], Aug. The memory of those of the congregation who died as Christians often gives my soul much pleasure, especially when I re-read the things that were recorded about their edifying conduct while they were sick and dying. This very morning the example of the late Mrs. Geschwandel has been so refreshing and impressive for me that I was greatly encouraged to submerge myself deeper into Christ and His very great Grace. I shall never forget what God did for me while I was associating with her. Just when my soul was filled with these thoughts, Geschwandel came to me to talk about some worldly matters. I took the opportunity to tell him a number of things for his own good and urged him to follow the footsteps of his helpmate.

As agreed recently, the Salzburgers left this morning to repair the bridges which had been damaged by the high water. They will find it necessary to do a particularly great amount of work on one that is halfway between here and Abercorn. Once this is done, they will work together to build a slaughter house, for which purpose they have had to use the guard house until now. They are also making preparations to build a baking oven for the entire community. The clay needed for this must be fetched by boat from some other place because none is to be found in this vicinity. We should have had such an oven much earlier, but the river could not be used this summer because of the low water, and consequently no clay could be obtained. In the meantime we have baked our bread in iron pots just as well as it could have been done in an oven.

The 19th [20th], Aug. Mr. Oglethorpe has written me a very kind letter which confirms our opinion that he still has very fatherly feelings for us. Among other things he writes that he wants very much for me to learn the Indian language, saying that Mrs. Musgrove will give me a good opportunity to do so. I am to show her this letter and assure her that he will reward her for her troubles with this labor of love. I know this woman very well and have made the proposition to Court Chaplain Ziegenhagen to learn this language from her. As I see from this letter, he has talked to Mr. Oglethorpe about this. Mrs. Musgrove became a widow a short time ago, and, as has been suspected in England, she cannot come and stay with us in Ebenezer for any length of time because she has too much to do with her large household. Thus it would be necessary for me to stay with her for a while, but for the moment this would involve many difficulties.

The congregation is especially close to my heart, and frequently things occur which make even a one or two day trip very difficult. [If I should tell of their most uncommon love for me that binds me to Ebenezer, it would all be the pure truth, to be sure, yet it would be incomprehensible to some people and perhaps appear affected.] The truth of the matter is that both of us teachers have such close inner associations with our listeners that even our enemies can see, and we cannot praise God enough for it. Even if I went there only once a week and used the available boat it would take two days going via Abercorn. Via Purysburg it is further still. To be sure, the land route to the house of the said woman is shorter, but after a rain it means risking one's life because the horse must swim through deep and broad swamps and other watery places. Perhaps the roads will be improved after Mr. Oglethorpe's arrival, as they should be, because it is the mail route from Charleston to Savannah. In that case we could get there in four to six hours, spend the day, and return to the congregation. We could learn from her and write down so much in a few hours that we could spend several days studying it alone. May God bring our worthy Mr. Oglethorpe to us soon. I hope then many difficulties will be overcome more easily. When I showed her Mr. Oglethorpe's letter recently, Mrs. Musgrove promised me every possible assistance with the learning of the language.

The 20th [21st], Aug. Yesterday afternoon we again had a very heavy rain and violent thunderstorm which lasted until late evening. But God graciously prevented all damage. [While I was in Bacher's house this afternoon, Mrs. Bacher told me that her oldest daughter had become very frightened by the heavy lightning and thunder because she thought Doomsday was coming and she was not yet pious or devout. To be sure, the mother advised her to pray; but this did not calm her because the Lord Jesus looks only for a believing heart and, when He did not find one in her and many other people, they would fare badly. I took this opportunity in the presence of the mother and her two children to tell what one should do if one wishes to await Doomsday and the Last Judgment with joy. I also reminded her what I had told her and other children about a pious maiden who said that she had no more heart, that she felt her heart no more, that she had long ago given it to her Lord Jesus, as a result of which she was very comforted in all sorrow, even in death. This girl is well behaved and gives us good hope.]

Schweikert, the former servant of Baron von Reck, has become sick and very weak. We learned only the day before yesterday how serious his condition is and we now are making every effort to do something for his soul. He has paid close attention to the Word as given to him so far, and it seems that his heart contains some good seed. He gladly accepts good advice, is humble, regrets his sins, and wishes to be saved through Christ as a miserable and penitent sinner. When I visited him and asked how he had used his time, he told me that he had presented his sins to the Lord Jesus and that he had asked forgiveness and had prayed for the right preparation so that he could die a Christian. As he lives in my neighborhood, he promised to visit me in my room whenever his strength would permit. We care for his physical well-being as best we can and he acknowledges this with many thanks. [I hope the Lord Jesus will receive this soul too.]

The 21st [22nd], Aug. Mrs. Schweighofer came to me to talk about her physical and spiritual condition. God has let her and her husband be sick almost constantly, and whenever they got better they had to bear a cross either with their unschooled children or with some other matter. She wanted to conclude from this that God was angry with them because of her sins, etc. She shed the bitterest of tears and accused herself violently because of her unfaithfulness and sins. At the same time she expressed regret that her two older children were not really getting better, although she and her husband prayed for them, gave them advice, punished them, and did everything they could. Her humble words and expressions, coming as they did from a deep understanding of her misery, affected me no little.

I prayed to God to give me the wisdom to conduct myself with this person, who may be very worthy and lovable in the eyes of God, as God wills it in Isaiah 35:3-4. I remembered the two verses which I had applied last Sunday, the second after Trinity, namely, Isaiah 57:15 and 66:2; and I told her about the answers the children gave me yesterday in school when I asked some questions about these verses, namely, that God, to be sure, lived on high in holiness with the angels and the chosen ones, but that He also dwelled among the believers here on earth with all His gracious and loving presence. But there are two kinds of believers, the strong and the weak. The latter are like a weak and miserable infant who is not hated or cast away by his mother because of his weakness. Instead, his miserable condition constantly draws the eyes of the mother to the child, even ties her, so to speak, to the cradle and sickbed. In the same way our heavenly Father has maternal and loving feelings for His miserable children who sigh under the burden of their sins and crosses.

In said verse, Isaiah 66:2, it is written that the hand of God has made everything that exists. But among all the beautiful things that His hand has made, He likes best of all those who are miserable and of broken spirit, and who fear His word. He may overlook others, but He always looks upon them with kindness and love, etc. The Father likes to have the miserable sinners come to His Son, and for that reason He makes them feel their sins and imposes upon them many worldly hardships, so that they may flee to Him as they are, naked and bare. For it is great honor for the LORD JESUS that He can and will save the poor and lost sinners and make them welcome to the Father.

Because I found the preface to the appendix of the *Golden Treasure-Chest*[77] so impressive this morning I decided to read it to her, and I observed that this preface as well as the verses gave her spirit some benefit and contentment. I also showed her that God, who is the true Father, did not mean any harm when imposing the worldly cross which she has had to bear: God marks

His children with the blood and cross of His Son, just as a shepherd marks his sheep, so that all will know to whom they belong. I referred her to nature and to the weather we have had so far, saying that we do not always have sunshine but also rain, wind, etc., and all of these things that appear to be unfavorable actually help the fruit grow and ripen. Psalm 126. And in order to make her feel more at ease about her children I told her about Monica, the mother of Augustine, and how God, after many long prayers, had finally saved her son from his miserable condition and converted him to Christ after he had grown to be a man. I told her she and her husband should do what good parents must do and commend everything else to God. The children have cost Him more than they cost them and He will not abandon them.

At last, upon her request, we gave her some medicine and something else for her sick husband and she returned home in fairly good spirits. She also grieved that the weakness of her body had affected her memory so that could retain only very little of what she read and heard. This, in her opinion, was a disadvantage for her further development as a Christian. But I showed her that memory also was a gift of God and that He would not demand from her what He had not given her: if she could not remember much she could at least remember the one thing necessary and adjust her thinking accordingly. And I told her that it makes no difference to God, moreover, how much we remember, as long as we, like Mary, select JESUS, the only good, and in fact the best. She must have already learned, I continued, that the Holy Ghost will come to the aid of her memory in time of need and will remind her of many a verse that she needs but has not been able to think of.

Today we again had a great deal of rain and a heavy thunderstorm, and, because it lasted until late in the evening, we have again been prevented from holding our evening service, as was the case on the previous days of this week. Shortly before night a Salzburger came to me to report on the progress of the board cutting which some of them have wanted to start in the last few days. On this occasion I was able to engage him in a very edifying conversation which suited his circumstances. [His name is Peter Gruber, a man of little religious knowledge but of great loyalty and honesty, and a very industrious and untiring worker.] Like Mrs. Schweighofer, he was very much concerned about his sins, and he was particularly depressed and worried that he was not thankful enough for the inestimable grace of the Gospel. He regretted very much that he had spent his youth so wickedly; and now he was not making enough progress in his Christianity, despite his age, and he wondered whether God did not want him because he had not come to Him sooner. I gave him some examples of grown people who were converted to God after they had reached manhood and were as old as he was, even though they had spent their earlier years in sin, frivolity, or hypocrisy. Among others, I used the examples of the publican, from the Gospel recently heard, of the first chapter of Paul's first epistle to Timothy, and of the thief on the cross. Along with that I showed him that the Lord Jesus, during the days of His incarnation, accepted all people without discrimination as to age or rank. Whoever comes to Him will not be refused, for He still calls out: Come unto Me, all ye that labour, etc.

When I quoted the last verse, he testified that it had frequently given him a great deal of encouragement and was still very dear to him, etc. Besides, he believed that God would still have mercy upon him, and he thought so because God moved his heart every time he heard the preaching of His word. He also reported that a number of Salzburgers had decided to send a letter of thanks to Senior Urlsperger not only because they had received so much in the way of worldly benefits and spiritual love through his good offices, but especially because they now enjoyed in abundance the Word of God, for which they had left their fatherland. As he is very poor, I promised to have some necessary articles of clothing made for him. I also was able to learn from him which of the Salzburgers especially need material assistance. Some of them are still so shy that they will not tell about the things they lack, and we have to send for them and offer them the things they need.

The 22nd [23], Aug. Since the very rainy weather has made it rather cool and the air has become damp, the people are again taken with various weaknesses, diarrhea, dysentery, a feeling of exhaustion in all their limbs, etc. [Therefore they beg us so movingly for our medicines that it would be contrary to love to refuse it to them, especially since the results and the help they have received so far has brought our dear Lord much praise and thanks.] We are sorry that our supply of medicines has become so small that we can help only the few who have become seriously ill. May God Himself be our doctor and helper. [We are now beginning to answer the letters we recently received from Germany and London, and we plan to send the answers as soon as possible to

Charleston.] Until now we have never known whether or not our
letters would reach their destination; but, as we can see from the
news we have received, God has held His hand over them so that
none of them have been lost. We still have no one in Charleston
whom we can entrust with the delivery of our letters. It also is a
little difficult and risky to send them to Charleston when an opportunity presents itself, especially now that the mail service has
apparently stopped again.

When visiting the sick Schweighofer I learned that the medicine he received yesterday had done some good, but his entire
body was still weak and miserable. His wife soon handed me a
Bible so that I could look up and mark for her husband the
verses I had given her yesterday, and also to say something for
his edification. I did so in my conversation; and he said with
tears in his eyes that he knew that God would forgive all sins,
but that he found it hard to believe in the forgiveness of his own
sins because they appeared too great to him. Hereupon I looked
up the beautiful words of 1 John 2:1-2 and explained them a bit.
I also showed him that it was not his task or the task of mere
humans to recognize sin as sin.

As he knew and could see by the example of many frivolous
Christians, it costs our dear God a great deal to give people a true
knowledge of their misery. God does this so that man will crawl
to Christ as a miserable and heavily burdened worm, for Christ
came into this world for the benefit of sinners. Because of Satan's
deceit and because of his own wicked heart man often reverses
this and will not come to Christ with all his misery because he
does not feel his sins as he should, or because, in his own opinion,
he has become a better man. But this is as false as it would be for
a sick person to deny himself the use of a doctor or medicine
until the sickness is passed or until he does not feel it so much
any more.

Going further in this comparison I showed him that it is er-
roneous to think that Christ cannot help everyone, even the
greatest of sinners, and that it is a particular honor for the doctor
to cure even the most desperate illnesses. If God has done so
much for him as to bring him to true recognition of his misery,
He surely will not let him perish, because His works are never
left unfulfilled. I also reminded him not to worry about his lack
of feeling of divine comfort derived from the forgiveness of his
sins; and I again told him what had been said in detail about this
last Sunday in the application of the truths presented in the ser-

mon. All this, he said, had been very dear and useful to him at that time.

He reported that in Salzburg his heart had tasted the Grace of the Holy Ghost and divine comfort. This had given him the courage to confess freely what he believed to a number of people; and this in turn had made his heart much stronger and willing to suffer anything for Christ's sake. He had come to the true knowledge of the Evangelical doctrine through a small book of verses which he showed me and which he had purchased for a few pennies during his wanderings. This conversation again made me see how careful one must be in his sermons with *Usus epan-orthoticus*[78] if one does not want to depress timid souls. This experience will make me pray more for wisdom from God so that I can give each listener his right portion of the Word.

The 23rd [24th], Aug. The damp, cool, and changeable weather has made Moshammer's body weak and miserable. He came to see me after dinner and made me very happy by talking about various instances of active Christianity. Among other things, he spoke about the great misery of this life and the good purposes GOD has in mind, and he stated that He visited a great part of this misery on His children. I told him what had been said last night during evening prayer-hour about the believers and their happy state in death, after death, and in eternity; and this gave us an occasion for wholesome conversation. He remembered the last words of the late Madereiter, who had told him shortly before his departure from this world that it would not be long until the two were together again and would remain together for ever. He told of an honest [Catholic] innkeeper in Salzburg who said in his sickness that, if he had the choice between getting well or dying, he would not choose either himself but give himself over completely to God. Hereupon I said that God is greatly pleased by such resignation on the part of His children and by their complete surrender to His will, which is ever good, but that He is not displeased if they long for rest and release, as can be seen from the examples of some of God's best loved children, especially of Paul, who always wanted to be released and to be with Christ, in whose company alone he considered himself blessed. All of them were worried about their sins; and, since they wanted to love and praise God and their Saviour without sin, they all wished to go quickly to the abode of the saved.

The 24th [25th], Aug. After today's morning service the sick Moshammer requested Holy Communion, which was given to him by my dear colleague since I could not do it because of the weakness which I usually feel for several hours after each sermon. When I visited him after the afternoon service I found him weak in body but comforted and happy in his Saviour; and his expressions, which are always full of power and meaning, were again very edifying to me. How he humbled himself and accused himself violently because of the sins of his youth, unfaithfulness, and impurity! But how great was to him Christ and His ineffable Grace, which he could truly feel in his heart! We came upon the 84th Psalm, which I read to him while spending some time on an explanation of the last words, verses 12 and 13.[79] After praying with him I commended him to Christ, the healer of soul and body.

Kalker also has been sick and miserable for several days, but God has blessed the use of our medicines so much that he could come to my room and talk with me about his physical and spiritual condition. Like Moshammer, he is a good man who works with all seriousness for his salvation and who furnishes a good example for everyone with both his Christian attitude and the execution of his worldly duties. Our dear God has blessed for him very much the evening prayer hour, during which we have been studying the main doctrines of our entire Lutheran religion in question and answer form. He knows how much he is still lacking, and his present struggle for the ineffable Grace of God in Christ is much greater now than we have ever seen. His tears and words give testimony of his good insight into his corruption and into the immeasurable kindness of Christ. This example too shall drive me on to be quite faithful to my Saviour from now on and to dig deep and to fight for the jewel of salvation and race for it in competition with my dear congregation, so to speak. O GOD, teach us to see more and more our original sin and the depth of human corruption that comes therefrom, as well as the richness of the Grace of God which Christ has gained for the poor and miserable sinners through His merit. That is the cause toward which we have striven so far, with our own Christianity as well as with the guiding of young and old through our office. Thank God! it has not been without success.[80]

[The 25th, Aug. A short time ago Mrs. Brandner had a very severe diarrhea, of which she was cured by the use of a few medicines. Not long thereafter she suffered other serious attacks, which must have been largely due to the wet and cold weather to which she has been greatly exposed both by night and day in her poorly protected house. Finally she had violent dysentery;

and, because even the best medicines would not help her, we compelled her and her husband to move into another Salzburger's house that is better protected. This comfortable lodging suits her much better, of course, but her sickness is so acute that no medicines have any effect but the griping is still continuing in her lower stomach even though there has been no lack of necessary care and warm drinks. She is an upright Christian, and we will cordially praise our dear Lord if she can be kept alive. There are again many sicknesses and we have run out of most medicines. This drives us all the more to prayer in order to bring our patients to our Lord Jesus, the true physician of both soul and body, for which purpose we were also encouraged through an example in yesterday's Sunday Gospel for the 12th Sunday after Trinity.]

Our one orphan has been seriously ill for several days. It seems to be a hot fever and we do what we can, and at the same time we commend everything to the Lord, the Physician for all the wretched. She has been an unhealthy girl since birth. May God show particular mercy for her soul. [During her sickness we have observed some effects of the Divine Spirit in her.]

The 26th [27th], Aug. In last Saturday's evening prayer hour we finished with our consideration of the main doctrines of our Lutheran religion; and in this too we say: Ebenezer, the LORD has helped us so far. Truly, in this work of teaching He has helped many to a better understanding of the saving doctrines of the Gospel and the order of salvation and also to an increased seriousness in their Christian endeavors, all of which we must acknowledge for His glory. The blessings derived from this have made me decide to set aside about two months every year in which to go through the articles of faith and the duties of life, using this method with the children in school and with the entire congregation during evening prayer, and basing it in the future on the compendium of Pastor Freilinghausen.[81] Perhaps God will incline the heart of one of our benefactors so that we and our children can be provided with a number of copies of this book.

During our sermons we often quote from the small catechism of our dear Luther and use its words to explain and elaborate the matter under discussion. In our catechism exercises it has been my practice to work in similar fashion, namely, by way of explanation to lead young and old to the catechism and to make them understand unknown terms and expressions by using the equivalent words from the catechism. Through the Grace of God,

we now understand the peculiar expressions contained in this
small catechism more easily than formerly. Last night we again
took up the Psalms of David, which had been so useful to us
earlier, starting where we had left off. May GOD bless everything for His glory and our edification. Since Mr. Causton is
very insistent that my dear colleague's house be built soon, our
carpenters have started on it today, [even though we would have
preferred to wait until Mr. Oglethorpe's arrival.]

[The 27th [28th], Aug. Mr. Causton has sent some people here
who are to take back to Savannah ten of the oxen that were sent
to us for fresh meat. Fresh meat is lacking there, and they cannot
get any live cattle right away. In his letter he promises to send
us others soon in their stead so that we will not suffer any loss.]
The Salzburgers who recently started to cut boards are making
very good progress. They sold someone a few of them which had
been cut extremely well. As the heat is still very great and they
are not yet used to this work, they cannot do more than twenty
to thirty feet per day. We have urged them most earnestly to
spare themselves as much as possible at the beginning.

The 28th, Aug. So far the sick Huber girl has been under the
care of the good Moshammer and his wife, who care for her as
if they were her real father and mother. Today GOD so arranged
it that Mrs. Bacher and her husband offered to take the sick girl
into their house and to care for her until God should change her
condition. They did so because they felt sorry for Moshammer
and for his wife, who is also in bad health. We want very much
to reward them for this deed of love. In this way Moshammer,
his wife, and a single Salzburger who is also sickly can get better
care in his own well built house. All the people in this house fear
the LORD; and they are now experiencing the benefit of a true
fear of God, much to the great comfort of their hearts.

Among other things, Moshammer told me that during the
night, when he was at his weakest, he learned the meaning of
the words: The Lord is the strength of my life. And, even if his
mind is sometimes so weak that he can hardly remember anything, he still feels in his heart Christ and His comfort, and this
brings him the best of rest. The weak Schweighofer sat by his
bed and looked up some verses for me from Sirach which had
been particularly comforting to him in his miserable physical and
spiritual condition. They are chapter 2, v. 1 and chapter 17, v. 28.[82]

Many Salzburgers have asked my dear colleague to write letters

for them to Germany, for which they have given him the material
and in some cases the words.[83] Now they are much more used to
this land and the manner of living here than they were at the
beginning, and they recognize more and more the spiritual and
worldly benefits as well as other advantages they enjoy as compared to other Salzburgers and other people. This gives them a
great deal of material for praising God and for writing letters to
Germany, which, it is hoped, will also provide edification.

The 30th, Aug. Moshammer and his wife are very weak of body
and we lack the medicines for the sort of care they require, yet
what little we can give them from the available supply helps to
relieve them of some discomfort and to improve their condition.
I cannot express how much they praise God for this medicine,
the effect of which they have felt previously and also feel now.
They are pleased that these medicines do not react with violence
and strong movement but instead are mild and work gradually,[84]
following the course of nature; and they describe this in simple
and very well chosen words. They also trust that the Lord, who
looks down from heaven upon the needs of His children, will
supply us with more medicines in the future.

The wife expressed surprise over the great goodness and love
of God, who acts like a mother who imposes upon her child only
a small and light burden while carrying the heaviest portion herself. She mentioned that she had heard this comparison a number
of times in sermons dealing with the fatherly love of God. She
had also been told by a pious woman that a few days ago I had
attempted to instill in a Salzburger woman a childlike love and
sweet trust in the friendly Lamb of God by using the parable of
the lamb in John 1:29 and by telling her that a child is not
afraid of a lamb but likes to play with it, etc. This made her very
happy. She accused her distrustful and unbelieving heart, but her
husband reminded her that she must not pay too much attention
to her heart and what it says but, instead, she must consider the
Word of God. Let Your Word make me more certain, etc., I John
3:20. Before leaving I read them the verse Psalm 68:20-21, which
they liked very much.

The 31st, Aug. Although Moshammer and his wife are still
weak of body they are very happy in their Saviour. He spoke
very impressively about the nothingness of worldly joy and pleasure. He also recalled the words from Psalm 91:14-16, which say
emphatically: I will, I will, etc. These, as well as the words from
Isaiah 41:10, 13, 14, gave him much comfort. Today he had some

bitter struggles and temptations within his soul, but he overcame them with Christ's help. He complained very much about reason which sometimes fights against belief.

The 1st, September. Until now I have seen N. N. more often sad than gay and happy. Today I had him come to see me about his worldly affairs, and at this opportunity God made him open up his heart to me. He told me very sadly that the sins he had committed in his youth weigh so heavily on his conscience that he often thinks he is lost. To be sure, he remembers the examples of the great sinners in the Bible who received the Grace of God, but this did not give any comfort to his spirit because his repentance and penance were not to be compared with theirs. He said that he was right with God and that his heart experienced the comfort of the Gospel when he left Salzburg. But after that he had served a master who not only kept him from hearing and studying the Word of God by overburdening him with work but also laughed at him and called him a Papist whenever he knelt down to pray or read. Thus it had gradually come about that he had lost all the good, and especially the zeal that had been in him. He considered it a very great and kind deed of God to have let him out of these conditions and to America, where he has more opportunity to work for his salvation with fear and trembling and without being interfered with by anyone. He also said that he still has a brother in N., whose master treats him very well, but he is afraid that all is not well with his soul.

Praying to God, I made every effort to comfort this man, who was so downcast and sad over sin, by telling him what I had experienced during my conversion and by reading him some selected Bible verses as well as some examples. Among other things I told him that, when God was about to convert me from this world and its sin, I had read about the lives of several people and about the way God had guided them during and after their conversion. Here I had found that the others had experienced a very hard and fearful struggle; and, when I compared my penitence and penance with theirs, I could hardly find any comparison. This gave me much cause for worry, but in my distress I went to a pious and experienced teacher at the University (it was the late Dr. Anton) and told him about my troubles. He gave me approximately this answer: I should examine myself to see whether my remorse was such that the sins I had committed so troubled me that I wished I had never committed them and that I would rather die than to commit them again. Whatever I seemed to lack in remorse and heart-felt sadness at the beginning, God would grant me as I progressed further in my Christianity and strengthened myself in goodness. From now on the most important thing for me was fidelity and faith.

I applied this to his condition and at the same time referred him to some verses such as I Timothy 1:15, which shows that Paul considered himself the greatest and grandest of sinners and still did not despair but added that he had received mercy as an example for subsequent great sinners who should consider: If GOD gave Grace for the conversion of this terrible persecutor of His flock, etc. Also Matthew 11:28, Come unto me all ye, etc. I explained that He does not call unto Himself only one kind of sin-burdened sinners but all of them, even those who have the greatest burdens on their souls. And since during last week's prayer hours some people were moved by the expression that the greatest sinners have the greatest share in Christ, the exterminator of sin, and must not be afraid of Him, I explained this to him by using a parable about a doctor who always sees his weakest and sickest patients first and most often and who is pleased when such very sick persons call for him.

I told him that he only had to look into the New Testament and he would find that the Lord said that He would not send away anyone who came to Him. Furthermore, he would not find an example of any suffering and miserable person that had been chased away or treated harshly by Christ: on the contrary, He always sought out the greatest sinners and acted kindly toward them, and He had great patience with the shortcomings of His children, as can be seen especially well from the example of the disciples of Christ whom Christ continued to comfort, although they swayed from one side to the other, so to speak. He also should know what is written in Luke 15 about the prodigal son and the very loving attitude the father showed toward him, which is not a description of a man but of Christ himself who used this to show the heart of His Father, which He knows best, and its attitude toward repentant sinners.

I advised him to take heart and to approach his sweet Saviour and to put more faith into the Gospel and its beautiful verses than into the outbursts of his heart. With this, I explained to him the words from I John 3:19-20 and asked him whether he would believe his heart if it told him that he was good enough and did not need to prove his righteousness through Christian conduct. When he answered "No," I applied this to his present condition in which his heart wants to deny him the grace of God and lead him to desperation. I explained that he did not have to wait any longer for the distinct feeling of comfort which he formerly had because God preferred us to look upon and trust the Word He gave us sinners rather than to rely on the feeling of our heart. At last I gave him a hymn to take home: Away, my heart, etc. Upon leaving he testified that God had strengthened and comforted him and that he would come to see us more often. He also promised to pray diligently and to come to Holy Communion more frequently, especially since his last attendance had given him noticeable strength.

[Continuation of the Diary

Tuesday, 2 Sept. 1735

Our diary and letters are now packed together and, because the post no longer goes through our place, one of us in person will have to go to Savannah and ask Mr. Causton about an opportunity to send the letters to London. He has too much business, and therefore we cannot accomplish as much by letter as we can orally.]

The 2nd, Sept. Today about noon Moshammer passed happily away to JESUS. As his leave from this vale of tears had been anticipated during the morning hours, a number of pious people of both sexes went to visit him. At first my dear colleague, and after his departure I prayed with them and thanked our dear God for all the good deeds, spiritual and physical, which had been done unto Moshammer while sick and while dying, and we commended him to the wounds and arms of his Saviour. A few days before his end he was so weak that he could barely move his limbs and the fever had become so hot that at times he could not use his mind very well. At one time the pains in his body were so great that he thought he could stand them no longer. He constantly prayed to God for patience and he was granted it in rich measure.

Once, when I went to his bed, his pious wife said among other things that God had given her husband a great cross but also great patience. O how good it would be, if people stored away the good during their days of good health. Another man who had sat up with him during the night and watched his attacks told his wife that he had never seen such a patient man. Just as his illness was very painful, it was God's pleasure also to let him have a hard [death] struggle. But even during the worst attacks he continued to look steadily and faithfully upon Jesus, whose heart he had learned to know well during his lifetime, and he

made good use of all the things we called out to him. All his life
he was particularly fond of the hymn: LORD JESUS Christ, light
of my life, etc., which I read to him a few hours before his end
when he still had his mental powers (although somewhat weakened) and could still affirm the blessing I spoke over him with
Amen and by nodding his head. He was very happy when we
prayed with him; and he used what little strength he regained
during the cool morning hours for prayer, thinking, and constant sighing.

When he realized that his head was becoming weak, he told
those who were with him that now they had to pray for him all
the more because he would soon lose his mind. Christ's intercession at the right hand of the Father, and the intercession of the
faithful on this earth meant a great deal to him. And he liked
the Lord's Prayer very much because in it one believer prays for
another. Just before his end certain verses were worth more to
him than all the treasures of this earth. Some of them were: It is
done, etc., I know that my Redeemer liveth, etc. His wife noticed
that he would frequently stretch out his hands with eagerness
and then fold them again as if he wanted to embrace the Lord
Jesus and draw himself quite close to Him. When doing this, he
would say: "O how worthless are all things. Nothing matters,
absolutely nothing except the suffering and death of our Lord."

He was a great admirer of Arnd's *True Christianity* and he
knew some of the lessons in it so well that he often quoted the
most strength-giving words and expressions from them, much to
my edification. He particularly liked the fact that the late teacher
put so much emphasis on the renunciation of the world and the
self. He himself had learned how necessary and salutary this is,
although it is a bitter cross for the Old Adam. His mind was
always filled with edifying thoughts and he always knew how to
say the right thing to people, depending on their condition, and
he did so with all humility and simplicity. He worked on his
neighbor without being overly zealous in his efforts to convert;
and he knew how to be patient because God had shown so much
patience and forbearance with him. All of those who came to
him, an experienced Christian, with their inner struggles or trials
cannot give enough praise to his fine understanding and good advice. All of us in the congregation lost something very precious
with him.

The 3rd and 4th, Sept. Because I had to post our letters to
London and also to speak with Mr. Causton about several im-

portant matters, I had to take on the trip to Savannah this time. We went via Purysburg. Because of the great heat about midday I stopped at the house of a pious man where I usually lodge; and again this time I was told in moving terms about the plight of their young people who are becoming wilder and wilder by the day because they have no school. And the smaller children are a burden to their parents at home, at a time when they could very well go to school because they have time for it, but when they get bigger they will not have the time. I had set out with the very weighty words Paul wrote to the Colossians, 3:12, ff., which God had blessed so much for us during last night's prayer hour, and before we arrived in Purysburg I had talked them over with the Salzburgers traveling with me. Therefore, when the need of these children was pictured to me, I was so impressed by these words that I thought God wanted to give me an opportunity to put them into practice.

I sent for the man whom they had proposed to be their schoolmaster and agreed with him to try him for a quarter of a year and, if he applied himself, to give him two pounds sterling per quarter so that the parents, who are very poor, would have to contribute only a little. The man is well regarded by the people, he is their Sunday reader, and has a good understanding and the gift to deal with people and children. Besides, he is not without fear of GOD. I cannot describe how pleased the parents were over this school arrangement. A certain benefactress from Hanover has sent a gift with the request that some of the money be used for the spiritual benefit of the Indians, but since there is little opportunity for that at present we will let her gift bear fruit meanwhile in this manner. But we shall report this to our benefactors and ask for their views in the matter. With this in mind, we have engaged the schoolmaster for not more than a quarter of a year. He will deal with the children in every way in accordance with the methods we have promised to give to him in writing. And since we have occasion to go to Purysburg now and then we will soon be able to judge his diligence by examining the children. May the heavenly Father let this undertaking be commended to His blessing. [Whoever knows the miserable circumstances, both spiritual and physical, in which many people in Purysburg are caught will have a heartfelt pity for them.]

In Savannah Mr. Causton received me in most friendly and loving fashion. The Salzburgers that were with me also enjoyed such good treatment that they were amazed. He himself took our letters for posting, hoping to be able to send them off very soon. He showed me what remarkable things the Indians had to say when they recently received some presents here. They had had an interpreter write it down on a buffalo hide in the English language. [They were very remarkable circumstances that will certainly be well received in England and Germany. A copy was sent to the Trustees with Captain Thomson.] I took care of my affairs as quickly as possible in order to get back home soon, for I am not happy or content anywhere except in our beloved Ebenezer.

The 5th, Sept. Yesterday and the day before the heat was greater than any we have had this year. Last night it changed and it looked as if would rain, but it did not. This morning I returned to Ebenezer via Abercorn and arrived there fresh and in good spirits. God be praised for all the good deeds done unto me and ours.

The 6th, Sept. [Schweikert is, to be sure, somewhat healthier; but, because he cannot get entirely well, he imagines that he cannot stand the air here. Therefore he has asked me for a recommendation to a planter he knows in Carolina so that the latter will make him chief overseer over his black slaves. But I shall not let myself get entangled in this. He asked Mr. Causton for permission to live in Ebenezer with the Salzburgers and also enjoys provisions; and therefore he must take his request to Mr. Causton.] In the month of June we received a supply of Indian peas for planting and we have distributed them from time to time to the Salzburgers. Like Indian beans, they grow in a variety of soils. They are much smaller than German peas, but they have a fairly good flavor.

The 7th, Sept. Mrs. Moshammer, who is still weak, receives visits from many Salzburgers, and she derives much strength from their conversation and from reading materials from the Bible and from other spiritual books. She has always been a particularly great lover of the Word of God. As she has always prayed diligently, she has acquired a large treasure of verses and edifying truths during the days of her good health, and it gives you great pleasure to listen to her. All the dear people whom I found at my [her] house today agreed that God could not have given them anything better than to bring them into this wilderness where He gives them so much sweetness through the preaching of His word that the denial of all earthly goods is very easy for them and gives them very little trouble. They said they had never once regretted it that they had come here [and since God has so far done us the mercy of not letting a single person of our congregation go unconverted into eternity, we may hope that God will still keep carving and working on the remaining impenitents until He has them accord to His will.] One of them reported that he and some others were very much moved during last night's prayer hour when they learned about the pitiful condition of some people in this vicinity [in Purysburg]. They had agreed that they did not acknowledge it enough and gave too little thanks for the good which God did unto their bodies and souls. The LORD does all of this, He must be praised here on earth and in eternity. Psalm 46:5-6.

The 8th, Sept. Since Saturday we have had such cool weather that we are rather anxious. It is rarely this cool in Germany at this time. The people are now busy planting turnips, radishes, and cabbage, in which they had been hindered until now by the great heat, which was greater at the beginning of this fall than it was in the summer. Schweiger has brought his bride from Purysburg to us and he will be married to her tomorrow. Their banns have been published three times, not only in Ebenezer but also in Purysburg, and the pastor there has given me written assurance that there is no objection on their part. In matters concerning holy matrimony it is necessary in this country to exercise every possible caution with people whom you do not know.

The 9th, Sept. I brought a good supply of coarse linen back from Savannah so that the poor among us can make themselves trousers, shirts, and other very necessary things from it. Those who still have some money do not want to take away this benefit from those who are poorer, and this is a good sign. [Rauner and his wife and child will get something even though they are not Salzburgers. They are all behaving very well, and we hope that this benefaction will be well spent on them. When those who are not Salzburgers conduct themselves in their lives like upright Salzburgers, they are treated like other Salzburgers too.] Recently many members of the congregation have been supplied with very much needed shoes, which they wear on Sunday. This morning Schweiger was married to the woman he had brought to us from Purysburg. It is our custom to give some instructions to the people who are to be married and to tell them what holy matrimony means and how one should conduct himself according to the instructions of the divine word. In order that they may better remember in later life the duties that are impressed upon them we usually select a well known verse as a basis for our instruction. Schweiger's bride is the daughter of a schoolmaster who died soon after his arrival in Purysburg. Her mother still lives in Purysburg with three more daughters, two of whom are still quite young. [But she would rather move with all her family to us than to remain there.]

The 10th, Sept. For some weeks Rauschgott has been sick and bedridden and he has gradually got so sick that now there is little hope for his recovery. As soon as I received news of his illness I not only recommended the use of several medicines (until now he has faithfully followed Mr. Zwifler's advice and taken his medicines), but also arranged for better bodily care for him and engaged a woman who is to wait on him day and night. For some time his illness has been accompanied by loss of hearing and near deafness, which makes it difficult for us and other pious people who visit him to work with him properly. You must talk very loud if he is to understand everything. [He is one of the lax and lazy Christians in the community. He has always made good resolutions but has not kept them. For some time he appeared to have become more serious, and led us to believe that his eyes were beginning to open and that God was showing more mercy to his heart.]

A good man who waited on him during the night told me this morning that he had begun to pray in great earnest and had presented himself to God as a great sinner. When I started to talk to him this morning in an effort to move his conscience he struggled to get his hands out from under the cover and folded them as well as his weak state would permit. He showed by his expression and with words that he is sorry about all of his sins and that he intends to ask in prayer that they be forgiven him for Christ's sake. I reminded him of the story in the 4th book of Moses [Numbers] 21:9 and, by way of application, used the words of Christ from John 3:14-15 and those of Paul from I Timothy 1:15. This is a faithful saying, etc. Upon my request, he recited this power-verse in a weak but audible voice, to the words: Of whom I am chief.

While I was writing this about Rauschgott, my dear colleague came from him to report that he had just died. After my departure his ability to hear and speak had dwindled more and more. Thus my dear colleague could do nothing but to pray for him with the people present. He himself had kept his hands folded, with his eyes looking straight toward heaven and his lips constantly moving in earnest prayer. A pious Salzburger who had read to him and prayed with him a few days ago assured us that he had found in the late Rauschgott a great love and longing for everything that is good and that he was always happy when he came to see him for such purpose. And we know of him that he liked to have us with him and liked to pray with us. He believed that he had contracted this illness not long ago when he had to ride through some deep water in order to follow the oxen he was herding. When he sat down in his wet clothes he felt the ill effects on his body almost immediately.

The 11th, Sept. Mrs. Kalcher has been sickly for some weeks and bedridden at times, during which period God has shown her soul much mercy. Yesterday evening she came to see me in order to talk about the condition of her soul. Both of them are very serious about working for their salvation. Mrs. Bacher was not happy on her sickbed because, as she said, she did not know how she stood with her Saviour. She knew, she told me, that God had given her Grace for her conversion and that she had tasted the fatherly love of God in other ways: but this taste had disappeared and now she could feel nothing but sin and shame, which made her afraid to go into eternity. We have found in many members of the congregation that they pay more attention to the feeling of their hearts than to the promise of God. For this reason we must be careful while preaching of the Gospel to avoid showing them only the taste and noticeable enjoyment of the Grace of God which the heart experiences after conversion.

In such cases we usually show such persons the characteristic signs of true conversion: 1) since in this state they feel sin with all of its bitterness, it is a good enough sign if they find within themselves a true hatred of sin, and if they dislike themselves because of the sin that is within them which prevents them from truly loving and serving God. 2) We usually give them some of the well known verses of the Gospel in which GOD offers His grace to greatest of sinners and actually bestows it on those poor and miserable ones who drag themselves with their burden of sin to the Lamb of God, Jesus Christ. O, how often we have offered thanks to the true Merciful One for offering grace and forgiveness not only to those people who follow His order, but also to the poor and miserable ones who are burdened and pitiful, afraid and fainthearted, and that He is particularly friendly toward these simple souls. 3) Since such examples make a deep impression on the mind, we usually show such grieving souls the persons described in Holy Writ as great sinners but also as favored children of God who are not cast away by God even if they show many faults and weaknesses after they have been converted and forgiven. When talking to Mrs. Bacher I recalled, among other things, the example of the late Arnd who prayed on his deathbed, shortly before his blessed demise: LORD, do not pass judgment on Thy servant. I opened up this passage in his book *True Christianity* and used the occasion to tell her various things that fitted this example.

Upon my request her two daughters recited a verse for their sick mother which applied to her condition, namely: Lord thou hearest the cries of the suffers, etc.; and these words contributed not a little to her comfort. Her husband had sung for her a hymn from Schaitberger's book,[85] which she could not praise enough. And, because it was also very edifying for me, I will include it in this diary for our further edification and, it is hoped, for that of others: 1. My Jesus is well disposed to me, [I was baptized at His command. At that time I drew Jesus to myself and He redeemed me for death. I am joyful and comforted because my Jesus has redeemed me. 2. I wish nothing but to die soon so that the cool earth will cover me: God will surely make me an heir of His grace when He awakens me. Therefore give me only the epitaph that Jesus' death is my life. 3. Praise God! My end is near, my greatest struggle is now done. Jesus is stretching out His hand to me, for it is He who brings me bliss. Therefore I ask again through the blood of Christ: God give me a blessed end. 4. In this hope I shall live, and so I shall die, and not otherwise. My Jesus will give me everything that my weakness is now lacking; and if I die with Jesus here, Jesus will still live with me. 5. So be comforted, dear soul, for thou art in thy Jesus' hand. If thou leavest the cave of the body, thou shall come into thy true Fatherland; for here there is nothing but trial and tribulation, while there there is eternal joy. 6. Thy suffering is nearly over, hold still, dear soul. After it will come a blessed ending and bring the last goal of life. Upon this period of suffering now follows the crown of heaven and splendor. 7. Help me willingly to bear the cross Thou hast laid upon me, and let me, Lord, not despair under my heavy burden of sin. Oh God, my sin is great and heavy, yet Thy mercy is still much greater. 8. I know Thou shalt remain with me as long as I am here in this life. I shall inscribe Thy name on my heart and on my gravestone. Even in my last death-throes Thou shalt be with me, my Jesus. 9. Jesus, life of my soul, stay with me in my plight. I have willingly resigned myself to live and die in Thee; for if I have Thee as a protector, then I shall defy death and the devil. 10. Let me die in faith when I depart from this world; and make me an heir of thy grace there with thy chosen ones. And grant me, Lord Jesus, that I die in bliss.]

This song fits the melody: Whoever lets the dear Lord rule.[86] Oh Lord Jesus be Thou our One and All in life, suffering, and death, and in all eternity of eternities. Amen. I selected for her and her husband another hymn, which resembles the previous one a great deal: As nothing is more common than death, etc.

[The 12th, Sept. Schweighofer is so run down by his almost constant physical weakness that he sometimes seems to lose his mental faculties and become rather childish. Therefore he sometimes does something without reflection that he greatly regrets afterwards when he sees the harm it has done. Recently his wife shed many tears about this at my house. A few days ago he intentionally drank more strong drink than he can hold in order to vomit and relieve his stomach of the pressure and illness he felt. He did succeed in vomiting; yet, because the excessive drink, especially since he got drunk from it, was not only a sin in itself but also offended some neighbors, I summoned him to me and reprimanded him of this sin through God's word. He was so humbled by this that he not only rued it heartily in my room but also, contrary to all my expectations, went to his neighbors' house and asked their pardon for it. To be sure, he well knew that drunkenness is a grave sin that the dear Son of God had to expiate on the cross with painful thirst and a drink of vinegar and gall. Nevertheless he felt that God would not count it against him because he had used it as a means of vomiting and thereby getting well. That this honest man had humiliated himself even before other people who knew about the sin is especially pleasing to us because now we can better handle Ruprecht Zittrauer, who some time ago got completely drunk in Purysburg and more recently here. Also, we can talk with him as seriously as his customary life deserves, for we will not have to suffer any reproaches from him or from some others of the congregation who consider us partial. Sins are sins, no matter by whom they are committed. Meanwhile they must be judged and remedied according to the circumstances of the case.

[Recently another case occurred that would seem very paradoxical to anyone who did not weigh the circumstances. On the Sunday when he wished to receive Holy Communion, the late Moshammer sent to me to say that wine was very repugnant to him and that he therefore wished to take water in its place. Since I well knew his weakmindedness, which fluctuates in him, I gave the messenger the answer that this could not be his opinion because Moshammer was much too well instructed in God's word and that one could in no way deviate from the institution of Holy Communion and the external means that are ordained for it. Rather I believed he meant that, because of his weak condition, we should use not pure wine but wine with water mixed with it. When I visited him after Holy Communion, the first thing he did was to confess his error to me and ask for forgiveness. He had sent me this message during his mental weakness; yet he felt great distress about it because he was afraid that, although we had to be sure worked on him and others a great deal up to now, we might still find little good and such crass ignorance. I tried to disabuse him of these ideas and worries and assured him that I did not attribute such ignorance of the teaching of Holy Communion. I hope that these two examples will not be known by anyone who cannot comprehend them.

The 13th, Sept. [The boy from Purysburg who was sent to us some time ago to our school is, to be sure, right stupid; yet he is industrious and willing so that he is advancing somewhat in reading and in knowledge of divine truth. He gladly accepts the admonitions we give him privately for the good of his soul and promises much good so that we hope he will someday surrender his heart to the Lord Jesus.]

There is a kind of chestnut that grows around our place which in our opinion has a much better flavor than that which is sold in Germany. They are only half as large as those in Germany and they grow on small, low bushes. It is possible to gather a large quantity in a short time.[87]

The 14th, Sept. Yesterday toward evening three of the Lutherans from Purysburg came to see us. The recently engaged schoolmaster was among them. He asked for some books for the poor children and also for advice regarding the right manner of treating the children. We were happy to serve him both orally and in writing. Our method pleased him and he promised to follow it faithfully. And since we had recently received a number of ABC tables as well as a good supply of ABC books and catechisms from Germany, we gave him some of each so that he would have some books in his school which would help the children very much in their studies. He is to keep and take care of these books at all times and must not let the children take them home. [This man, like the other people in Purysburg, wishes we would take charge of this school and arrange everything there according to our desires; yet for good reasons we can not agree to this even though we do not refuse to help with advice and to visit it whenever our official duties take us there. The schoolmaster also agrees with us to take into the school the orphaned Reformed children who are straying around, if it is requested. This time I repeated what I had recently mentioned, namely, that I can contribute something for the establishment of this school only in so far as it is approved by our benefactors when it is reported to them.]

The 15th, Sept. Although Mrs. Moshammer is a little better she is still very weak in her entire body and we lack the medicines which have helped her and others in a similar condition. [One cannot speak to her about Mr. Zwifler and his cure, especially since she has a good example of his unsuccessful cure at home in the pious Herzog, who vomitted blood after taking one of his emetics and has been miserable ever since and seems to have an internal injury. For want of medicines from Halle we have advised the people to use the medicines that Mr. Zwifler prescribes for their sickness in God's name and with heartfelt prayers. Some of them have done this but they have obviously experienced the contrary effects on their bodies and have complained very much about it during our visits. We tell him that very clearly and beg him to adjust himself to their weakness, but he denounces this as fault-finding and obstinacy and is very angry. In these circumstances we can no longer expect the good people to make use of his advice and cures. Some of them have become stronger and healthier after discarding his medicines. We try to serve them with warm drinks, especially in the case of diarrhea and dysentery and contribute to their bodily care as much as possible. This is accepted with much praise of God and has sometimes been of value to their physical condition.]

The worthy Mrs. Brand has had to struggle with dysentery for some time. We were able to supply her with medicine at the start but it was soon used up. Through God's blessing her sickness has finally been cured with the administration of much tea and coffee. Mrs. Bacher has become much better after using a household remedy which some other woman had given her, and warm drink helps her a great deal. We have used some money from the poor box to get some tea, coffee, and sugar for the use of the sick. We would be able to do without these things much more easily if it were possible to get the other things necessary for good bodily care.

Mrs. Moshammer frequently offers thanks to God that she is not suffering any pain during her sickness; for this makes it possible for her to prepare her spirits more calmly and steadily for eternity, and she spends her time in constant prayer and supplication. Her contentment with divine government is uncommon and she speaks and sings about nothing but divine benefactions; and she marvels that God does so much good unto so great a sinner. She often recalls the words which she recited to me with great emotion: I am satisfied as long as I am going to heaven and am not separated from Jesus. Everybody that visits her derives edification from his visits because the Grace of God is revealed in her in a most unusual fashion. We would be happy and would thank God for it if we could keep her in the congregation for a long time.

The 16th, Sept. A Salzburger, Herzog by name, returned to me Wudrian's *School of the Cross*,[88] which he had borrowed some time ago and had made good use of in the meantime. When I asked him about the condition of his body and soul he gave me a very fine reply. Among other things, he said that he could not work very hard because he lacked the physical strength. God was now calling him to use his perhaps short period of grace to prepare himself for eternity, and he considered this his dearest occupation, for he experienced the love and friendliness of his Saviour very sweetly while his former scruples and legalistic representations were losing themselves more and more. If it were God's will he would like to live amongst us longer, but he thought it might be better to die because a longer life might make him sin more, as his heart was very wicked, etc. But he is still afraid of death, he says, and does not know whether he might not deny God in the end, when sickness and other suffering become too much for him.

I quoted him the words from last Sunday's Gospel, Matthew 6:34: Take therefore no thought for the morrow; and I told him that I too had burdened myself unnecessarily with these sorrows for some time, fearing that I would not remain steadfast and would perhaps be disloyal in the future. But when I told a good Christian about this worry, he gave me the following answer: I should make use, in prayer and inner struggle, of the present day and of the grace at hand, for God would take care of the morrow and of future times. This explanation made him most happy and content. And to help him rid himself of these terrible thoughts of death with God's blessing we gave him the 57th chapter of John Arnd's *True Christianity* to take home. We also showed him in this chapter the words of a patriarch who said: O LORD, let me die so that I may sin no longer. During the sermons as well as at home this dear man has been showing a special longing for the Word of God. When visiting him you cannot do him a greater favor than to pray with him and to tell him something about our Saviour.

The 17th, Sept. Recently our days have again become very hot, but at night it is so cool that we have to take care to keep warm for the sake of our health, which is easily damaged by a cold. I must have committed some oversight that has caused me to suffer an indisposition [a very violent diarrhea with many pains]. However, by following the advice Professor Junker sent us some time ago in writing and by keeping my body warm with an abundance of warm drinks and staying quietly at home while doing so, I have been quickly cured of this evil [that is often very dangerous here in this land. At the same time I took some pulver antispasmodicus. We are lacking the pulvis contra acred. that is usually prescribed for it. Today the post rode again through our place from Savannah to Charleston. Time will tell whether or not it will continue. It would please us very much, for then we could send letters to Charleston and Savannah.

[The 18th, Sept. A few weeks ago Mr. Zwifler caused many people in the community a great annoyance, which has caused us much trouble until now. Recently he swore most dreadfully that he would no longer care externally for the people who did not wish to take his internal cures, and the —— might take him if he did. We have often presented this sorry affair to God in our prayers so that He will give us wisdom and strength to dispose of this vexation; and we have not reprimanded him for it until after having thoroughly prayed about the whole matter. Today I sent for him and remonstrated with him about this dreadful cursing that is in itself a dreadful sin and therefore causes a vexation which is greater in his case than in that of other people because in certain ways he is considered a leader in the community and as well as a doctor and has lost his standing in the community even more through such unreasoned actions.

[I told him I was much afraid and did not know what to do,

and I asked him to make me some suggestions as to how we could dispose of this sin that was now public. To be sure, he well acknowledged that he had used such hard expressions and had committed a sin; yet he thought that I and the people were to blame for it because they had scorned him in his cures and had used our medicines. I showed him very clearly what efforts I was making now that our medicines were consumed and how I heard from the everyone just what he was learning from his patients, namely that his suggestions were more harmful than helpful, as had been the steady complaint even of the first Salzburgers at the very beginning. I also told him what was said by the board-cutter who had cut boards here, namely that his medicines had been the reason that his wife had brought a premature child into the world. He could not stand my rebuking him for the sin of cursing and swearing so dreadfully; and he blamed me for making mountains out of mole hills, of which, however, he could not quote me any data.

[And, because I well observed that he was aiming at his wife's offense, which we did not wish to pass over in silence, I told them that both their excesses were so crass that I could not forget them but would use my office for their salvation in due time because they had not yet done penance for it. This cannot be held against me or my dear colleague, with whom, before God, I weigh all matters that occur in the community, because we must some day give an accounting to our Chief-Pastor. To that he said spitefully that I am intelligent enough myself so that he neither can nor will give me any advice concerning his transgression. I might announce it to the congregation if I wished, and he would ask nothing about it. After all, he would not have to go there to ask the people's pardon. I advised him to pray, I would do the same, and I would be happy if he would suggest how to remedy such a great excess. We could not stand annoyances in the community. This is the first step that one must take, and later on one must do whatever else God wills.

[It seems to me that in the case of his cures, as in the case of his bloodletting, cupping, and bandaging, there is much external damage. He has never studied surgery, but he wishes to learn it now by practicing on the Salzburgers; and this, as I myself have experienced, has occasionally turned out badly. If he only now wishes to learn the art of medicine by practicing it (for he is no more than a druggist by profession), then he can cure many more to death. He uses Weisbach's medical book and the recipes prescribed in it. But because he does not have all the ingredients, he must replace them with substitutes that seem of equal value. And because he seems to approve of the principles of those who have *mechanismus* in medicine and wishes to be an eclectic, he can make a hotchpotch. And it seems to me that he needs a lot of *Martialia* and strong laxative and emetic drugs (?)[89], about which, however, he does not wish to talk with me because, as he says, medicine is not my métier.]

The 19th, Sept. Our people have been told that the sweet potatoes in this country will grow in all kinds of soil and, consequently, will do well at our place. But now they have learned different, for the roots they put into the ground have grown a lot of leaves but nothing else. When we asked a planter from Carolina for the cause of this he answered that potatoes do not require the best but have to have good rich soil and can not grow at our place without fertilizer. This is a sweet and very tasty root, which the people have been looking forward to because it can be eaten in the place of bread [which is still lacking in this country].

[Ruprecht Zittrauer came to see me again, and I remonstrated with him about his drunkenness, in which he has let himself be seen both in Germany and here. He showed remorse about it and assured me that he had already apologized to some of those whom he had vexed. He also promised to attend divine services both on weekdays and Sundays as often and as diligently as circumstances would permit. We would like to have more opportunity to teach him privately the Catechism and basic essentials of the Christian religion, which he is greatly lacking. Since he is now guarding the cows of the entire congregation, his way of life prevents him from making use of our private instruction.]

The 20th, Sept. Today God gave us a fruitful rain which, we hope, will benefit the recently planted seed. The land has been needing rain for several weeks, and therefore our river has again become so small that it cannot be traveled by boat. As soon as the water rises again some of our people will go after some clay, some of which will be used to build a fireplace in my room so that next winter will not be like the last one when the cold made us suffer much discomfort and interfered with our work. We would have looked after this during the summer and would have asked Mr. Causton for some fire brick if we had received assurance whether or not we would stay here. My dear colleague's house was finished by the carpenters today and now he can at last have decent living quarters. Until now he has had to put up with a poor and very small house. Thanks to God's protection it has done no harm to his health.

The 21st, Sept. We had a rain that lasted the entire day, which we hope will be very useful for the people's gardens. Praise God! Mrs. Moshammer has become so much better that she was able to attend services today, although she still lacks strength. Because medicine is in short supply we have been able to give her only an occasional dose of antispasmodic powder, but we supplied her with warm drink and, with God's help, she eventually benefited from it. She often expressed the wish for good health for the sole purpose of being able to attend the sermons and prayer hour because God had used them to refresh her greatly and to prepare her for His heavenly kingdom.

[The 22nd, Sept. Within eight days the people have lost three milk-giving cows from their herd. Two have died and one of them has been shot accidentally by a Salzburger who wished to shoot a deer. In addition, several calves have previously died. To be sure this grieves the owners, but they know how to resign themselves to it so well that we find no fault in them. The cow that was shot was butchered and distributed, so it will probably be replaced by Mr. Causton. He will be told about this and the others, and he will gladly do whatever he can to make up the loss.]

The 23rd, Sept. The rain keeps on almost constantly, and last night it was so heavy that the river became quite swollen and a large part of our garden was flooded once again. It is very low, and the water cannot be drained off into the river or anywhere else. The people who have fields close to the river are having the same experience. [Bach has guarded the cattle for some time together with Ruprecht Zittrauer, and in doing so he has damaged his health not a little. And because he has become slovenly and frivolous through such a way of life, I sent for him a couple of times and warned him with moving words of the great danger to his soul as well as of the obvious ruin of his body, and this seemed to do some good. Now he lies sick and is taking all the drugs prescribed by Mr. Zwifler, whereby we see to his care as best as we can. Now in this tranquility he seems to ponder better God's word and good admonitions. Measures are being taken so that he will not be needed to herd the cattle again even after he gets well.]

The 24th, Sept. The Salzburger Herzog is now quite burdened and troubled; but, through the grace of the Holy Ghost, he is learning to know his Saviour better and better and finds refreshment and peace with Him. He is hungry and thirsty for the Gospel; and, when it is impressed upon his heart and preached to him, he is so strengthened by it that he cannot hold back his tears. [A thing that he did during his apprenticeship and which he especially wishes to reveal to me troubles him greatly and at times robs him of all divine comfort. He would like to make it good again if he could return again to his master; but, since that is now impossible, he would like to recommend it to Him who will surely make it good. Meanwhile he hopes to reveal it to me in the next few days.] When I wanted to look up a verse in his own Bible he pulled it quickly from a barrel that was standing close by his bed, saying that he did not want to keep the Bible and other good books far away because they were his refuge now that his attacks prevented him from attending the sermons and the prayer hours. I found for him the words of Psalm 36:6-8 and applied them to his condition, and at the same time I instructed him in the proper behaviour during those hours when his mind was dark and confused, a condition which he had often deplored and to which he could not become accustomed.

Mrs. Moshammer, who was present, was so full of joy over the goodness and grace of God that she felt in her heart that she begged me to help her pray to God to preserve this comfort for her, for she could not wish for anything more beautiful or magnificent except being in heaven. I told her that she must accept everything from God's hand, both the sweet and the sour. Trials and chastisement are also very necessary for us. She soon agreed to this and said she knew from experience that God did not try beyond one's capacity, etc., and that this was comforting to her.

One more thing she had to tell me, she said, namely that before the death of her husband God had let her learn the hymn: Jesus, Thy holy wounds, Thy suffering and bitter death, etc. Ordinarily she did not learn easily; but God, in His mercy, had let her learn this hymn quickly, and she had derived heavenly pleasure from it ever since. The words she spoke about the dear sacrifice of the LORD JESUS, which is so well described in this hymn, were so powerful that they made a deep impression on me. God be praised for His inestimable grace that He has given to this woman, who is simple in the eyes of the world. According to Psalm 19:8-9, no one is too simple to recognize and experience Christ and His mercy. Her example made these words particularly impressive to me.

[Today Mr. Vat made it clearer than usual how much he dislikes me and my dear colleague and how much he wishes to harm us; but by this he just alienated the Salzburgers' hearts even further. Not long ago Mr. Gronau had received permission from Mr. Causton himself to have a fireplace built in his house in order to keep himself warm against the wind; and this was told to Mr. Vat. Yesterday he had two people begin the work, but today Mr. Vat sent Mr. Zwifler, whom he had appointed constable, along with two Salzburgers who have had to accept the office of tithingmen, to us and, as delegated Commissioner of both Societies,[90] ordered us to cease our construction at once, regardless of Mr. Causton's permission. The people, as well as we, were most amazed not only at the unexpected protestation but also at the procedure that was so unusual among us. However, we were pleased that the people were obedient and carried out his wishes. We sent him word that he did not have to be so ceremonious, but rather he could have forbidden the matter privately, if he had sufficient grounds and authority, since we had more than once offered to come to him as often as he demanded.

[Meanwhile I sent word that I would like to come to him now myself if it would not be inconvenient for him. When I came to him I found him trembling with anger. He justified his procedure with English customs and laws, as he has always done up to now, and he vowed he would oppose this construction as well as that of a fireplace in my house to the very limit and with emphasis even if we had permission from Mr. Causton. He kept referring to the commission that was expected from England; and he said that he would soon speak about the matter with Mr. Causton. Mr. Gronau himself went to him and asked him not to cause unrest and strife among us, but he could get no further with him than I could. Thereupon we told him that we were compelled to report his protestation and his recent behavior to Savannah this very day, for which purpose there was, by the Providence of God, an opportunity at hand. My dear colleague had resolved with good reason, and especially for the sake of some people who wished to have Holy Communion in Purysburg, to travel there; and for this purpose some Salzburgers were already engaged to take him there. And because this matter occurred just before his departure, he will have to go the whole way to Savannah.

[This time Mr. Vat did not wish to go along, even though we at once offered; but he prefers to go to Savannah on October 13 in order to complain copiously to Mr. Causton because, as he claims, I encroach on his office and make the people disobey him. And in order that Mr. Causton might know the sequence and context of the things that he has undertaken among us so far to the harm of the people, and their consequences, I wrote them down briefly and gave them to Mr. Gronau pro memoria. Yet at present we have only reported in a general way how he has behaved toward the people and us. We consider it necessary to incorporate his entire conduct in more detail in this diary so that our benefactors in Europe will also see how he has acted toward us and we toward him.

[At first he behaved very well and was able to give a good appearance to all the things about which the people complained on the voyage. Therefore we gave him credit for much good and gave him much good testimony in the diary. For we greatly prefer to report good things and are accustomed to hold back as long as possible from quoting unpleasant circumstances, especially personal matters. He held back all sorts of things from the Salzburgers that had been donated by the benefactors and applied it to his own use (of which I shall report some details) and he also wishes to rule over the poor people with great severity and great obstinacy as he sees fit, and this we could not countenance in silence. His greatest vexation at us is that people take refuge with us in all spiritual and material matters and accept our advice; and he denounces this as a contempt of his person and of his commissionership. To all appearances he was especially vexed that I could prove in writing that the ox that Mr. Bryan gave the last Salzburgers belongs not to him (as he wishes to maintain against me and others) but to the people.

[From that time on he has turned much more bitter toward us. I have asked him several times to release the things that were given to the people, for example two kegs of butter, several kegs of brandy, sugar, soap, etc. Likewise he should at least open the wine that Mr. Causton sent for refreshing the sick and give it to the thirsty people. But in this he cut me short as if all matters pertaining to provisions were entrusted to him alone and I should keep out of them, etc. He was free to distribute to whom and how he wished. We would have to respect his words and his orders as from the Trustees themselves because he was sent here by both Societies and in their name. We should concern ourselves with nothing but our office, it was his task to give orders.

[I showed 1) that we had never had things done through commands and had never demanded blind and servile obedience of the people, but rather we had assembled the people in a conference and showed them their duty from divine and human grounds and explained to them the necessity and value of this or that thing that was to be done. This was always accepted with love and willingness by the dear people, and I knew of no case of insubordination. It is no great art to lord it over poor people with severity and obstinacy. Rather the important thing is to pity the people because of the many hard conditions in which they have been and to a large extent still are to show them love and to correct them in their weaknesses more by means of forebearance, patience, intercession, and good advice than through rough and hard methods. If one were to act in anger and obstinacy, then it might come about that the one or the other might fly into a passion and thus commit a sin; and not only would this cause us much annoyance but the name of our Saviour would be disgraced and blasphemed.

[Our conferences, which we have continued to hold even with the increased congregation, he has never approved, even though he has never wished to say anything directly against them, especially since he heard that our benefactors approve of this method. He once said that we should not take the people into counsel with us but rather show them that we can command them. 2) I asked him frequently to give it to me in writing that he should rule at our place without us and that we are thus relieved of the care of keeping public order and other arrangements. Yet he did not wish to do this. And when I showed him the purpose of Mr. Oglethorpe, as Mr. von Reck left it to us in writing and sealed, he rejected it with very contemptuous words and said that, even if we had it in Mr. Oglethorpe's own hand, it would no longer be valid, because he is out of the country. Likewise, if Mr. von Reck were here himself as commissioner, he would have to be under him.

[I showed him that we would be obliged in our consciences to espouse the people's cause in every way and to prevent them from suffering any harm as long as we are not relieved from London from the performance of these duties. And we were amazed that he had not brought any warrant from London to be our superior in Ebenezer. Already at the time that I spoke of this with him I requested him to accuse me before Mr. Causton if I were encroaching on his office. If Mr. Causton recognized him as the chief authority in Ebenezer and freed me of such a burden, I should be very well contented, even if the people were to be pitied for it. Nor did he wish to do that, but rather he showed me a good number of letters which had been written to him not only by Mr. Newman in the name of the Society but also by Mr. Urlsperger; and out of them I was to recognize his good reputation and the trust they had in him and thereby draw the conclusion that it was their wish that he alone should command in Ebenezer.

[After I had read all the letters through and he had expounded the one and the other to his advantage, I told him freely that I could see from these letters that he must have behaved himself better formerly than now. If Senior Urlsperger knew about him what we are now experiencing, he would no longer give him such recommendations. 1) He thought little or nothing about religion here with us: we noted that he had bothered to go to Holy Communion only once in the long time that he was here. In Purysburg there is a minister whom he knows well and whom he highly praises, and he appeals to him because he is a minister of his confession.[91] 2) He has no Bible but passes his time, both on weekdays and Sundays, in reading secular books or with his accounts, to the scandal of those with whom he lives. 3) For a long time he has not visited our divine services at all, whereas at first he used to come from time to time. The people knew all these things and even more, and they were offended by them. What sort of trust would they have in such a commissioner, especially since there are additional matters that run contrary to Christianity.

[Despite all these representations, he steadily rebuked me for being to blame for his miscredit with the Salzburgers and said they had become indignant at him and disobedient because of me and my actions (even though I know of no disobedience). Therefore he had to give me some details, whereupon the following came out: Once, not long after his arrival in America, when he had journeyed to Savannah and had remained too long, I had distributed 6 lbs. of rice and a half lb. of powder to each head. The people came to me with Mr. Zwifler and complained, for some of them were in want of food. They also declared that, according to the orders of the Commissioner, six of them had to stand watch and had no powder. I never imagined that after his return he would make so much to do about this distribution of necessities first behind my back and now in my face and so very often. He considered it an encroachment on his office that I persuaded the people at the conference to repair the way to Abercorn, to build a slaughter house, etc., that we both told the carpenters that Mr. Causton wished them to build my dear colleague's house, etc.

[I was very amazed at these complaints, especially since I had conferred with him about these points before calling the people together and had asked him to tell me what else I should call to their attention on this occasion. Also we had considered with him all the circumstances of the house that Mr. Causton wished to have built so that he too contributed some suggestions. Our fault was merely that we summoned the carpenters and asked them when they wished to begin, whereas this was, in his opinion, his business. It was a great crime that I gave Schweiger permission to fetch a bride from Purysburg and bring her here; yet I had already reported it to Mr. Causton and had already received written authority from him to do as I saw fit. He was also offended that several people by mistake announced not to him but to me that they wished to travel to Abercorn or to Purysburg.

[He knows of no other complaints nor does he believe that the above quoted points are of such slight importance that one can hardly think about them. Had we known that this or that was offensive to him, I would have gladly abstained from it through love of peace, as is now the case. I offered several times to serve in any way to further good order among the people. If he thought he could not succeed in this or that, he should just commit us; for we hoped God would let us succeed through his great mercy as He had always done in former times. Yet he did not like this offer, because he thought that he would not enjoy much status. It was his right to command, yet he would ask us for advice some times and in some cases. If the people did not wish to obey him, he would have them bound and sent to Savannah. I showed him that he had no authority to do the latter. And, as far as the first was concerned, I had so far experienced from many test cases that he would in no way and through no representations let himself be dissuaded from anything that he had once gotten in his head; and therefore our counsel would just be sham.

[When he asked for an example, I gave him one. 1) He had plagued the people so long with the watch. It was proper that there be a watch, but the circumstances were difficult: e.g. that every night 6 men had to mount guard, that 2 men had to visit the entire place every hour, that the rounds were assigned in a military way, etc. When Mr. Zwifler approached the watch he placed his naked sword against the corporal's chest, to say nothing of the insolent shouting that is customary among soldiers and which we have to hear every evening because the guard house is very near our houses. With how many words and with how much earnestness have we not had to oppose this order (or this disorder) of his, since he absolutely insisted that the 6 men whom he assigned to the guard must present arms to us and make all sorts of movements. 2) How often had I not asked him to distribute the late Glantz's clothes among the poor or else to sell them at a low price? But he wished to auction them and first asked in London, as a result of which they are rotting. 3) How often have I not urged him to give the sick people some of the wine that Mr. Causton sent here for that purpose but which he has held back from them for over two months. And there are more examples of that kind about which we have had to sigh so far. I shall not mention other circumstances now.

[It remains to be seen how Mr. Causton will like his last protestation against Mr. Gronau's construction. We have obeyed his command and have discontinued the construction until further orders from Mr. Causton in order to deprive him in this way of the opportunity of sinning further and prohibiting anything more. We would be most happy and would thank God if a conscientious Christian man would be sent to whom the civil government could be entrusted; we have already made this heartfelt desire known in our letters and diaries. The poor people would be in a bad fix if this man were to be their authority, as everyone among us recognizes. We know no one at our place, unless possibly Mr. Zwifler and his wife, who is pleased with him and his behavior.]

The 25th, Sept. The water in our river has risen higher than we have ever seen it. It has spilled over the banks so that not only our garden was covered by water a yard deep but also that the cow stalls of several people were filled with water, many cellars have been spoiled, and the fields all along the river have been flooded. The bridges to Abercorn, which had recently been repaired and lengthened, are said to have been ruined. And the bridge across our river will be in a bad way if the water rises only a little higher. During the night we had a rather heavy thunderstorm, but God let it pass without damage.

[The 26th, Sept. Since losing his pious wife several months ago through death, Geschwandel has been bad off because of his still unreared child and also because of his entire household. Today he complained to me of his hardship and asked for advice as to whether he might marry Mrs. Resch, whose husband was lost in the forest. I told him that I would not begrudge him this pious and honest woman as a helpmate and that I believed he would be very well provided with her. However, I could not yet give my approval because we have no definite evidence that her husband is really dead. I told him I would do nothing about it myself because I had already reported it to England and asked for good advice and that I would also speak about it with Mr. Oglethorpe when he arrived.]

The 27th, Sept. This afternoon my dear colleague returned from Savannah. God willing, he will go to Purysburg next week to hold Communion service there because circumstances did not permit him to do so on this trip. [Mr. Causton was distressed on account of Mr. Vat and promised to come to Ebenezer himself and hear the grounds that moved Mr. Vat to his recent protestation. Meanwhile he sent up some nails, which are to be used in the construction of the fireplace.]

Herzog came to see me to get some comfort from the Word of God, for which he shows a great longing. [On this occasion he told me of the thing that he had done in his apprentice years and which had often caused him much unrest and worry. He had been badly treated by his unscrupulous master, and this misled him to calumniate and speak evilly of his master before another man who was his enemy. These two, although for other reasons, got involved in a legal entanglement before the authorities, as a result of which his master suffered embarrassment and was reduced to beggary. On the one hand I reminded him of the verse: Remember not the sins of my youth, and on the other hand of the example of St. Paul in I Timothy 1:13 ff.: I did it ignorantly in unbelief. He was also assured that God had forgiven him this and all his sins; yet he had considered it profitable to reveal it to me. He complained greatly at the malice of his heart, whereupon we got into a very necessary and useful conversation which was, God be praised!, edifying for both of us. Now all his efforts are going towards preparing himself properly for eternity; and he thanks God very much for his physical weakness, since in this way God took him away from other people and brought him to greater reflection.]

The 28th, Sept. A Salzburger had to report something to me [to report a boy's misbehavior], and on this occasion he could not give enough praise to the great mercy and guidance of God which had caused him to work seriously for his salvation. Physically he had been extremely well off in _____ [Memmingen] and while there had enjoyed so much in the way of kindness and good deeds that he could wish for nothing better in this world; but his soul had been in such a precarious position that he could not express it with words. He often longed to get away from this situation and he had prayed to God about it from time to time; but making a change had been made very difficult for him, because people reproached him that he was ungrateful, that he received the very best of treatment but was not satisfied, etc. But at last God had so arranged it that the Salzburgers there [in Memmingen] had been given the choice of either going to America or staying there, and he had quickly decided upon the voyage. He could not deny that he was worried when he saw our place and our condition upon his arrival and even when he had heard about them in Savannah; but now he was well pleased with the guidance of God and he could not marvel enough at the goodness and righteousness of God which he had experienced within himself after hearing and reading His word.

In accordance with the Gospel for the 17th Sunday after Trinity we spoke today about the proper behaviour of believers in their dealings with the Godless. In order to impress this important matter particularly well on the minds of our listeners, I used the review lesson to read them some of the *Rules of Life*[92] of the late Professor Francke and repeated for them everything that applied to them, according to the grace God had given; and in the great mercy that God extends to us, He has once again given His blessing to this simple method. We pursue this matter with great diligence and earnestness so that our congregation will always conduct themselves in a Christian manner, as prescribed by the Word of God, and that they do so not only here in Ebenezer but especially in their intercourse with people who do not belong to our congregation; for everyone watches us closely and the name of our Saviour can be very much blasphemed by uncautious behavior or even by the appearance of evil.

For that reason no one should blame us when we refuse to consider lightly but reprimand some excesses which others may think of as insignificant and common among Christians. A righteous teacher must have more concern for the glory of God than for his own life or comfort. He must try to save and to defend himself by watching, praying, exhorting, chastising, etc., if he does not want to be an unfaithful servant of his LORD. But the glory of God also often requires you to show gentleness, patience, and forbearance, with everything, depending on the particular circumstances. May God have mercy upon us and grant us wisdom.

[The 29th, Sept. Today Mr. Vat distributed provisions to the first Salzburgers, and at this opportunity he wished to take revenge on the Salzburger Schweiger by giving nothing at all to either him or his wife. This Schweiger took a wife from Purysburg after having considered the matter with me several times. Afterwards he presented himself to us with his wife three times here and in Purysburg. I reported his intention myself to Mr. Causton and also told Mr. Vat that this Schweiger was going to get married here in Ebenezer. Since I had foreseen the Commissioner's treachery (for with no good reason he is more hateful to the first Salzburgers than to the last), I had my dear colleague report to Mr. Causton that the marriage had now taken place; and I was asked whether Schweiger's wife was also to have provisions. Mr. Causton was entirely in favor of this.

[We reported this to Mr. Vat soon after my dear colleague's return; but then he revealed his anger that we had presumed to marry and accept a strange woman here without his consent. I told him that we had Mr. Causton's permission both orally and in writing and that we had not imagined that he would claim that the permission must be sought from him too. He should not impute this error, which he esteemed so great, to the poor man but to me, since I had not told him to ask his permission for his plans. Today he refused him shamefully, after having already treated him unspeakably a short time ago. I sent him word in a most friendly way that he should not cause any difficulty in this because he would remember that Mr. Causton had allowed provisions. But he let me know that he would not do it until he had spoken to Mr. Causton himself.

[I consider it necessary to record some pertinent words out of a letter from Mr. Causton: "As to Mr. Zwifler's Desire to be joyned in Wedlock, as you mention, I have no objection to that matter, nor to anything else of that nature with respect to your Congregation, that Shall be agreeable to your Judgment. His intended Wife Shall be accepted after matrimony as one of your people." We can do nothing about this now but to pray and to remain very passive, especially since the one and the other of his violent acts and his obstinate behavior have already been reported to Mr. Causton, who is now expected any day among us. Among other things he used this expression against Schweiger in front of the other people: he would give him no provisions because he had turned to an outside authority for his marriage.

[If Mr. Causton should remain away longer than we expect, we would let this Schweiger and his wife receive victuals during the interim so that he would not suffer distress. He shows the same vengeful and hostile attitude toward the people in the case of the beer and wash cauldrons that he bought with the Society's money yet handles as his own property and gives only to those who practically fall at his feet. And that is the way it has been with almost all the benefactions that have been given for the people. En route he has badly mismanaged the wine that Court Preacher Ziegenhagen provided for the people on their voyage, and he applied the bottles that he brought here only to his own use.]

[Just as he had been so friendly to the people from Augsburg to London, he proved himself just as merciless towards them, especally towards the children, at sea. When we first heard such complaints, we did not wish to believe them because of his good public conduct and appearance, even though we were always grieved by his holding back the things that belonged to the people. May God convert him! Not long ago he defamed our Salzburgers in Savannah by telling Mr. Causton, upon his asking how they were faring, that they went to work as if they were going to the gallows. Mr. Causton was shocked at this, especially since he said it in the presence of other people, and since Mr. Causton had praised the Salzburgers' diligence in front of other people after having seen it here himself.]

The 30th, Sept. When my dear colleague passed through Purysburg last week on his way to Savannah, the Lutherans there again begged him to hold communion service for them; and, since he could not stay for it at the time, they asked him to return soon for that purpose. He set out today in order to satisfy their want. [Since my dear brother has often had to undertake such uncomfortable trips, I would gladly have undertaken it this time if Mr. Causton had not been expected here every day according to his promise; for he might take it badly if he did not find me in Ebenezer.] As trips to Savannah and Purysburg are frequently necessary, we have had to purchase a light and fast boat. The boat belonging to the congregation is heavy, unsteady, and so full of leaks that it is almost useless. For this reason Mr. Causton is having a wider and longer one built, in which a large quantity of provisions can be transported at one time. But this will not be of much use for us when we want to make a quick trip.

On this occasion a boy from Purysburg, Johann Jacob Metzcher, seventeen and one half years old, will be dismissed from our school and sent back to Purysburg. His father, who is a tailor, sent him to our school some time ago; but now he is dangerously sick and needs help in his household. Recently we have had him come to us privately in order to prepare him for Holy Communion, to which he will be admitted in Purysburg at this time [even though he is stupid.] In the short time that he has been here in our school he has, through God's blessing, learned the basic truths of the Christian religion, Luther's Catechism, some Biblical verses and some Psalms and even to read. But, best of all, we find that his heart has acquired a great love for GOD and His word, and that it is his serious intention, as he has promised to continue to think about the good he has seen and heard here, to pray diligently, and to show the people by his Christian conduct that he did not listen to the Word of God in vain.

Although his parents' poverty required him to live very frugally, he was always happy; and he would have liked to stay with us longer if the condition of his parents had permitted him to do so. While here he received a number of things to fill his needs. He hopes to come back during the hot summer days when he will not be able to work in the fields, in order to get further instruction in the Word of God as well as in writing and arithmetic. God be praised for His help and blessing. We could dismiss three more boys from school if the people had been assigned some land and their parents could give their children some work in the fields. We are anxiously waiting for the arrival of Mr. Oglethorpe because then we will know where we are to stay. Toward evening Master Schielaender's[93] wife gave birth to a son who was christened a few hours after birth because the parents thought their child to be weak and not out of danger. [The last time, not long after her arrival in Ebenezer, she brought premature twins into the world; and, because she later experienced some unusual and serious attacks during her pregnancy, she prevented any new trouble, through God's blessing, with essentia dulci, with which we were then still supplied.]

The 1st, Oct. Yesterday Mr. Causton sent hens and roosters here, 60 in all, which Mr. Vat is distributing today among the new Salzburgers [and thereby skipping over the old ones in the division. A short time ago he was present in person when I asked Mr. Causton again to send the first Salzburgers their long-promised poultry, as he wrote down pro memoria. Likewise I read to him out of Mr. Vernon's letter that the Trustees were of the opinion that the old Salzburgers had already received chickens, ducks, etc. Up until now he has not been able to stand having me be concerned with such external matters and has referred me to my spiritual office. Had I not feared to anger him again, I would have advised him to make no differentiation but to distribute the chickens we received to them one and all, for this would cause less sensation and jealousy. For no reason at all he is less well disposed to the first Salzburgers than to the last, even though they suffered the greatest misery. A few days ago he distributed pots for brewing beer, and here again the first Salzburgers went empty handed. And thus it has gone in several other matters.]

In their common fields as well as in their gardens the Salzburgers have harvested little corn but a good many beans. We were told earlier and we have now learned by experience that they grow in different soils, even in the poorest soil that is not well prepared. Even the weeds do not keep them from growing although they frequently grow up with them. These Indian beans do not climb up on poles as they do in Germany but they spread over the ground and bear plentifully. When they are still young and green they can also be eaten with their pods, but their flavor is not as that of the French or German beans. The high water has done much damage to these beans in our garden as well as in others. In addition to these there is a broad colored variety which blooms and bears fruit all summer. But this is different from the former in that it cannot be eaten with the pod when young, unless it is picked while very small and very young. This latter variety did not grow as well as the former beans, which are also called peas.

[The 2nd, Oct. Our orphan girl is, to be sure, cured of her sickness; yet she seems to be in such a condition that she will probably not live long in this world. We have earnestly petitioned God to make her well; because both before and during her sickness her soul was in a very bad condition, in which she could not have died a blessed death. She is well tended both night and day and provided with all necessary care. Mrs. Moshammer has taken her back again, now that she herself is well again, and proves herself in every way more than a real mother.] A Salzburger killed a rattlesnake which had thirteen rattles on its tail. It was seven and one half feet long and its circumference measured one and one half spans. Such a monstrous snake had never before been seen by any of us.

[The 3rd, Oct. I have pursuaded the disorderly Ruprecht Zittrauer to leave his former hut in which he has lived together with the boy Ott and to move in with a family where he will have supervision and a chance for edification. Also, upon my urging, he has entrusted his little money with me to keep for him so that he will have no opportunity for dissolute excesses. He is still rather blind in Christian knowledge and zeal because he has had to guard cattle from childhood on. The other herdsman can read and must often read him the principal items of the catechism out in the field. Perhaps he will comprehend them in this way. As much as his situation will allow, he must come to us privately. The boy Ott is again becoming naughty and does not want to obey the pious people in his neighborhood who admonish him. Therefore we are of a mind to put him too under the supervision of a Christian Salzburger.]

The 4th, Oct. The night and morning air is now so cool that we must be very careful to watch our health. The days are very hot. [Schweikert is now healthier than previously. He comes to me occasionally and protests much good. He says that nothing gives him more joy than to hear much about Christ and the Grace He won for poor sinners. He diligently pictures the good that is prepared for the blessed in heaven, and this gives him much pleasure and a desire to die. Time will tell whether this protestation has a firm foundation. The truth is usually revealed when one is assailed by trials, tribulations, and unpleasantness. Up to now many a person has been revealed to us on such occasions. Schweikert diligently visits the divine service and the daily prayer hours. In order not to be contradicted by Commissioner Vat, I asked his consent concerning the boy Ott, whom we consider it most important to put under the guardianship of a pious Salzburger. On this occasion I asked him if he would tell me the doubts he has with regard to the building of our fireplace. Yet he refused this again and referred to the arrival of Mr. Causton. I requested him to report such doubts to Mr. Causton in a letter, since possibly after promising to come he might be prevented by the bad route or by too much business.

[We now have fine weather, and the fireplaces which are to be made of clay could dry out; and the morning winds are very cool and are getting cooler, and therefore we would like to advance the construction. But neither of us wished to do anything against his wishes so that he might see that we would gladly be submissive to him and thereby set a good example to our people because he presumes an authority and mastery over us. Yet he also refused to send his doubts to Mr. Causton in writing, and therefore we must be patient until his arrival. I notified him at this time that we were compelled to report his procedure to London. Moreover, we endeavor with God's Grace to treat him with forebearance, patience, and love so that they will find no cause to blaspheme.

[The 5th, Oct. The vexation that Ruprecht Zittrauer caused in both Purysburg and Ebenezer was disposed of today. After the morning service I called him to my room with the people who were with him in Purysburg and also the people whom he offended here. There I called to their attention what I and my dear colleague had been attempting with our office, namely to prepare our congregation for a blissful eternity and, through the Grace of God, to put them in a position here to set a good example for everyone through their pious and inoffensive behavior.

[While doing this I cited examples of why I had insisted so zealously on the last point. Just as we had had much joy from many in the congregation because of their Christian behavior, there had also been no lack of those who had given us great grievance and heartfelt sorrow both through their unrepentance and their persistence in trusting to public respectability[94] and even public scandals. Thereupon I applied this to the present *subjectum et factum* and showed what should be done by every pious minister who means well by his Saviour and his congregation in the case of such scandals, namely, when good admonitions and remonstrances do not suffice, he must not be an Eli but rather resort to discipline, and that 1) according to the will of God and example of the Apostles, 2) as a warning to the remaining members of the congregation, 3) for the salvation and betterment of him who has sinned.

[Finally I asked the man whether he wished to acknowledge his remorse even before this assembly as he had already done several times before me. He not only affirmed this with his mouth but also, with outstretched hand, and begged me and every one of the people present to pardon him for the scandal he had committed. Hereupon we fell to our knees and prayed together for this Zittrauer and for the whole community. Before his departure he thanked me in a most humble way for the trouble we had had with him and assured me that such correction was very welcome and salutory. Finally I admonished them to pray diligently for this man and to tell others who might have heard of his crude offense that the scandal had now been done away with. However, I told Zittrauer that he should hold to pious people and to ask the one and the other to keep watch over him and set him straight if ever he should commit some fault or do some wrong. I myself shall tell some pious Salzburgers who know him well that they should help him with good admonitions and instructions.]

The 6th, Oct. Yesterday as well as a week ago it was announced to the congregation that we intend to have Holy Communion next Sunday. [We have postponed it this time somewhat longer because we have need time to remove several things from the congregation beforehand.] Today the communicants will start to report for it and this gives us an opportunity to speak with them about their Christian beliefs and to reprimand them for the deeds we have noticed that were not right. The Salzburgers among them take this very well. This afternoon my dear colleague returned to Ebenezer from Purysburg with some people who had accompanied him back. God not only kept his body in good health but He also placed His blessing on the word he preached publicly and during visits to sick persons and others. [He cannot express in words the physical and spiritual misery of the people and their children, which our listeners well know and because of which they praise God for His excellent Grace.] The schoolmaster has started school and proves himself to be very faithful; [for God is working loyally on his heart toward his and his wife's total conversion, as I was told in some detail.] The place where he has his school is too far for the small children, besides being too wet and out of the way. We must look for a more comfortable hut for him, [and also accept the poor and almost abandoned Reformed children into the school].

[The 7th, Oct. Mr. Zwifler and his wife announced their intention to take Holy Communion and, upon my question, he testified, to be sure, that both he and his wife heartily regretted the scandal they had committed and that they had already made amends for it with God. But when I insisted that they both also make amends for it before the people and thus settle the matter, the latter being evidence of the truth of the former, he became very refractory and sinned with many words uttered in anger. But, because he heard that I would not be misled in the performance of my office and could not allow them to Holy Communion in this way, he gave in and accepted my suggestion. I wished, namely, to summon those people whom he had offended by his horrible cursing and swearing and whom she had offended by her squabbling for precedence in the church to come to me so I might ask them in the name of both to forgive them their trespasses, since they had both expressed their remorse to me and had settled the matter with God. But I did not wish to deceive these people, but rather it had to be true of both of them and they had to wish this procedure. I could not settle this scandal any more gently. They both have a hard and bitter disposition, about which we have warned them. God have mercy upon them! They are in dangerous circumstances. We are treating them both so gently so that they will have all the less cause to be embittered, even though their excesses, particularly those of his wife, deserve something harder.

[In contrast, what a joy we have with the dear Salzburgers, who fear the Lord and, as often as they visit us, bring a heart full of desire to hear and learn something. If we begin a conversation with them, they give in their simplicity such a testimony of the good that God has put in their souls through the Word of Truth that we are heartily pleased and edified. Such hours sweeten all the bitterness that we otherwise have to swallow in our office. We make private observations about the godless and the hypocrites in the congregation as a bridle and a means of hindering their godless ways and in order to prevent many a scandal. In this way one also learns about many things that one has not previously known but that one should know.

[The 8th, Oct. The boy Ott has accepted my advice and has moved in with the Salzburger Pichler; and therefore he does not only live in our neighborhood but also with a man by whom he will be well cared for in physical and spiritual matters. The young unmarried Salzburgers who came with the last transport live almost all together, five persons in one hut; and, because some are still frivolous and mischievous, we have long wished for a change and separation. Indeed, some of those who applied for Holy Communion this time wish it themselves. But they can not build now for themselves, but hope to receive certainty soon whether we shall remain at this place or not. As far as possible we keep an eye on them and are right behind any disorder.]

The 9th, Oct. The German shoemaker from Purysburg, Reck by name, who worked here some time ago, has returned in order to serve the people with his trade as long as they need him. He earns a great deal of money from us and we like his work much better than the shoes we have had to buy in Savannah until now. He also announced his intention to have Holy Communion with us since he was prevented from going in Purysburg because of sickness among his children. [Christian Schweikert again asked me to speak a good word for him to Mr. Causton so that he might receive liberty to seek his livelihood where he wishes. He detects very clearly that he is losing his strength more and more and is therefore afraid he may soon die if he does not have a change of air and way of life. I have promised to do whatever I can for him. But even more I directed him to Mr. Vat, as the one who brought him here.]

The 10th, Oct. For the glory of our ever faithful and merciful God we must acknowledge that this week we have again discovered some people in our congregation whose eyes have been opened to the fact that they had not been truly converted to God heretofore but have carried on with Christianity of the mouth and with outward worship of God. Through God's mercy it will now be different with them. The Father reveals His beloved Son to many wretches amongst us and shows them from a distance the good which they shall attain through their faith in His name. This makes them eager to pray, search, and knock. [Also the two Ortmanns are making a good showing. They did not go to Holy Communion this time because they needed more time for a proper preparation. Some among the Salzburgers were so worried and depressed by the multitude of their youthful sins when they applied for Holy Communion that the comfort we try to give them from the Gospel would hardly stick with them. But God, who is rich in mercy, never forsakes such souls; for He loves them far too much. The words of Psalm 111:18-21 were, among others, very impressive for some of them.]

The 11th, Oct. The very cool nights have let up again, and now it is once again lovely and pleasant during the night; but the days are very hot and the fields in which the people have planted turnips and other autumn plants need rain very badly. People and animals, particularly those who have to work in the forest, are now badly tormented by gnats; but we in our houses are spared this. Last year, when we lived nearer the river where there are many deciduous trees, we had to suffer much discomfort, especially at night. In addition to these large and small gnats there is an untold number of other vermin in this hot, still uncultivated and wild land, most of which are similar to those in Germany. [Toward evening today it appeared as if the devil would cause us new unrest and distress. However, since we received word of it in time and prevented it, everything took a happy ending through God's blessing. People who prefer themselves to the simple Salzburgers try all sorts of things, and then it generally falls upon us when they cannot advance in their petition and disorder.[95] But who can harm us when we are pursuing the good?]

The 12th, Oct. Forty-six of our dear congregation came to Holy Communion today. Not only did God give us much spiritual pleasure on this day, but we also noticed how the words of truth which had been preached last week during our preparation have had a good effect on a number of souls. Hallelujah!

The 13th, Oct. [Poor Schweiger, whom Mr. Vat recently excluded from the provisions, would suffer hardship with his wife if we did not help him as best as we can. Today Mr. Vat is planning to distribute to the new Salzburgers, and we are afraid that the foodstuffs that have been sent up may run out so that nothing will be left for this Schweiger and his wife, because then he would have to fetch the victuals that are due him from Savannah with great effort and difficulty. Therefore I found it necessary to send our boat down to Mr. Causton with a letter to report this matter, which I would have preferred to give orally if Mr. Causton had come to us according to his promise. At the same time I reported the unequal and partial distribution of the newly received poultry. Also, I again asked whether Mr. Causton would still give his permission for the construction of the fireplace, the construction of which had been hindered by Mr. Vat.]

That which was reported on the 19th of September about the sweet potatoes in this country must now be supplemented as follows. People who dig in their gardens with diligence are now finding more of these potatoes than formerly. Where the soil is very sandy there are few of them and they are small; but where wood has been burned and the soil has been mixed with ashes or a little manure, or where it is naturally good and black, they grow well, fairly plentifully, and large. Our own garden produced cabbage but no potatoes because it is too wet. [Some of those who try to justify the sandy soil say that the long-absent rain is to blame for that and also that the people did not understand the way to plant them.]

The 14th, Oct. When visiting the good Ruprecht Steiner, who has been sick for several days, I found him in such a fine state of mind that I was very much edified by his strong and meaningful talk. He and his wife often thank God among other things for the blessing of poverty. If he had been rich it would have been as hard for him to leave Salzburg as it was for his relatives. Besides, in good times he would not be very serious about his Christianity because his heart is too deceitful. He opened up for me the verse from Jeremiah 17:9-10, and I compared it with Proverbs 30:7-9. This pleased him very much and gave us material for further good conversation. He seeks to dig very deep in the knowledge of his wretchedness, as it were, but he likes to hear or read of nothing more than of Christ and the great salvation He gained for us. He could not express how much he had come to love the hymn: Immanuel, not to count the good, etc., and how beautifully it fitted his condition. [N. N. B. The Salzburgers have a great longing to work in the fields, yet no land has yet been surveyed for or assigned to them.]

Nevertheless some Salzburgers are working some pieces of land near the river although they have no assurance that they may keep them or that we will remain here. The best time is now approaching because the cooler weather permits one to work hard. For this reason everyone is anxiously waiting for the arrival of Mr. Oglethorpe. [Should the people get good land of their own, everyone would certainly take joy in his serious work.] If the people have to remain here many will be discouraged, and this should surprise no one who gives due consideration to all of our circumstances. [It is said that the Salzburgers should not be so choosey and obstinate with regard to their land but remember what benefits they have received, etc. They respect these benefactions very much and thank God for them cordially in public and in private, but they know that good land was promised to them orally and in writing above all else.

[And since the benefactors are not in a condition (as Mr. Vernon himself writes), to supply the people with provisions for more than two years and they would rather nourish themselves with the work of their hands, no one can rightfully hold it against them if they earnestly desire that which was promised to them and is necessary for the maintenance of their physical life. They are now being comforted that people hope to find them good land, but that the city can not be removed to any other place. Good dry land is not to be found around our place, except for a few places along the river, the larger part of which has been innundated by the rising river water. Therefore they may be directed a few leagues farther away as it is done in Savannah, where the people have their house and yard in the city, five acres of land a few miles from the city for a garden, and the remaining fields several miles away. With our Salzburgers such a distance between the fields and the dwellings is unfeasible for several reasons. I shall now mention only the daily prayer hours and the Word of God, for which they departed from their fatherland and which for most of them has been the dearest and most valuable thing. How many times could they come to hear the Word of God if they had to walk two, three, four, and more hours to their fields and from there back again to their homes? Even if they returned home every evening they would be too tired to participate in devotions. I will not mention other difficult circumstances of which these good people could be relieved if Ebenezer were moved to a more convenient and fertile region. Our help is in the Name of the Lord who has created heaven and earth. This great LORD who does not deny anyone who puts his hope in Him can easily guide the hearts of our worthy benefactors to that which is good for the bodies and souls of these poor people. May He also guide the hearts of those who can help our cause by speaking for us to the Trustees in Christian fashion so that they will consider this point sympathetically and seriously.

[The 15th, Oct. Mr. Causton has, to be sure, again written to Mr. Vat in answer to the questions recently asked him; and among other things he reported that Mrs. Schweiger should be supplied with provisions just like the other Salzburgers. Nevertheless he (Vat) remains determined to give nothing to the man or to his wife until he has first spoken himself with Mr. Causton, who, as he again promised, wishes to come to us in the near future. We can well note that Mr. Causton does not wish to offend Mr. Vat, for which he has his good reasons. Meanwhile Mr. Vat's behavior up to now has been of such a nature that all our benefactors in England and Germany who have seen the points we have written down will already have recognized his intentions, even though he, like an advocate, can give them a good color and appearance. We surrender everything to the Lord, may He do in this what He pleaseth.

[If he (Vat) is confirmed in his intentions and his present procedure of being the ruler of the people and of treating the people roughly and obstinately, then we must be patient and be a good example to the others in submissiveness and obedience, as we have previously told him. Meanwhile it grieves us when too much happens to the people and when that which God and the benefactors have granted them is taken away from them. We are very much afraid that, if he should not succeed in his petition to Mr. Causton to rule despotically in Ebenezer and to show his authority, he will refer to the commission he is expecting from the Trustees and therefore not relent from his hard and inflexible disposition and thus cause even greater offense. We have an example in the matter that occurred between him and Mrs. Ortmann. (See the note under June 26.) He compromised the woman enough. She had to go to Savannah twice and received there a harsh reprimand. But Mr. Vat testified several times against me that he was not satisfied with the judgment of Mr. Causton but that he would refer the matter to the commission of the Trustees so that she would be really punished, he would be dismissed from his office, and both of them be expelled from their house. This is a disgraceful bit of private revenge and all the more sinful because he himself has given the occasion for these squabbles, as we have shown him often enough.]

The 16th, Oct. All day yesterday we had a very cold north-westerly wind, which was followed last night by a heavy frost. The cold is already giving us much discomfort in our wooden houses since we have not yet been able to build any fireplaces. We had hardly expected such cold weather at this time, [and because of it we could not hold school this morning, especially since Mr. Vat would not allow us to build a little fire in the guard house, where we hold the school. According to his order, six men must stand watch every night; and they are in a bad way because they cannot build a fire in the guard house even though it does not do the least harm except that the shingles would become smokey and somewhat blackened. Because Mr. Vat again had an ox slaughtered, my dear brother Gronau asked Mr. Vat in the most kindly and moving way to show mercy to Schweiger and let him get something in the distribution of the fresh meat. But in this too he could not be budged. And because he again made several severe and unfounded reproaches, e.g., we did not yet understand St. Paul, we were seeking our

own interests, we were alienating the people and making them
loath him, etc., my dear colleague could not help but point
out to him a few points from the teachings and example of St.
Paul and to test his and our behavior by them. But he accepted
this just as evilly from him now as previously from me whenever
we have spoken with him for the good of his soul. He even
says that his soul is no concern of ours, he is not a member
of our congregation, we do not have to account for him, etc.
But this matter is without rhyme or reason. The man claims
to be the head and leader of the congregation in Ebenezer and
yet is not a Christian member of it, as he has shown well enough
so far through words and deeds; and he has vexed the people
with whom he lives, for he lives in Ebenezer without God.]

The 17th, Oct. In addition to the chickens he had sent
recently, Mr. Causton also sent some geese and Calcutta hens,
which have been distributed among the last Salzburgers. Some
people have been made sick by the cold weather, which is still
lasting. Schweikert too is again bed-ridden and very weak. We
are now making arrangements for him to have his own hut
and a better place to sleep. [Mr. Causton justified Mr. Vat for
recently distributing the chickens only among the last Salzburgers and said that he had no exact order to give any to the
first Salzburgers. Concerning this we showed him the last letter
from Mr. Vernon that specifically states that the Trustees think
they have already received some poultry, to say nothing now
of what he himself promised in regard to this point. Time will
tell whether Mr. Vat's other crass misdeeds will likewise be
painted with such a good color. In our prayers we seek nothing
more than that the Lord's will be done and that the Lord give
us wisdom to work on the poor man for the salvation of his soul
as long as he is with us so that he will not be lost. If Mr. Causton
does not come to Ebenezer, Mr. Vat will go to Savannah himself
next week concerning the accounts, for then hopefully our
suffering Schweiger will receive his provisions.

[We would like to inform Mr. Causton of the great need and
complaints of all the people at our place, if we were not afraid
of even greater harm from Mr. Vat's contradiction. The things
about which we hear complaints are as follows: in the spring,
out of an ungrounded fear of war, Mr. Vat had such a quantity
of grains, such as corn and rice, brought up here that the last
of it has only now been distributed. But because it remained
in the store-house all summer, the corn and rice have been

entirely eaten out by the worms and have almost become empty hulls. At the very beginning I was not pleased by such a supply. Also the people asked him rather to give it to them in advance since they wished to try to preserve it by constant cleaning; but he was not willing to do so. I advised that some of the men go to him and respectfully request him to champion their need with Mr. Causton when he visits him; and this they wish to do. Also, instead of rice, he gave three people who have children some 30 lbs. of corn that was so miserable that it could be used almost only as cattle food. On the other hand, if the rice is sifted and washed, it can be used better, especially for children.

[The cause of such unChristian behavior is this: Originally he went to Savannah and remained away longer than he or we had expected. Because of that the poor people became famished (for it was then his custom to distribute for only fourteen days). Mr. Zwifler and some of the people complained to me of their need and asked whether they might not distribute a few lbs. of rice, because it was required by necessity and by excessive absence of the Commissioner himself. I consented, whereupon Mr. Zwifler distributed 6 lbs. to each and noted it all down. At the same time the people, who had until then stood watch without powder, were given ½ lb. of powder.

[When Mr. Vat returned from Savannah, he acted as friendly towards me as before but cursed and scolded me behind my back and threatened the people. And now it is these three families' punishment that they have to take miserable and unusable corn in place of the rice that they received at that time. They would gladly accept corn in place of rice if only it were usable. They can get along with this provision all the less because they have children, all of whom eat as much as adults even if two are counted only as one grown person. In addition the parents are annoyed that he has recently deducted meal and rice for 16 weeks because at first he had erroneously given the same amount to their children as to the grown people. I asked him at that time to reveal this error to Mr. Causton and to request that nothing be deducted from the parents because they had already consumed it and would have to suffer want from such a great deduction. But in this and similar matters he reproaches me for thinking only of the private interest of the people and not of the public good, as has always been his way.

[The good people are greatly amazed how it is possible for the man to have changed so completely. On the first trip as

far as London he conducted himself in such a way that they had
to praise him and could not have asked for any other or better
commissioner. But as soon as they went to sea he sided more
with the Englishmen than with them and was severe and un-
merciful towards them; and he dispensed the medicine, Schauer's
balsam,[96] and other necessary things either not at all or in very
limited quantities. And he has continued in that even among
us, especially recently, whereas he had at first acted better and
had taken some trouble in caring for the people. I also advised
these parents to go to him even before his trip to Savannah
and to move him to mercy towards their children through their
petitions. We shall do our best too through prayer and representations.

[The 18th, Oct. Since taking Holy Communion Mr. Zwifler
has behaved himself so well toward us and others in the congregation that we have great hope in him with regard to his Christianity, and we praise God for it. Today a Salzburger said that
he had seen a great reverence and humility in him during Holy
Communion and during the preaching of the Divine Word, as
well as an emotion not previously usual in him. We are very
pleased that God had looked upon our miserable prayer with
grace and has averted that which we feared, namely an animosity
against our office because of the proceedings we recently had
with him. God grant that this overtly good behavior has come
from a good foundation; for otherwise it may cease again in
times of trial and opposition.]

The 19th, Oct. It has been the pleasure of our heavenly Father
to impose upon me, Boltzius, a great weakness of body which,
although not dangerous, prevented me from taking care of the
duties of my office today. It was an attack of fever which I sought
to combat in every way possible. After taking some medicines I
felt their good effect, and I have hopes that the fever proper
will no longer give cause for worry. May God strengthen my
dear colleague who did his duty today, as always, in good health
and in good spirits. It is now quite cold during the morning
hours, and since we do not wish to waste this noble time in bed
but rather to use it for the glory of God and the good of the
congregation, it is easily possible for us to contract various bodily
weaknesses.

[We do not know what the reason is that Mr. Causton does
not visit us according to his promise; yet we do not worry about
the impeded construction of the fireplace, for in this we look

more to our beneficent Father than to men.] A Salzburger visited
me during my weak spell and testified among other things that
his eyes were being opened more and more and could see that
he could not have been saved if he had remained in his former
condition with its imagined Christianity and faith. He also related how difficult it had been for him to leave his fatherland
of Salzburg and later his job in Germany. When he had become
suspect he and other people in Salzburg had been locked in a
room as prisoners and were later led away by soldiers who were
very rough and hard with them. When he was still in the room
his own mother had come to him and knelt before him and
thrown her arms around his feet. In this heartbreaking position
she begged him in moving terms to stay. If he went away, she
said, she would no longer hear the Word of God because her
husband, his stepfather, was a Papist. Until then she had been
able to hear some of it when he read to her and prayed with her.

When he had nearly reached the border and felt sure that
no one would know him there, he was tempted again in a border
village by some acquaintances he had not known before, particularly by two women and a man who tried the most extreme
means of keeping him from emigrating. In the course of this
he received the most attractive promises for the flesh, promises
which usually succeed easily with young people. But it seemed to
him that he would rather go through fire and water than to
give in to such temptations.

He added that he as well as others had made a great deal of
their courageous conduct at that time; but he had really been an
unconverted and very wretched man when he left Salzburg [as
he had revealed through impudence and wild behavior after he
had departed from Salzburg]. After that his physical well-being
had become so great that everyone considered him very lucky;
but his conscience had continued to give him trouble whenever
he thought to place himself on an equal footing with others
and even with his master. In periods of quiet his wretched condition had become clear to him and he realized that this kind of
Christianity could not save him because his own actions and
those of other people were contrary to the Word of God. When
he let it be known that he longed to get away from this condition
he was told that he was foolish, for he had what others wished for,
namely, a good master, good days, good pay, etc.; but he showed
that these things were only for the flesh and that he also had
an immortal soul which was more important to him and which

he could not save in this manner, etc. Praise God, he said, that he is now in this wilderness where our dear God lets him learn things which he had not been able to imagine before, for the spirit of the flesh could not grasp the good in Christ.

The 20th, Oct. [Because of a few cannon shots that we heard at our place Mr. Vat assumes that Mr. Oglethorpe must have arrived; and this, among other things, may have caused him to journey very early this morning to Purysburg in our boat. If he should hear there that Mr. Oglethorpe has not yet arrived, he intends (as he said to other people) to spend some eight days in Purysburg with his very special friend Mr. Pury and afterwards to go to Savannah. Late last evening, after we had been advised of his departure, we both requested him with great emotion to do us the kindness and show the suffering Schweiger the mercy of transmitting to Mr. Causton in writing the complaints he had against this man and his wife because Mr. Oglethorpe had perhaps not yet come and because he (Mr. Vat) might remain for a long time in Purysburg, in which case the poor man would suffer even greater hardship and difficulties. But in answer he let us know that he could not do it in writing and that it would also be to our harm if he did it.

[And thus the man causes us nothing but trouble and, through his unChristian behavior, is forcing one of us to go down again and help poor Schweiger to his rights. It hardly happens to a delinquent and criminal that people start out with him *ab exhecutione* (sic!). And even towards the evilest people one has enough mercy not to deny him all food but at least give him bread and water in his prison. That Mr. Vat begins *ab exhecutione* and does not wait for Mr. Causton's judgment comes perhaps from his fantasy and imagined authority, which, according to his own assertion, is as great as that of the Trustees themselves. He told some of the people that he was more in command in Ebenezer than Mr. Causton because he was authorized by both societies but Mr. Causton only by one.[97]

Kalcher, who, along with his wife, lives with Mr. Vat and serves him, told us yesterday evening that, in addition to the matter of his unauthorized marriage (which was reported above), he wishes to bring two other accusations, which he has kept silent from us. 1) When he had returned again from Purysburg, where he had gone with my permission because of his marriage business, Mr. Vat summoned him to himself and, among other things, threatened him that he would have him bound and taken to Savannah as a disobedient person if he dared to go away again without his permission. Thereupon Schweiger stepped up to him and said that he was right there and that Mr. Vat might do it if he had the authority. He did not recognize him as his superior because only the two pastors had been presented to him and the likes of him as superiors, he should show his plenipotentiary power in writing. 2) Mr. Vat had visited the guard during the night and found this Schweiger along with the other five Salzburgers sleeping and had taken his musket away to his room. But the good people are to be pardoned in this, just as I excused them before him at that time. During the day they had been in the forest to find the lost Resch, as a result of which they were exhausted and overcome by sleep. If Mr. Vat, who has intelligence and cunning, presents everything he knows about the Salzburgers to Mr. Causton onesidedly and with the circumstances omitted, this could cause damage. But the Lord is with us, so we are not afraid. What can man do unto us? Psalm 118.]

As it has been two years today since the first Salzburgers left Augsburg and the two of us received and accepted the call to go with them, we asked a number of them whether they wanted to come to us this evening to join us in prayer. This was done, and not only the first Salzburgers came but the last ones came also to increase our company. First we sang the hymn: Praise be and honor to the highest good, etc. Afterward I, Boltzius, expressed in a few words why we had gathered together, namely, to remind each other of the good which the Lord has done unto us during the last two years, to praise Him for it and also to ask Him for His mercy. Thereupon we fell on our knees, prayed together, and especially requested our Father in heaven that His will might be done in regard to our land and a possible change of location. At the same time we asked for His blessing for the voyage to Savannah which is to be undertaken tomorrow. It always gives us great pleasure whenever we can get together with our congregation in this manner. We also did this a week ago yesterday and we hope that it will happen more often in the future, for we are sure that the Lord will not let it go without His blessing.

[The 21st, Oct. My dear colleague, Mr. Boltzius, undertook the trip to Savannah in order that he himself might speak in greater detail with Mr. Causton about Mr. Vat. It grieves us that in Mr. Vat we have a commissioner in whom we cannot live in any brotherly union. If he would try with us to go through the narrow gates of heaven and act as it behooves a true Christian, we would agree with him in all matters, even in external ones; and we would be one heart and one soul. To be sure, he thinks he is doing well; yet, if we try to show him what is right, he does not know what to answer. And now that he has such a good opinion of himself and his spiritual condition, he no longer uses the means to salvation, diligent prayer, contemplation, or the hearing of God's Word. The Salzburgers are very scandalized at this and can not get used to it.

[The first time that fresh meat was distributed, I recited to him the proverb: Blessed are the merciful, for they shall obtain mercy. He should consider these words of Jesus and give something to poor Schweiger and his wife, especially since Mr. Causton had given him permission. In answer he said that he could not do it: his bowels were full of mercy, but he could not show it in these and those matters. But I showed him whence this came, namely from the fact that the foundation of his heart was inadequate. He had not yet experienced what St. Paul and every man who wished to get to heaven had to experience, namely, that he could say: Mercy has been shown unto me the greatest sinner. To this he again could answer nothing, but he merely said this and that as an excuse.

[Once the dear man has resolved upon something, he will not let himself be turned from it, let us say what we will. If we then show him whence it came, then he answers that, as we know, he is not seeking anything, he is getting and asking nothing for having come here and taken care of the people. Therefore no one could think in the least bit that he had the wrong intention or was seeking his own interest in carrying out his duty. But if you look at the matter in the light, then he has interest enough, namely, his own prestige. When the Old Adam has this pabulum, then he is very content. May the dear Lord have mercy upon him and save his poor soul, which certainly seems in much danger, and all the more danger because he does not wish to recognize it or believe it.]

The 22nd, Oct. With a heartfelt prayer I, Boltzius, left early yesterday morning to go to Savannah via Abercorn, together with several Salzburgers. I left there with much praise of God toward evening and, through divine blessing, returned this morning to our beloved Ebenezer in better health than before. The light boat which we acquired recently speeds up this trip considerably. God is still LORD of this earth and the hope of the poor. This belief is often confirmed, and the blessing which God gave to this journey has confirmed it again. As I was about to enter the boat in Abercorn I met an Englishman who brought me greetings from a merchant and Indian trader and said that he had sent me a few bushels of peas as a present which I might pick up in Savannah at the next opportunity. This new proof of divine care awakened in us great joy and praise of God during the boat trip.

[The real reason that forced me into this trip was Schweiger's and his wife's lack of provisions, but on this occasion the intended construction of our fireplaces was not only permitted again but all the more furthered by Mr. Causton. He was amazed that we had heeded Mr. Vat's protestation so long and had not begun this so necessary construction with his (Mr. Causton's) permission. I told him the reason, namely, that we would have just embittered him more and perhaps given him occasion for very great excesses by really beginning the construction, which would have scandalized the congregation even more. For he had very brazenly told our Salzburgers that he had more power and authority in Ebenezer than Mr. Causton, likewise that his commands were to be looked on as the commands of the Trustees, and that he had uttered threats against me because of the construction. Therefore it is easy to suppose that he would have done his utmost to show his pretended authority publicly; and, if no one had obeyed him in this, he would have torn down the construction with his own hands.

[In addition we were afraid he might punish the Salzburgers who were used in such construction, just like Schweiger, by holding back their provisions. This would just cause us new troubles and Mr. Causton annoyance and embarrassment. He was satisfied with my arguments and, to remove the last worry, he gave me full authority to engage a mason at once from Savannah or Purysburg, whom he would pay. I considered this authority as a new blessing of God, for we know a German man of this profession in Purysburg who is not only extremely poor but who is also in such circumstances *ratione animae et Christianismi* that he surely has need of our private company and also of frequent hearing of the Word of God, and also desires them. His name is Tullius.

[Mr. Causton let Schweiger's and his wife's provisions be given them from the store-house in Savannah. The man will, to be sure, have to bring his food here with some effort; yet he does so with joy because at the last distribution the other Salzburgers received the meal only to a half, some things not at all, and the grains eaten out by worms, whereas he received everything completely and also fresh. For Mr. Causton has the good practice (which I did not understand a year ago when I described our lack of provisions and wrote that there was but a small supply in the store-house. See under   1734[98]) of dispensing the old provisions early in the fall, especially those that soon suffer damage in this country; and then acquiring everything fresh after the harvest. The people who need provisions shortly before the harvest must be patient for a short time, but then they receive it all the better. I especially admonished Schweiger to be heartily grateful and also severely warned him as well as the other travelling companions not to boast about the blessings received as a reproach or insult against Mr. Vat but to behave with all humility, caution, obedience, etc., as behooves Christians. And since he is generally inclined to discourteous manners and to anger, I gave him some especial lectures.

[Mr. Causton entirely disapproved of the authority that Mr. Vat had affected and will refer everything to Mr. Oglethorpe, who should arrive soon. He merely testified that it was indeed the will of our benefactors that we too occupy ourselves with external matters in the congregation and be concerned with their plight. At our request he again offered to serve our congregation in every way that lay in his power. At my request he gave me full power to do what I wanted with the old things in our store-house and to apply them as I wished, whereas Mr. Vat had made great commotion and difficulties about almost every rag. Also, he was not at all content that Mr. Vat had kept the late Glantz's few clothes in the trunk until I had written to London in order to be able to auction them. He should, Mr. Causton said, have come to Savannah with his scruples; but this would have been against his principle, in which he sets himself above the magistracy in Savannah.

[I also revealed that almost no one had any faith in Mr. Vat because he had treated the people so obstinately, annoyingly, and with severity and that this had aroused even more his feeling of indignation and anger. As he (Vat) himself knew, I had done my best in the community with admonitions, representations, persuasion, etc.; yet the desired effect was not achieved because he would not desist from his former method of lording it over the people, and finally he could not stand it for the people to make use of our advice and assistance. It is, I continued, no great performance to rule over poor people with strictness and severity. Rather the thing to do is to bear with new colonists and their various difficult circumstances, which are never lacking at the beginning, with gentleness and patience and try to lead them in their frailties and shortcomings back into the right path.

[To be sure, Mr. Causton would not recognize Mr. Vat's attitude, which we have particularly observed of late, from his public association with him but rather presume the opposite because of this and that (as it fared with us for a good while). However, if for example he used him for some business in his store-house, he would easily recognize the same things as we did. Even the two matters, our construction that was hindered and the Salzburger's provisions that were held back, reveal much about his disposition. Only about the poultry that the first Salzburgers have not yet received do we need not worry, for it will soon follow. It is said that a man has long been entrusted with supplying them. In fact Mr. Causton showed me every possible kindness. And because I had expedited all my affairs, I departed already the same evening for our Ebenezer, but came only as far as Abercorn.] Just as I was getting in the boat, I was greeted by an Englishman who brought me greetings from a merchant and Indian trader and said that the latter had sent me . . . bushels[99] of peas which I could have someone pick up in Savannah at the first opportunity.

All these examples of Divine Providence that we experienced awakened us on the boat to joy and the praise of God. I also received letters from Mr. Causton, some of which he had received from Charleston and some from Pennsylvania. [The letters from Pennsylvania were from a merchant named Gemig, who was in Ebenezer a while ago with Mr. Weisiger. In them I was again asked to make the trip to Philadelphia for the benefit of the Lutheran people there, and also to answer the letters that the congregation there had written me. However, I know nothing of such letters, except that Mr. Weisiger referred to them some time ago in his letter.] The letter from Charleston came from an English pastor named Dyson, who told me about the death of the English pastor, Mr. Fullerton, near Charleston. This Mr. Fullerton had come to Savannah on the boat with the last Salzburgers; and, since he had a special fondness for the Salzburgers, he went to the trouble of visiting us here in Ebenezer before leaving for his congregation near Charleston. He was very much pleased with the arrangement of our services, and he wished with all his heart that he could bring his congregation to the point of wanting to come to him often in order to pray and listen to the Word of God. And since in my dealings with him I saw in him a spirit which was not in tune with this world but strove for something better and more magnificent, we not only had a very enjoyable time together but also stayed in touch with each other through quite intimate correspondence, which, unfortunately, never proceeded very far because the postal service stopped.

The letter he wrote me after his arrival in Charleston confirmed the judgment I had formed of him when he was here. The entire letter is very edifying and shows what he thought of our services and our efforts on behalf of the congregation. We hesitate to write down his own very nice expressions because it could be considered self-love on our part. Because of his good, Christian, and upstanding character we could wish nothing better for him than constant intercourse with good teachers who have Christ and His mercy in their hearts. We regret very much his early departure from this world, particularly because here in America there is a great lack of such teachers who have in their souls a true love for Christ. This blessed man preached several times in Savannah with good effect, as I was told on this last trip.

For several days Mrs. Rottenberger has been in quite difficult circumstances [and has always expected to give birth, but has not been successful. Today everything appears to be even more dangerous, so that we are in great worry and fear for her life.] May God have mercy upon her and hear our prayers for her, for Christ's sake. We would gladly comply with her and her husband's request for certain medicines if only it were in our power to do so. Formerly her use of them had a very good effect on her symptoms.

The 23rd, Oct. Late last night God helped Mrs. Rottenberger over her dangerous condition and child-bearing difficulties. She gave birth to a boy and a girl both whom were baptized soon after birth because they were weak. One of them has become stronger and more alert, but the other one still suffers from great weakness. During the afternoon we had a sudden shower and thunderstorm which passed by quickly. We have had constant drought for some time, the weather being hot during the day and cold at night. Today the mason from Purysburg arrived here.

God willing, he and a few Salzburgers who want to help him will start building a fireplace tomorrow. [The clay that was recently brought here is not much good; but it so happens that better clay has been found in our schoolmaster's garden, for which, however, one must dig very deep.

The 24th, Oct. [Mr. Bryan drove a good number of oxen through our place that he is to take to Savannah. He knew, to be sure, that Mr. Causton had recently taken and slaughtered ten head of ours; but he hesitated to leave us ten others in their place because Mr. Vat had not left behind him Mr. Causton's order as to what was to be done.] Upon my return from Savannah I had told some of the Salzburgers that a bridge on the way to Abercorn had been damaged and made useless by the high water. Now six men have gone there to build it up higher so that Mr. Oglethorpe will have less trouble if he wants to come see us. We often think of our dear Mr. Oglethorpe, and we pray to God to guide his heart in regard to our land as He has decided with loving counsel since eternity. We also urge the congregation publicly and in private to pray with all their hearts that God's will may be done. If it is done it will be for our best, whether we stay on or are sent to some other place. If we pray the third supplication in truth and earnest: Thy will be done, then surely the Lord will not let us lack what we ask for in the fourth supplication, even if we have the very worst of soil.

[The 25th, Oct. Mr. Vat has, to be sure, wished to prove his authority; and upon his departure he again wished to show that the people in Ebenezer depend on him. For that reason he securely locked up the wine that Mr. Causton had sent here for the sick and feeble and took the key with him. But God has previously provided for the suffering people in the congregation by granting us good wine through the friendly care of the Society, of which we are to give some to the needy members of the congregation. We have often had to use many words to urge the people to go to him and to request some wine as their situation might requires, because they were made shy and timid by his attitude and unnecessary hesitation.]

The 26th, Oct. In yesterday's evening prayer hour as well as today we spoke about the cross of the Christians and its usefulness to them, basing our discussion on the Gospel of this Sunday, the 21st after Trinity, and applying it to the congregation in accordance with their circumstances. Instead of repeating this matter in the form of question and answers in the review hour, as is usually done. I spoke to the listeners, who come to this review as frequently as they come to the sermon; and showed them in the most simple fashion: 1) that in the Old and the New Testament, God always led His dearest children along the path of the cross, and shaped them in the fiery furnace of misery into useful vessels and tools of His mercy. 2) If God is to purify and choose us (Isaiah 45:10-11), and if we wish the name of the Lord to be glorified in us and through us, we must not be afraid of the cross.

I explained that it is my true belief that we did not come to America by accident but that God has plans for us which the human eye cannot yet see. It has always been God's way, I continued, to start with something small and insignificant and to lead this small beginning through the cross, as can be seen in the case of the apostles and what was accomplished by them, also in the case of Luther and the magnificent work of the Reformation. If it should be God's wise and merciful intention that we, too, should be made into something for the praise of His magnificence, we certainly can not be without sorrow and various outer and inner crosses. We know what we have experienced so far, and we praise God for the benefit of the cross whenever we think back to our earlier and often very difficult circumstances: we do not really know what we may experience in the future; but as disciples of Christ and true Christians (Luke 9:23), we can expect the cross with more certainty than anything else. Yet we must not be afraid of it because the Word of God, many examples, and our own experience prove that this yoke of Christ does not bring damage but instead brings many spiritual and physical benefits. I explained that we would soon be over it and partaking of the joy of the Lord, just as some souls from this congregation, who had been especially purified and chosen under the cross, had preceded us. Now these are surely thanking our ever faithful God for the benefit of the cross which they had to bear in this wicked world.

After this I showed them more clearly my real purpose of this sermon, namely, that as Christians they must be content with anything that God may decide in regard to their land and that we will probably learn more about this after the arrival of Mr. Oglethorpe. I told them that people who have the best interest of the Salzburgers in mind have done all they can in this matter and that now everything must be left to the Lord who does everything well. They should remember the following points:

1) That a complete and clear report on the land and on their circumstances has been sent to our benefactors in England and in Germany. 2) That these benefactors have done everything they can by calling on and writing to the proper authorities. 3) That our condition has moved them greatly and that they have sent heartfelt prayers to God in our behalf. 4) When Mr. Oglethorpe comes back to this country we will also do our best through representations and intercession. We will tell him that the houses built for us should not be a deterrent to change because we would not expect new houses to be paid for by the Trustees, etc. These points and others which cannot be mentioned now should show them that people have done what they could and have neglected nothing which could serve the best interest of the congregation.

Now it would be proper for them (the Salzburgers) to 1) pray to God together and in private that only the will of God be done and that He guide the heart of Mr. Oglethorpe to do as He wills it. And, as they had already begun, they should continue to come to my room on Sunday and weekday evenings so that we can present these and other matters to our merciful Lord in song and prayers. 2) They should be completely satisfied with the will of God, no matter what comes and whether we are left at this place or transferred to another. Not to mention the fact that it is a great sin to ask for something contrary to the will of God and to insist on the fulfillment of one's own wishes, they should know from their own experience that it would have done harm to their bodies and souls if they had had their own way in everything since the days of their youth. Whenever they have worries about the future they should conduct themselves like the nobleman in the Gospel who followed the unfailing Word of God: The man believed these words and went.

We added that God had given them preferential treatment over many thousands in America and that they must continue to be satisfied with His guidance. We have many reasons for dwelling at length upon this matter at this time. Besides, it is our duty to prepare our congregation for all eventualities, in accordance with the Word of God. After supper many men and women came to us for prayer. After singing the hymn: Entrust your ways, etc., we again told them about the great benefits which all of us derive from the crosses and manifold trials of our youth. May God let us commend all of our simple efforts to His blessing.

The 27th, Oct. Yesterday and today we had a fine, misty rain and last night we had strong wind and rain accompanied by considerable cold. The Salzburgers have built themselves a hut in which they can keep warm by a fire when they have to be on watch at night. [Shortly before his departure Mr. Vat wished to make their guard duty easier for them by telling them that they might be relieved of inspecting so often at night, yet six men would still have to stand guard duty and sit by the fire. Perhaps he was afraid that there would be a change in this after his departure, for they had long ago asked him for this many times but not received it.] During the last few days the people have gathered a great many acorns which are to be found some miles from here along the river and also on the so-called Red Bluff. Some of those I have seen are larger than those in Germany. Squirrels and turkeys eat them frequently. In the same region there are also some nut trees which bear fruit, but the nuts have a very thick shell and little meat.

The 28th, Oct. [Because our diary has become very thick in a short time and we suppose that ships are now sailing directly from Charleston to London all the time, we plan to send it to Charleston at the first opportunity. Recently, namely at the beginning of last month, we wrote several letters in which we reported the condition of our congregation. For that reason we now plan only to address our diary to Court Preacher Ziegenhagen and to give brief reports about this and that.] This evening a [drunk] man came to see me and brought me a letter from Mr. Causton which, however, was wet and torn. Perhaps he had fallen off his horse and into the water. From what we could read, Mr. Causton reports that he has sent some chickens to Abercorn which the Salzburgers are to pick up tomorrow. He has also sent us a draft horse and will provide some more.

[The 29th, Oct. The strong wind continues day and night, and it is almost as cold as in mid winter. I am more inconvenienced now than usually by diarrhea, to which the cold weather, which one feels very keenly in a house of planks, may well contribute. The people are working hard to complete the fireplace. Christian Schweikert, Baron von Reck's former servant, is now miserable in body and soul. He is at odds with Mr. Zwifler, who will no longer give him any medicines. His spiritual condition required me to reveal to him emphatically his great corruption, which he does not wish to acknowledge, and to admonish him to penitence. The Rieser family and others in the congregation show him all possible love; yet there is little gratitude in him but rather defiance and obstinacy. God have mercy on him! He has very severe dysentery.]

The 30th, Oct. Yesterday and today the Salzburgers went to get the poultry that Mr. Causton had sent to Abercorn for us. Most of them were hens and roosters, but there were also a few geese, Welsh chickens, and ducks, numbering eighty-seven altogether. These last chickens are bigger and better looking than the first ones. Thus those people who did not get any from the first distribution did not suffer any loss. We have so distributed them that now both the first and the last Salzburgers are equally satisfied and all of them are giving praise to GOD for this latest good deed. Some of the hens and roosters that were received earlier had died since then but they were replaced at this time. [The Salzburgers are very pleased when one of us two is present in person at the distribution, and we gladly do this with good reason. Through Divine Grace much unnecessary talking and laughing can be prevented; and during the distribution we see to it that the people receive these benefactions with pleasure and are aroused to greater praise of God and hearty prayers for the benefactors.]

Construction of our fireplace led to the discovery of so much clay in our region that all of Ebenezer can be well supplied with it. It is said to be better than that which we formerly had to bring here by boat and which we could not get at all during periods of low water. The chimneys are being built of wood but they are so lined and guarded with sun-dried bricks and with clay that the houses will not be in any danger. They will not cost very much, and the first one that is nearly finished is so well built that Mr. Causton and others will doubtlessly be pleased by it.

The 31st, Oct. Approaching childbirth has put Mrs. Kalcher in such a state that she earnestly asks for, and needs, the prayers of the congregation. Those Salzburger women who have some experience show her every care and consideration, and what they do for her they do with heartfelt sighing and prayer. May the GOD who, for the sake of Christ's intercession, graciously heard our poor prayer for Mrs. Rottenberger, look upon us with mercy in this case also and send us aid when human aid ceases. This woman has given so much proof of her Christianity that we are sure she will get the rest promised to God's chosen people if God should impose physical death upon her. [Since neither of us could go to her] we let her husband tell her that she must not lose courage even under the worst conditions. Instead, she should strengthen faith in the Son of God who suffered the greatest pains for our sake, and should commend everything to her truly merciful Lord, no matter what His decision for her may be. Even her body would benefit from that, whereas both body and soul would suffer damage from despondency. We sent her the hymn: In all my deeds I follow the advice of the Highest who has and can do everything, etc. She is a great admirer of edifying songs.

Rheinländer intended to travel to Charleston by land, but he had to return after having covered half the distance because the way was too bad and dangerous. Meanwhile he had an opportunity to see the plantations in Carolina, which are said to be in good condition. [However, as he describes it, both the masters and the servants appear so miserable and live in such monstrous sins that one is horrified at it. He added that he could now understand what Ebenezer is and that he was now resolved to remain in Ebenezer with water and bread rather than to live well in a place where people walk the straight path to hell.] From this experience of his own he intends to tell all of our people about the advantages they have and how they could not thank God enough for the benefits they have received so far. We are often surprised that so little efforts is made to preach the word of God to the people in this country and to instruct the children in the ways of Christianity. In most cases the people on the plantations in Carolina are like the nobility in Germany and have means enough to employ theological students, as is done in Germany, for their own benefit and for that of their children. In England there are a number of societies established for the glory of God; and, if GOD would lead some of them to help conditions here with good advice and suggestions, it would be very advantageous for the Kingdom of God.

There are not nearly enough pastors in the cities, and they usually have plantations and large households so that they cannot do much for the people in the country. May God have mercy upon the poor provinces of America, where most people seek only worldly goods and in doing so provide for their eternal misfortune. Whoever can pray should pray to the Lord of the Harvest that He may send faithful workers for His harvest. We believe that good servants of Christ would not lack in suffering and adversity, but neither would they lack blessings. Good teachers have always had the most blessings on the path of the cross (1 Corinthians 16:9). If it were possible to establish a seminary here in America in which talented children could be taught piety, knowledge of the English language, and other necessary things, we could in time hope for many spiritual benefits from it. Perhaps God will give us an opportunity to speak with Mr. Oglethorpe about this. We shall do what we can with our children, with God's help. We believe that such arrangements open up a shorter road to the conversion of the heathens.

The 1st of November. Yesterday and last night the cold was so great that ice was formed. We are often surprised at this weather, especially when we think of how it usually is in Germany at this time. [Of the three boys who were sent to us some time ago from London by our benefactors the one who belongs to my dear colleague is the naughtiest and is inclined to every wickedness. In addition he is very sly and cunning and all the more dangerous because he has little to do at his house and is moreover very harmful for my two boys, particularly for Bishop. Therefore we have resolved to send him to a fine Salzburger for a while, under whose supervision and with whose help he is to clear out a piece of land and prepare it for a little garden, which will then fall to Mr. Gronau and be planted as he wishes. To be sure, this does not please the boy, who would rather assist our two boys, especially Bishop who is very attached to him, in our household chores. But it is to his own advantage to be held to, and instructed in, regular field work. Not only will we get on better with the two other boys, but we also hope to work on them with all possible diligence and to prepare them for the service of the Lord.

[Bishop has a quiet docile disposition and is loyal and diligent in all things, yet rather shy and timid. He attends divine services regularly and gladly, and he understands German rather well even though he does not yet speak very much. The other boy, by the name of Nicolas Carpenter, is not worth much, to be sure, but he does have a flexible and at the same time cheerful and clever disposition and would be capable of much good work, if he feared the Lord. I am very fond of them both; and, even though I could easily spare them from their work in our household, I would not like to dispense with them because of the hope I have in them for the service of the Lord; and I would not regret the costs that might have to be spent on them.]

The 2nd, Nov. Rottenbergers little daughter (one of the two twins) died this morning. She had been very weak since birth, and we rather expected her death. Last night and this morning the cold has been so severe that people say they hardly ever had it more cutting or penetrating in Salzburg. Mrs. Kalcher has improved and her seemingly dangerous condition has improved. She desired to speak with one of us, and my dear colleague went to see her and talked with her about the matters she reported. [Her heart is very disquieted, and the sins she previously committed assail her conscience so intensely that she can not express it sufficiently with words.] One can see that the Holy Ghost is chastising her and stripping her so that she will come to Christ naked and bare, troubled and burdened, [which is more necessary for her than for other people.]

Although it again turned very cold toward evening, a number of Salzburger men and women came to my room to pray with us. This pleased me very much. In the main we sing and pray, and the dear souls show great devotion and eagerness for both. Before prayer we usually speak to them about some edifying matter, for example, we tell them something about the Kingdom of God for the edification of all of us; we speak with them about matters that lead to the inner aspects of Christianity, showing them how, in His great mercy, the true GOD has let us experience His ways and guidance. Some have noticed that this simple exercise has already done much good for some who formerly had been satisfied with the outward aspects of Christianity. Everyone is free to come or to stay away. We only spend about one hour together.

[The 3rd, Nov. We would be ready now to send our diary to London, but we lack an opportunity to send it to Charleston. A few weeks ago the mail passed through our place en route to Savannah, but it has not yet returned. Even though some people travel through here on the way to Charleston, we can not entrust the letters to them too safely because we do not know them. We almost regret that in July we entrusted a thick diary together with many letters to a man who inspected our place and offered to forward them. His name is Savy. He travelled with Captain Thompson to England, and from there to Geneva. Only later we were informed that he stood in bad credit in Carolina and also with the magistry in Savannah and would have been put in prison if he had not saved himself in time. It will be easy for the Lord to dispose with His providence in this matter as He has done in the past. The letters were addressed to Secretary Newman.]

The 4th, Nov. Last night we had a south wind and with it we got warm weather, which does us a great deal of good after all the cold. Toward midday we had a violent thunderstorm and heavy rain. When visiting Mrs. Kalcher I found her to be still rather weak of body but very much strengthened in her faith in the Son of God and His precious redemption. At last God has looked with favor upon her sighs and tears by giving her assurance of the forgiveness of all her sins and by giving her over to much joy and praise of her magnificent Saviour. She has placed her hard and seemingly dangerous condition into the will of the Almighty and is determined, if God will save her life and rescue her from danger, to honor Him with serious Christian conduct and to continue asking for His grace and diligence. I took this opportunity to speak to her about the wise intentions of God during the troubles and trials of His children, and His great faithfulness. This brought me to two examples of pious women who had experienced in an exceptional way the helping power of the Lord Jesus during times of physical distress. We give whatever we can in the way of good advice and care of the body, but the rest we entrust to the LORD and His government, in this case as we have done in others.

A Salzburger made us a present of a turkey which weighed fourteen pounds. He had shot it on Red Bluff where he and other Salzburgers had been gathering a great many acorns. There are many such turkeys in this country, also a large number of wild ducks.[100] This Red Bluff is a high bank on the Savannah River, near the mouth of the Ebenezer river. This is the place to which the people wish to be transferred for a number of good reasons. There is a large strip of fertile soil there and it is conveniently located on the river, which would furnish easy communication by water with Purysburg, Pallachocolas, and some of the plantations in Carolina. There is grass and nourishment for pigs, cattle, and fowl there.

A little further downstream toward Purysburg there is another high bank which the Salzburgers call Indian Hut. The land there is also good, but Red Bluff is said to be better. The name Indian Hut does not come from the fact that Indians actually live there. Rather, the first Salzburgers to go there built a hut of posts, as the Indians do, and they had no other way of distinguishing this spot from other places and, consequently, this high ground has been called Indian Hut ever since that time. We are reporting this because I was told a few days ago that people in England were of the opinion that this land belonged to the Indians and that Indians lived there.

The 5th, Nov. After the people received their poultry and found that the recently distributed corn was bad, some of them found it necessary to go to Pallachocolas in our light boat, where corn and beans are said to be for sale. None can be purchased in Purysburg or anywhere else in this colony. The mild and wet weather changed again last night and it is now windy and cold again. Rottenberger's young son is very weak and gives little hope of getting better. In our prayers we have already given him back to the Lord Jesus, and the mother was very well satisfied with that. [Both twins were so weak immediately after their birth that we could not imagine that they would live this long.] In these circumstances we always give the mothers the best physical care available in this wilderness; but for the rest we must patiently resign ourselves to the will of the LORD, who so far has let us have some very bitter and hard, but well meant, experiences.

The 6th, Nov. Yesterday evening God released Rottenberger's weak child from this vale of tears through timely death. The father, who reported it to me, spoke in moving and edifying terms about this act of God. [Since we still have no news as to whether Mr. Vat is still serving the Salzburgers in Savannah, I was compelled to write a letter to Mr. Causton that only half the meal was distributed to the first Salzburgers by Mr. Vat, and likewise that the people had received no molasses, butter, or cheese, which important things he was requested to send up soon. Tullius, whom we let join us because of the fireplace construction, understands how to make tar and pitch very well; for he was used for this purpose a short time ago. Some of the Salzburgers wish to learn it too, and he is showing them how today so that in the future they will be able to make as much as they need for their households. We need pitch now to prepare and preserve our boat better, and this gave the occasion for this work.]

The 7th, Nov. Late last night our boat returned with the purchased corn. As it is very fast it covered 40 English miles downstream that afternoon while only two oarsmen were used. The people like to ride in it twice as well as they do in the old one. When the people were about to leave our place they met two men servants[101] who pretended they wanted to go to Pallachocolas but had lost their way. They asked to be taken along in the boat, which was done. But on the way it was found out that they had run away from Savannah and intended to cross over into Carolina. They were delivered to the captain at the fort. Two men on horseback had ridden through our place in an effort to catch them. It often happens that servants run away from Savannah and are caught again at Pallachocolas, and it is said that treatment which some of them get from their masters is responsible for such escapes. People here are accustomed to treat servants like slaves because there are negro slaves in our neighborhood, but some of them are very malicious. We are very happy to have made the acquaintance of several planters, from whom we will be able to purchase corn, beans, potatoes, chickens, butter, etc. at a good price; and, through God's blessing, they may be of use to us in other ways as well.

The 8th, Nov. A woman of the congregation[102] has been made very uncomfortable with pain and weakness which lasted for several days. When we expressed sorrow over this, she said that the LORD was doing the right thing for her, that so far her days had been far too good, and that such chastisement was very salutary for her; her pains were easy to bear because her heart could taste so sweetly the comfort of divine and fatherly grace and love. In Salzburg God had made her have pangs of conscience and soul because of her sins which pained her much more, and she had had no one to give her the least comfort. Instead, her relatives had mocked her and had been happy over her misery. She marveled very much at the goodness and wisdom of God, who not only so arranged it for her but had fairly forced her to go to America, where she was now receiving nothing but pure spiritual and worldly benefits through which God intended to lead her more and more to penance.

[The 9th, Nov. During the afternoon service Mrs. Rheinländer was churched with her baby; and this was carried out just as with Mrs. Pichler. In the case of the Rheinländers, both parents and children, there is not much progress with regard to Christianity. A short time ago the man evinced much good and claimed to feel something of the bitterness of sin and of the anger of God that hovers over it; but now he has slipped back very much. Toward evening they both came to visit me and let me tell them and read them many good things. They lived for several years in New York, Pennsylvania, and other regions thereabout and knew various preachers who were sent from Bremen and used their offices. However, they can tell many stories about their godless behaviour and shallow teachings whenever anyone wishes to hear them.]

The 10th, Nov. Yesterday we heard some cannon shots at our place, and we suspect that this means the happy arrival of Mr. Oglethorpe. As it means much to us to be certain about this, we sent our boy on horseback to Abercorn today to learn the reasons for the shooting. But he brought the report that the shooting had been done by the people of a certain plantation, probably for no other reason than frivolity and levity, [for in this colony much powder is shot up uselessly in this way.] Meanwhile our boy also brought the news that Mr. Causton had sent sixty-six fowl, among them geese, Welsh and other chickens, to Abercorn for our people. God willing, they will be fetched tomorrow. The stack of pine wood which the people had made last week for the purpose of making tar was lit today and the people got from it nearly one and one half barrels of tar. At the same time the mason Tullius showed them how to make pitch. The stock of wood was only five and one half feet high and six feet in circumference.

The 11th, Nov. Since the mason Tullius had finished his work for us, he was taken back to Purysburg in our boat this morning. My dear colleague found it necessary to go to Purysburg with him, partly to take care of some business and partly for the sake of the Lutherans there. It is always good to visit them occasionally and to help them in their physical hardship with instruction and comfort derived from the Word of God, and to do our duty in accordance with the nature of their needs. This time he will pay particular attention to the school that was started recently.

The poultry we received was distributed, and again the people were very much pleased and awakened to praise of God and intercession for our benefactors. As these creatures are sent to the Salzburgers by worthy benefactors, we like to distribute them in accordance with their wishes and opinions which we have asked of all of them. Prior to the distribution we have one of the most intelligent members of the congregation come to us in order to consult with him. After the congregation has assembled, we make them a number of propositions, and all of us choose the one that appears to be fairest and best. It has been necessary to have such consultations in this matter because all of the fowl are not sent at the same time or in the same numbers or in the same kind and quality.

The 12th, Nov. With the first quarter of the moon we are having much rain and very mild weather. Two Indians called here and requested us to repair their two flint-locks. I gave them breakfast and some uncooked rice to take with them and referred them to the locksmith in Abercorn. They were both handsome, and they conducted themselves with modesty. This evening my dear colleague came back home again and reported that the schoolmaster in Purysburg is showing much faithfulness and diligence, and that the children are profiting from his instruction. [However, he must put up with a lot of inconvenience, fault-finding, and contradiction from some of the parents; but to this he can accommodate himself rather well. Among the Lutherans there there is not much unity or Christian love; and one will have to use all means, with God's grace, to prevent perdition there, especially if ever they request Holy Communion again. They err and stray like lost sheep, each sees only his own path, as a result of which there can be only disorder.

The 13th, Nov. N. N. [Rieser] has become sick and he now seems to work more earnestly than formerly for the salvation of his soul. He spoke movingly about the evil of sin, about penance, faith, and eternity, and we could see from his words and tears that everything he said was coming from his heart and that the things I interposed were going to it. It is his intention from now on to prepare himself seriously for eternity and to pray sincerely for that purpose. His concepts and expressions of the ways to salvation were so thorough that they made me very happy and provided me with no little edification.

During our conversation his wife returned home from her field work, and she also thanked God with tears in her eyes for grace which He had shown her through the preaching of His gospel at Ebenezer. [This led her to what had happened to her in Salzburg. She grew up in ignorance and without instruction; yet she always had a desire to take the right way to heaven. When the persecutions began publicly and the Lutheran teaching was damned along with those who professed it, this confused her greatly, since she did not know to what party she should hold. From simple people she heard that she should hold to the teaching that Christ taught his disciples, but its content was still concealed from her. In her sickness she went to the doctor, from whom she had to hear that she had an incurable disease, namely, cancer of the tongue; so then she wished to go confess and prepare herself to die. She revealed to him her dilemma, namely that she was confused, there must be two gospels, and she did not know which was the right one. Thereupon he answered her that there were not two gospels but just one and that the Lutherans expounded it wrongly.

[After the doctor had warned her to prepare for death, she went to her priest at the auxiliary church, whom they called Cooperator, and complained to him quite openly of her troubles and begged him, please for God's sake, to show her the right way to heaven. She had children and much hardship, and how miserable it would now be if she missed heaven too. He then asked her what

she believed, whether she was Roman Catholic? She answered that
she would gladly believe that which Christ had taught his apostles.
He told her she should just remain in this faith and not drop
away. Others would hate her and persecute her if she only said
she was not Lutheran but Apostolic-Catholic. As for Purgatory,
about which she asked him, she just did not have to swear by it,
for it was not necessary. In addition, this priest comforted and encouraged her with moving words so that she was very comforted.

[Finally it came to the attention of the secular authorities that
she had a Lutheran husband, who had already been ordered to
emigrate. But because her Catholic friends did not want to let her
go, they got behind the priests, who then went to great efforts to
persuade her to remain. The Jesuit, who was sitting with the other
priests, first presented her with several articles of faith to which
she should swear, e.g. whether there was a God in heaven, and
whether she was ready to swear to it? Ans. Yes. Whether she would
swear that there is a Purgatory and that it is as true as God in
heaven? Ans. I neither can nor will swear that, the Cooperator
told me I need not swear that, it is not necessary. (The Cooperator had been removed because he was too kind.) The priests said:
"We are not asking what the Cooperator said. You should obey
our words." She answered: "After all, you gentlemen directed us
to the Cooperator and said: 'If you do not understand something,
then you have a good Cooperator. Go to him.' Likewise, our
pastor (who was present at the time) said himself in Sunday-
school: 'There is probably a Purgatory, but we do not know
whether it is a fire or water or snow or a deep pit.' Why then
should I swear by such an uncertain thing?"

[In order to please them, as her authorities, she was willing to
believe it because they wished her to, but she could not swear to
it. The priests got angry at that and referred her from themselves
to the Pope: she should believe him and not just to please them.
Ans. I do not believe the Pope, because he is a sinful person like
other men. I believe what Christ and his apostles have taught.
Qu. Whether she did not wish to damn the Lutherans along with
their teaching? Ans. That I can not do; I am much too simple and
do not know their teaching. The priests have the key to loosen or
bind, they have damned them, so it is not necessary for me to do
so. I am much too simple. Qu. Whether she believes in heaven
and hell? Ans. Yes. Qu. Why is she not too simple for this? Qu.
That is in my creed (Symbolum Apostolicum) and therefore I

must believe it. And if there were no heaven or hell then we would need no spiritual advisor.

[Afterwards they did everything possible to persuade her to let her husband emigrate alone; but she always defended herself with the assertion she had made before the Holy Sacrament at her marriage, namely that she would cleave to her husband in happiness and sorrow, in good days and bad, etc. They tried to convince her that that applied only if he remained Catholic, etc.; but she objected that these conditions were not added at the time and that she would remain with her husband, come what may. She added that she was very frightened before the examiners but that she became very courageous when she called upon her Lord. Her old mother could not go with them because of her age, even though she wished to; but her brothers and sisters had backed down through love of temporal things, and this grieved her in her heart.

[This woman is a particular admirer of the Word of God, which she practices diligently. So far she has been very helpful to women in various conditions, serving them by day and night, and even now she is helping the very sick Schweikert with great faithfulness and much hard work. May God reward her and hers for the good she is doing unto others.]

The 14th, Nov. Last night Mrs. Kalker was delivered of a healthy daughter. Her recent and seemingly dangerous condition had changed after a few days and she had recovered completely, so that she could walk about until almost the last hour. This is renewed proof that God answers prayers, which has served to give much strength to us and to the parents.

[Ruprecht Zittrauer wishes to marry the widow in Purysburg, whose daughter Schweiger recently married, if we can advise him to do so. She would also like to move to Ebenezer because she is faring very miserably in Purysburg with her two children. The chief obstacle to this marriage is her passage money from London to Purysburg, which, according to the statement of her aforementioned daughter, should run to 30 guineas. Even if she wished to sell her lot, she would not get much for it because it is full of swamp and water and therefore of not much value. It is a hardship for poor people in Purysburg that they are compelled to pay their passage money and, after a few years have passed, a heavy interest, namely 10 percent. If the family is large, then they receive much land, namely 50 acres per head; and for this, whether they have built anything on it or not, they must pay a ground rent after ten years (which are calculated not according to the time of arrival of each of the colonists, but of the establishment of the city of Purysburg).

[Among the people there there is such poverty, hunger, and misery that it can not be described. And because the Salzburgers in contrast enjoy a golden age in spiritual and physical things, many of them long to go from there to here. The Germans in Purysburg sigh for the arrival of Mr. Oglethorpe just as much as we do because they know that he is a great patron of the Germans and of the poor. Many more colonists are expected at Purysburg, and then the misery will become even greater; for provisions are lacking, and what is given to the colony goes through dishonest hands. We do not like to think of particular circumstances, for then the misery there would become even more apparent and palpable. The sighs that are made because of Mr. Pury alone are uncountable.]

It appears that Schweikert is getting closer and closer to death but also to blessed eternity. He considers it a particular benefit that God not only brought him back to Ebenezer from Boston, but that He also imposed upon him a long and difficult sickness which has given him time to think, and prepare for his salvation. One can see very well that his present talk about recognition of sin, trust in Christ, and hope for salvation is quite different in tone from earlier times when he was full of self-righteousness and piety and thought to get to heaven merely by reading and praying. He is happy to die, but he would like to enjoy Holy Communion one more time. However, he does not want to hurry this. Instead, he wants to prepare himself for it for several days because this act is very important. [To be sure, Mr. Zwifler had not wished to give him any medicine for a few days because of the patient's rudeness and unusual behavior; but afterwards he had cared for him again with all possible loyalty. Through his present good behavior this Mr. Zwifler is making good all his past conduct; and he would win the confidence of his patients if he should continue in this, as we hope he will through the Grace of God.

[The 15th, Nov. Three months ago Mrs. Ortmann took a little English girl from Savannah into her home to rear her and to teach her sewing and housework. But she soon got tired of her because she had to chastise and punish her so often and so violently that some people in the community were offended and complained to us. Therefore we took the opportunity to rebuke her for such mercilessness and advised her to send her home again rather than to cause further vexation. This could cause great calumny, as if English children were brutally treated in Ebenezer. She promised to send her back to her parents at the first opportunity, because, in her opinion, she was incorrigible in various ways. I also warned him especially how he could become suspected of being a tyrannical schoolmaster because of the severe discipline that his wife used on the child.

[We would have sent our diary to Charleston, but we had no opportunity to do so. The postman who has been expected so far is said to be lying sick in Savannah. Mrs. Rheinländer has again given occasion for disorder and misunderstanding in the community through her gossip, even though she still hopes to give the appearance of being a conscientious and circumspect woman and good Christian. Because we now know from experience that, in her case, if the fire is not stamped out at once at the first spark it can result in a great scandal, I had her come to me yesterday and not only rebuked her for the matter that had occurred but also revealed to her the wicked basis of her heart as best I could and showed her that she and her husband could not be saved in such an unconverted condition, etc. Should there be any more excesses or scandals, then she should know that we would perform our office very earnestly against her and her husband, since nothing had been accomplished through our previous way of love. Because her *opus operatum* and self-righteousness were now undone through God's Word, she became very angry; but in that she manifested new and very palpable tokens of her extremely miserable condition.

[Her husband also came to me this morning to discuss his and his wife's condition further with me. On this occasion, contrary to my expectations, he conducted himself so well that I can not help but believe that the good that had taken place in him for some time but had gradually become lax and dissipated was not hypocrisy but the Work of God. He complained to me of the domestic burden because of his wife, and how he endeavored as best he could to take her along on the right way. And, because he well knew her emotions and extravagances, he was noting the proverbs and verses from the hymns with great diligence that are precisely against her and her behavior, and with them he had so far accomplished something.]

The 16th, Nov. Today Schweikert received Holy Communion. He gave evidence which makes us believe that he was worthy of receiving it and that temporal death will soon bring him to the

Holy Communion of the wedding of the Lamb in Heaven. School-master Ortmann is serving him well with readings and with pray-ers, both of which the patient wants very much to hear. And Mrs. Ortmann cares for his physical needs to the best of her ability.

After the noon service it was God's pleasure to take away from us, through temporal death, our mother-in-law, Mrs. Rohrmoser (or, as she is properly called after her husband, Mrs. Kroher). For more than eight days she had had to suffer the most severe pain. This loss hurts us very much because in her we lost a truly pious mother-in-law who was also very well experienced in matters of the household; but, as she has now preceded us into happy eternity we will not begrudge her this precedence because, if we follow in the footsteps of the Lord JESUS with honesty as she did, we will surely find her again before the throne of the Lamb.

What we said on November 8th about a sick woman in the congregation was said about her. If we wanted to go into detail, it would be possible to report much that is edifying about the great grace of God which dwelled in her heart and governed her entire conduct, because we have always had her with us and we have loved her as one of the real gems of the congregation. She belonged to "the silent of the land" who prefer to keep their treasures in their hearts rather than let others see them.[103] Con-sequently, she lived quietly before God and tended to her affairs faithfully, being guided by constant prayer. Thus she partook of the blessing of the first Psalm: Whatsoever the righteous doeth shall prosper. She was nothing in her own eyes; but Christ, His sacrifice, and His [dear] Gospel were so great in her heart and mouth that her expressions often made me marvel besides provid-ing me with edification.

Because of her love for Christ she had tearfully but willingly left her husband, with whom she had had happy days in Salz-burg, and her children, one of whom was still nursing at its mother's breast. Since leaving her husband's house she has prayed earnestly for her family and has commended her small children to the care and supervision of her heavenly Father on innu-merable occasions. God could not have given her greater joy on this earth and a greater worldly treasure than to have arranged for her children to be brought up by her according to the Gospel and to be taught in our schools here in Ebenezer.

She was well aware of the general corruption [in Popery and also in the Protestant church] and could not marvel enough about the great mercy and guidance of God who arranged things so well

for her and brought her to this wilderness and to unhampered
worship. During her last sickness she did not speak much because
of her great pain. She only praised God, saying that He had given
her preference on her sickbed over many other sick persons and
that she did not deserve this because she was the greatest sinner
and the most unworthy wife. With all her poverty of spirit and
knowledge of her failings, her heart remained as it had been, and
thus was full of grace even in sickness, full of forgiveness of sins,
and full of love for the Heavenly Father in Christ, her Redeemer.
During her days of good health she had stored so much good
within herself that no impatience or complaints came from her
when she was in severe [excessive] pain. Instead, we could find in
her only contentment and eagerness to put the chastisement of
the Heavenly Father to good use.

Today, the day of her death, she would have liked to partake
of Christ's body and blood at Holy Communion although she had
received this benefit with the congregation only five weeks ago,
if she had not been prevented from doing so by constant vomiting; but in this, too, she resigned herself completely to the will
of GOD. Shortly before her departure her worst pains had let up
so that one could hear nothing from her except very short breathing. We knelt around her bed together and prayed over her. She
went to her Saviour during this prayer, with her eyes open and
looking toward heaven, her hands moving as if they wanted to
seize the crown, and her features showing love. Shortly before
that I had repeated for her several time the words: Jesus Christ
has loved us and has washed off our sins with His blood, etc. I
also told her that the Lord Jesus would like it very much if before her departure from this world she would bathe once more
in His blood so she would appear before the Father as a virgin
of the Lamb.

She was loved by everyone in the congregation, and her very
sincere and honest nature as well as her readiness to help inspired great respect in everybody. As all of the Salzburgers know
what I, my dear colleague, and our two helpmates, who are her
daughters, had in her, they all feel very strongly about the loss
which God made us suffer. As much as my grief permitted, I gave
warning to those people who came to evening prayer that they
must not postpone conversion until they are on their sickbed if
they want their end to be as happy and good as it was for this
saved woman in spite of all her pain [during which time we and
Mr. Zwifler exercised every possible care, but without effect, be-

cause she had received a bodily harm, I know not from where, which was incurable especially in our circumstances.

[Continuation of the Diary Monday the 17th of November 1735]

The 17th, Nov. [We have waited a long time for an opportunity for Charleston but have not been able to find any. Therefore my dear colleague has resolved to go tomorrow himself to Savannah to entrust our diary, which is addressed to Mr. Court Preacher Ziegenhagen, to a certain man. The first Salzburgers are still lacking half the meal for this quarter year, which is to be brought back in this way.] The present weak condition of my body has made it necessary for me to give up my instruction for the time being. Thus the children are now given only an hour of catechism by my dear colleague. This will not do any harm because their parents make them go to the daily prayer hours, and they learn much that is good besides.

The 18th, Nov. We have had cold and penetrating rains for several days. It is true that it cleared up last night, but the north-westerly wind has again made the air very raw and cold. We intend to hold Holy Communion next Sunday. As usual, this was announced to the congregation last Sunday as well as a week earlier. The people are to announce their intention during the first days of this week. Married people come together, but single ones come alone, and we talk with them and pray with them as their circumstances require. On such days we find reason for sadness and sighing in some of them, but most of them give us reasons to be joyful and to praise God on such occasions. This makes us forget, so to speak, all that is bitter and unpleasant and encourages us in the further execution of our office. But, praise God! most communicants come out frankly with the confession of their state of mind. They tell us simply about the hindrances and advantages they have in their Christianity, or about incorrect application of this or the other benefit; and all of this gives us very necessary and salutary *Monita pastoralia* which we can bring out during public service for the benefit of all the listeners.

The 19th, Nov. An Englishman called on me who had been sent seven weeks ago from Savannah to the Creek Indians who live some three hundred miles inland from Savannah. He complained that, although he had made this trip many times, it had never been so difficult or dangerous as this time because the rivers and swamps everywhere were high. I asked him the following questions: 1) Where do these Indians live? Ans. Not on the Savannah River but further up in the country, where they can be reached only by land. There are some rivers, to be sure, but they cannot be passed because of the Frenchmen that live on them. 2) How do these people live? Do they live together in towns and do they live more orderly than the Indians in this colony? Ans. There are a number of towns in which live perhaps four hundred men (not counting the women and children). The men go hunting and collect a great many skins. The women plant corn, beans, sweet potatoes, and tobacco; and they also raise many hogs and fowl, which can be bought at a low price. Of wine, beer, and the like they know nothing. 3) Are they, like the others, given to drunkenness and especially the drinking of rum? Ans. Yes, very much so, and they hold nothing more precious than a bottle of rum: but they cannot get as much of it as others because everything must be brought to them by packhorse and thus only small kegs ever get to them. 4) Do white people carry on trade with them? Ans. "Yes, many Englishmen live among them; I have lived among them myself for some time. They buy their skins from them and give them in return all sorts of ribbons, knives, guns, powder, lead, white woolen cloth, and also rum. They do not accept money." 5) Are the white people who visit them or live with them in any danger? Ans. "None whatsoever. When they are drunk they will cause inconvenience and it is better to avoid them but when they are sober they are very friendly and eager to help the white man." 6) Is any form of worship to be seen among them? Ans. None at all. Further question: Is there no opportunity for such even among the Christians? Ans. The Frenchmen may have it. 7) How is the soil there? Ans. Very fertile, there is hardly any comparison between the land there and the best land of Carolina. 8) How is the weather? Ans. Much hotter in the summer than in Georgia, but also much colder in the winter. During the hot summertime the people must often bathe in the river if they are to stand the heat. 9) What sort of clothes do the heathens wear? Ans. Much the same as the Indians in this country. They will not accept European dress. 10) Is there a regular road that leads to them from this colony, and is the trip dangerous? Ans. It is a regular footpath which is very well known by the Spanish Indians as well. This way leads through many swamps and also across rivers or creeks which have to be crossed on horseback. From Pallachocolas on there is no house along the way to give shelter, and you must sleep in the forest under the open sky at all times. You build a good fire and hobble your horse and

turn it loose with a bell on it to eat the very good grass. You have
to carry food for yourself, whereas there is enough drinking water
everywhere. There are many wild beasts in the woods but they
do not harm people. They are the same kinds to be found in this
colony. The only thing one has to fear on this journey is the
Spanish Indians who are roaming the country, they are cowardly
if you carry a gun and look them straight in the eye; but if you
are timid and afraid they tie you up, carry you away, and burn
you at the stake. As the man was in a hurry to reach Savannah
this very day, we were not able to speak with him further. He
had letters for Mr. Causton that had been written by the Englishmen living out there.

The 20th, Nov. My dear colleague returned home this evening
from Savannah, where he found a man who took on the task of
properly posting the letters to Charleston. The peas we mentioned
recently were brought back at this time; but they are not for us
alone, as we had heard before. Instead, they are to be a present
for the entire congregation from a benefactor in Charleston. People in Savannah are expecting Mr. Oglethorpe every day and
with him a number of additional ships with eleven hundred
colonists.

The 21st, Nov. Christian Schweikert died last night. It has
been very edifying to talk with him of late, for his talk dealt
with nothing except his soon-to-be-hoped-for release and the joy
of eternal life which Christ had gained for him and which he
would surely achieve because he was now quite sure that God
had accepted him and had forgiven all of his sins. During the
time of his great physical weakness he sighed constantly to God
and was overjoyed whenever we prayed with him or read to him
from the Word of God and other useful books, by day and by
night. The people who were with him and waited on him could
see a complete change in his spirit. He no longer was the old
Schweikert but a lamb of Christ and a child of God. The home-
ward journey of the late Mrs. Rohrmoser made a deep impression
on him and strengthened his longing for death. We do not doubt
that he, too, saved his soul and that he went to the Father through
Christ, who is the way and the truth.

It gave no little fright when I told him a few weeks ago I was
afraid that he would die in sin because of his imagined righteousness, etc. In the time that followed, God gave His mercy so that
he became smaller and smaller in his own eyes, while Christ and
His precious sacrifice became greater and dearer. And after the

Father had revealed His Son to him through the Gospel and had assured him of His grace, his longing for death became so great that, as he assured us, he would not consider it a favor if someone were to give him back his health. Schoolmaster Ortmann, who with his wife had done much for him in various ways, told me that once he had wanted to pray with him for the restoration of his health; but we would not agree and said that he would rather die because now, Praise God!, his house was in order. O how wondrous are the means God uses for the rescue of the souls of wretched men! One can see this very clearly from this example.

The 22nd, Nov. The rice which had been planted by the Salzburgers in communal labor as an experiment did not do very well because there was no rain for too long a period. But we see from our own garden and from the experience of others that planting it does not require much more labor than is required for other fruits of the land; and the rich yield makes all of the labors worthwhile. It is said that the hardest labor is required in threshing the rice to separate it from its hulls. It is firmly embedded in them, to all appearances as much so as the barley in Germany. Only negro slaves are used to perform this labor in Carolina. In time we will perhaps be able to use machines for this in this country, similar to the ones used in Germany for millet and barley.

The 24th, Nov. Our dear GOD has given His blessing to the preaching of His word on Saturday during preparation for Holy Communion, and also yesterday, as was made clear to me today through several examples. A man who until now had been a troubled and burdened individual, sighing and struggling for mercy, told me happily that he now knew for certain that he was a child of God. He did not trust his heart at all and knew that there was still much malice in it; but the testimony of the Holy Ghost was so strong that he now felt quite differently.

My circumstances do not permit me to undertake the journey to Savannah [which was recently reported under the date of Nov. 22,] and therefore my dear colleague is doing it in my place. However, I gave him a detailed letter for Mr. Causton in which I had to report a number of things. We and our congregation are now living together very happily in this community and we pray to God that He may keep out of our place all those who cause confusion and sorrow. But the will of God be done! Chastisement is often as necessary for us as other important things. Mr. Zwifler showed me a fish-otter which he had shot in our river. It weighed 19 pounds. There are many such animals in the river here in this region. They are frequently observed, sometimes in the water and sometimes in the trees, holding large fish, and especially eels, in their mouths or in their paws.

The 25th, Nov. The people now have much poultry but not enough feed for it. Those who have the money would like to buy some if only it were available in this vicinity. There is none in Purysburg, and it is very far to Pallachocolas by water. Besides on their recent trip our people have not been able to buy as much corn and beans there as they wanted. Yesterday three men went there by land in order to ask for some from another planter. If it is available at a reasonable price the boat will be sent up. I have added this point about the lack of feed to the letter which I wrote to Mr. Causton yesterday. The inclement weather has changed again. Yesterday we had a warm rain which, however, did not last long; and today we have had lovely summer weather. The three men returned from Pallachocolas this afternoon and brought the news that no more corn is available there. They learned that tomorrow a boat load of sweet potatoes is to pass by the mouth of our river and that the owner is willing to sell a few bushels to our people. Some of them will go there since they will be short of provisions because they must feed their corn to their livestock.

The 26th, Nov. My dear colleague returned from Savannah this morning; and we hope to be relieved of the need to travel from now until the time of Mr. Oglethorpe's arrival. This time I have had some coarse cloth brought back from Savannah in order to supply the poor amongst us with some clothes that are warmer than linen. God be praised for providing for us in every respect in this wilderness. On this trip my dear colleague and the Salzburgers spent the night in the house of the Indian King Tomo-chi-chi because they were overcome by darkness and could not reach Savannah. In his little house put together of long shingles this king keeps better order than the other Indians; but his clothes and manner of living are not much better. He accepted them into his house kindly and gave them a place to sleep.

The 27th, Nov. During my visit to their house, the members of a certain family spoke about the many benefits which have been poured on us, so to speak, partly by the Trustees and partly by the very praiseworthy Society. We rarely miss an opportunity to remind our listeners of these and to encourage their heartfelt gratitude toward God and man. Just now some of them told me about the edifying thoughts that are to be found in the late Dr.

Richter's little book about the nobility of the soul[104] which they had borrowed from me a few weeks ago for the sake of the hymns on the last few pages. In order to get some good material for conversation I read them the beautiful letter which the said Dr. Richter had written to his mother about the death of his brother. Through God's blessing this gave all of us edification and pleasure.

The 28th, Nov. The nice warm weather continues. Although turnips were planted at the beginning of the fall they are not growing because of the freeze. Now we are again having the same kind of seed put in our garden, for we want to try it in different ways and at different times to see if it will grow. In Carolina people have plenty of turnips, radishes and similar roots, as well as cabbage and greens during the winter.

The 29th, Nov. All day long today we have had a warm and heavy rain. Sanftleben came to see me in order to let me underline for him some of the main verses of the Old and the New Testament so that he can review and better remember them. On this occasion he told me how wondrously God had led him ever since his youth, and how He had furthered his physical and spiritual well being. He was born in Silesia, of poor parents who were able to send him to school for only half a year; yet through God's blessing, he learned to read a little during this time, and he considers this a particular benefit from God which was not received by any of his sisters or brothers. Since his parents were very poor he had to go into service with someone who kept him so badly that he would have lost his physical health and spiritual salvation if God had not freed him from his situation through sickness.

Soon after that he learned the carpenter's trade. After he had finished his apprenticeship his spirit was very restless but he lacked the knowledge of the right road to salvation. It was this restlessness which caused him to sign up as a colonist for America, and now he can see clearly the aim God had in regard to his soul. God has opened his eyes so that now he can see what salvation is and that it is not as easy to be saved as young people like him are apt to imagine. This man is well behaved and attentive during the services, he prays diligently in his little house, he sets a good example for everyone with his Christian conduct, and he is an industrious and skillful worker.

The 30th, Nov. We intend to do this year just as we did during the last church year, namely, to base our morning sermons on the regular Sunday and holy day Gospels. We like to do this very much because 1) the other beautiful texts that are in the

Bible besides the Gospels are read and applied to the congregation partly during evening prayer and partly on other occasions. 2) The Gospels are known to the people and thus they can more easily remember the divine truths presented to them. 3) Those who cannot read, or who do not have the time or the ability to learn to, know the content of these Gospels and therefore can understand more easily and remember longer the things that are said for their edification. Without that, they are very much grieved because they cannot remember as well as they wish the divine truths they hear. 4) Such well known texts give us excellent opportunity, on Sundays as well as on other days, for private conversations with children and adults, and it is easier to examine the people about them.

This year the afternoon catechizations are based on the regular Sunday epistles and the children are asked questions about them. The catechism, on the other hand, will be briefly explained and used for edification during the regular evening prayer hours as soon as the Psalms of David are finished. We are now at the one hundred and thirty-sixth Psalm. The congregation attend the prayer hours regularly and well. They will probably like these consecutive considerations of the catechistical truths better than hearing about them only once every week, because they may well forget in the interval what they heard the first time.

The congregation's great hunger for the word of God makes it necessary for us to continue the Sunday review through this winter, although it will have to be done by artificial light now that the days are getting shorter. The assembly of the dear people at our house after supper is becoming larger and they cannot praise enough the Grace of God which they are receiving in this simple way.

The 1st of December. Mrs. Schweighofer suffered a stroke yesterday afternoon and had to be carried to bed without being able to speak. I was called to her at once, since it seemed she would die immediately. After she was able to speak a little once again, she complained bitterly and very tearfully about her unfaithful Christian conduct. Among other things, she said: "Our Lord has suffered so much for my great sins, and I have been so ungrateful to Him," etc. Yesterday and today she was very anxious for some comfort; but, as He has done on earlier occasions, the LORD accepted her soul this time so that she would not perish.

Shortly before her stroke yesterday she had read a meditation from Schaitberger, page 47. As she related, God had blessed this very much for the refreshment of her heart, which prepared her for her present difficult condition of body and soul, as it were. The title of this meditation is: *The Comfort-Voice of the Lord Christ.* Today, after her mind had been cleared with the presentation of several comforting verses from the Scripture, I had to read said meditation again for her, together with the beautiful hymn: My Jesus is very fond of me, etc. The first verse which God blessed for her was Isaiah 54:10-11, through which I showed her that God called Himself merciful because He has the merciful heart of a father when it comes to the failings of His children. Such afflicted and uncomforted often think God is angry with them and will send them to hell and divert His grace from them, etc.; but He, the true God who does not lie, says: Mountains shall depart, etc.

With the verse Isaiah 49:14-15, I led her to the thoughts she herself had about her weak and still uneducated children. As she lamented again this time, she is very much grieved about having to leave wretched and still uneducated children behind who will be a burden. She cannot forget them and would gladly care for them in the best way if only she could do so, etc. We told her that God has the spirit of a father, that our grief grieves Him, etc. This woman is an old and good disciple of the LORD JESUS whom we would like to keep in our congregation longer, but there seems to be little hope for this life. She was bled today.

Last week the Salzburgers had been summoned to come to Abercorn to help launch the boat that has been built for us, since it is said to be very large and many hands will be needed for it.

To be sure that the people will not make this bad and wet trip in vain, I sent my boy to get definite news about the boat; and upon his return he brought us a letter which had been brought to Savannah by a ship recently arrived from London. It was the copy of Mr. Newman's letter of May 13th. But he had used the other side of the letter for some brief news which he wrote down on August 2nd, such as that Baron von Reck was on his way to London with 50 or 60 new colonists and that he would come to Georgia, that Senior Urlsperger and court chaplain Ziegenhagen are well, that Mr. Oglethorpe will go to sea about September and that he will try to alleviate a number of our difficulties after his arrival in Georgia. [My boy understood from the man who brought the letter that one of us should come to Savannah because things had arrived for us. But because no report was to be found in the letter and Mr. Causton had written nothing, we are remaining

at home, since the trip is more a burden than a pleasure for us.]
Tomorrow a large number of Salzburgers will go to Abercorn
to launch their boat and to take it to Savannah for hauling provisions. This morning five more Salzburgers went to Savannah in
the old boat, which they have patched once again, in order to get
the rest of the provisions for last year; [and they will be able to
bring us further news of these things.]

The 3rd, Dec. My dear colleague and I found Mrs. Schweighofer in such a magnificent state that we had to praise our truly
merciful God for it. From her face and her lovely expression we
could recognize a great calmness of soul. She spoke very little,
to be sure, because the weakness of her body did not permit her
to say many words; but what she said was heartfelt and strong.
Among other things she said: "I now know from experience that
God and His Grace are everything, while I am nothing and can
do nothing. This God has taught me in my trials. Praise God and
Thanks! They have been bitter and hard, but they have been
most useful. Now they are over and I know our LORD. Surely,
He will not leave me now but will take me unto Him soon, etc."

I spoke with her briefly about the example of old Simeon and
about his words in Luke 2:29. I also read her the first part of the
first chapter of the first epistle of Peter. This pleased her very
much and she made several comments here and there. Her special
calmness of spirit and her attitude so serene and content in Christ
were all the more impressive to me because on previous days I
had been able to see in her only struggles, and little comfort.
After our prayer I advised her to continue to penetrate into the
Lord Jesus with constant sighing and prayer during the perhaps
short period that was left her, and always to ponder some Gospel
verses in her heart. She answered that she was doing both and
that she needed to; for Christ, the LORD, told His disciples:
Watch and pray, that ye enter not into temptation; the spirit is
indeed willing, but the flesh is weak.

The 4th, Dec. The poor people for whom stockings and trousers
for this cold weather have been made from the cloth that was
bought recently are very happy about this benefaction and are
praising the Lord for it. They also promise to pray diligently for
their benefactors, and we remind them of this often. Today the
wind has been cold and so strong that we felt very sorry for the
ships which are said to be close to the shore; at the same time
we remembered the danger in which we had been, praised God
our Saviour, and prayed for others. Those who know our circum-

stances can guess very well how anxiously we are waiting for Mr. Oglethorpe's arrival.

The eagerness of the Salzburgers to work the fields is very great. So far, they have worked and fenced in the good and dry tracts along the river. But the building of fences has been rather difficult for them because the tracts are not adjoining and therefore every tract and even the smallest piece of land has to have its own fence. As the best land in this vicinity either has been worked or is still being worked, some of them want to go to work a few hours away from our place because they do not want to be idle but do not like to work the sandy soil. However, as they cannot return home every day and therefore have to miss the prayer hours, they find this rather difficult. We are hoping, meanwhile, that God will hear our prayer and not only bring the dear Mr. Oglethorpe to us soon but also guide his heart so that that will be done which the Father in eternity has decided for us.

The 5th, Dec. A few Salzburger men have had a cold fever for some time and they cannot get rid of it. Except for Mrs. Schweighofer, the rest of the people are now in good health and busy at work. Eleven persons have gone to Savannah, some having left last Monday and some on Tuesday, to get provisions in two boats. As the trip and the present weather conditions are very unhealthy, and the water is very high and swift, some of them will probably damage their health, as has been the case on earlier occasions, unless our heavenly Father makes it a point to prevent it. Most of last year's provisions were brought to our landing by Englishmen, at the expense of the Trustees: but since this required too much money the Salzburgers are to get them themselves now. Mr. Causton has had a large boat built for this purpose.

[The 6th, Dec. Of the cows that ran away from the first Salzburgers already last year two came back again today together with a large calf. We had otherwise been unable to find them even though they had been sought several times both by an Indian and by our people.]

The 7th, Dec. During the last church year, before singing the hymn: Dearest Jesus, here we are, etc., the schoolchildren were required to recite for the edification of the congregation a Psalm which fitted the Gospel of the day. This year we will omit these psalms and, instead, we will use a short quarter hour to repeat and catechize those truths about the regular Gospel which were presented the previous Sunday. With God's blessing, this will be useful for young and old, especially for the latter who often complain that they are apt to forget very quickly what they have heard and want to remember. In doing this we also have in mind especially those members of the congregation whose knowledge is still weak. This double repetition (for the first one occurs every Sunday toward evening) should do them much good.

In the afternoon service we do as we did last year. Before catechisation of the regular Sunday Gospel, and after the first hymn, we repeat either a main part of the catechism or a number of Bible verses, a great number of which the children have learned by heart. We alternate this from Sunday to Sunday. In this manner the adults learn a few things by heart through frequent repetition, and the children are kept from forgetting what they have learned. The eleven Salzburgers who went to Savannah at the beginning of last week to get provisions have not yet returned; and thus they have not been able to spend their Sunday in Ebenezer, although it means a great deal to them.

The 8th, Dec. Yesterday and last night we again had a very strong and cold northwesterly wind. This is not only adverse for the voyagers at sea, who are said to be close to shore, but it could also be dangerous for them. We now think frequently about the sea because, according to the letters recently received, our friends who want to join us may not be far off. May God be pleased with the prayers we offer for them in Christ.

The 9th, Dec. I have sent my boy to Abercorn to learn the reason for the long absence of the Salzburgers. Meanwhile, four Salzburgers returned home with the old boat, bringing some flour and corn. They had had to tie their boat in front of the big boat and pull it to Purysburg because it was too big and heavy and in addition was heavily loaded with provisions. Tomorrow four other men will go to Purysburg in the old boat in order to help the big one because it must go from Purysburg to Savannah once more to get provisions. And, since the six men in the new big boat are tired and half sick from too much rowing and from the cold weather, we will, in addition to the four, send six fresh men in our small boat to relieve them so that they will not suffer too much damage to their health. After all provisions have been brought to Purysburg, they will have to be transported from there to here. The trouble and inconvenience of this can be imagined only by one who has been in on it. We also received a letter from Purysburg asking one of us to come to christen a child there, and this we will not be able to refuse.

The 10th, Dec. My dear colleague has decided to undertake the

trip to Purysburg to baptize the child of schoolmaster Schoen-
mann Gruber there. This is the end of the quarter year in which
this man has held school, so we will take this opportunity to send
him the money that had been promised him; but the school will
not be continued. This Gruber is a good and able man whom we
could use very well with the children if only we had an opportunity to employ him. If it were feasible, he would like to move
to Ebenezer for the sake of the Word of God. [The late Schweikert's small trunk, which had been left in Savannah, was brought
here with the small boat that arrived yesterday.]

The 11th, Dec. On my visit to them, two pious married people
remembered the words from 1 Peter 4:12, which Senior Urlsperger had given the Salzburgers to take on their way. They were
full of joy over them in spite of the heavy crosses which God has
imposed upon them so far. Our dear God does His work especially on the married Salzburgers and it is very edifying to deal with
them. The six men who had been relieved on the trip returned
home this evening; and they thanked God with us for having
kept them in good health despite all difficulties, and for having
them back to Ebenezer. They were glad to be relieved, but they
would have been able and had wanted to continue the journey
because God had strengthened their bodies. [They suppose that
the others will be able to come to Ebenezer toward evening next
Saturday with the two boats, because the water has fallen again
and is not running so strong. Because the provisions could be
loaded, they will have to go to Savannah again.]

The 12th, Dec. Mrs. Schweighofer is still in very good standing
with her Saviour, and she is very patient with the cross she carries
with her body like a patient lamb. Her talks about the crosses
Christians must bear and about the way true followers of Christ
should bear them are very edifying and come from long experience. She and her husband have borne their cross as long as we
have known them, sometimes with tears, and sometimes with
praise of God. After she had been bled and given some medicines,
some of her weaknesses went away and her speech has become
easier to understand. But her right foot and arm are still almost
dead. Last night and today the northwest wind has been more
violent and strong than we have had it in a long time. [It is exactly
against our people who are dragging the provisions up with the
large boat.

[The 13th, Dec. The cows that came to us 8 days ago out of the
forest do not belong to our community, as has been definitely as-

certained after the arrival of some of the old Salzburgers. It could
be that they are some of the cows that ran away from us the first
time already in Abercorn; but this can not be proved by anyone
with certainty. We have sent Mr. Causton word that the people
are inclined to ride around in the woods again for a few days and
seek out the lost cattle. But there is too much water in the swamps
now. The corn that people should give to the horses from time to
time is now very rare. It is not to be had for money in either
Savannah or Purysburg.

[The 14th, Dec. Mrs. Kalcher was churched with her baby. The
people's circumstances will not allow them to wait six full weeks
before they go to church.]

The 15th, Dec. Last night the Salzburgers who had brought
the provisions to our landing in the big boat returned to us,
bringing orders with them to the effect that eleven other persons
should go to Savannah again tomorrow morning with the old and
the new boat to get the rest of the provisions and to bring back
Commissioner Vat. They will do their best to finish before the
Christmas holidays so that afterwards they will be able to celebrate
this joyous festival in a restful and edifying manner. [There is
still a good deal of provision in Purysburg that must be fetched.]
Today the people drove most of their pigs to Red Bluff because
they will have acorns and good feed there while they would have
to suffer here. Everyone hopes that they will be allowed to move
there themselves, but this is still very doubtful. At present they
are not at liberty to prepare any fields in that region. Instead,
they must stay within a circle of three English miles, which is
not quite an hour away. Red Bluff, on the other hand, is situated
two hours from us, on the Savannah River. It is a very pretty
and fertile region that offers a variety of comforts. But in this too
the Lord's will must be done.

The 16th, Dec. Late yesterday evening we heard bellows and
cries coming from the calf-pen as if the calves were being hurt.
When the men of the watch ran to see about it they found a wolf
sitting on a calf, in whose flesh it had already eaten several holes.
Such a thing we have never experienced before. When I went to
comfort the Salzburger, who had lost another calf recently in
addition to this one, I used the beautiful verse from Colossians
3:2, Set your affections on things above, not on things on the
earth, etc., to give him a good lesson; and his spirit was very calm
and quiet in spite of this loss. He remembered what he had once
heard his father say: a Christian must not be sad about a rough

foot (horses, cows, sheep) but must say with Job: The LORD has given it, the LORD has taken it, etc. Some people have remembered edifying examples and impressive sayings of pious men very well and they can recall them at the proper occasions to be remembered happily by them and others.

The 17th, Dec. The wind has again been so strong and violent today that we feared it would do damage to our houses, which are set up on only a few blocks, but even more to the huts of the Salzburgers. The people in the boat have this strong wind directly against them and must therefore have very hard work. When we do not have such a cold wind or when it does not rain, the winter days here in this land are very lovely and much preferable to the winter days in Germany. True, most of the mornings and evenings are cold, but we often have very pleasant summer weather after the sun comes up. Mr. Causton has let Mr. Vat inform the Salzburgers who were in Savannah the last time that they can earn some money by making shingles of cypress wood, as a ship will be loaded with some of them in the future. In this colony 14 shillings sterling are paid for one thousand shingles. Some of the people have started on this work already because they do not know where they stand in regard to field work. But they would prefer work in the fields, it being more necessary and useful, so that, with God's blessing, they will at last be able to eat their own bread.

The 18th, Dec. [We were told that the next time our boat was loaded with provisions in Savannah that Mr. Vat wanted to be taken to Abercorn in the small one in order to come back to Ebenezer from there. Therefore we sent a horse there yesterday because the trail is very wet for walking.] Mr. Vat arrived here today.

The 20th, Dec. Today the wind changed to southeast and brought us a lasting and cold rain. Toward evening it rained very hard and the wind became as strong and violent as it had been last Wednesday. The four Salzburgers about whom we were worried yesterday arrived in the small boat before the start of this heavy rain and wind.

The 21st, Dec. The big boat arrived at our landing this evening. Early tomorrow morning, by moonlight, a number of them will go to Purysburg once again to get the provisions left there. They will do their best to get back here by Wednesday evening, before the holy festival of Christmas. They had been expected to go all the way to Savannah but they could not and would not agree to this. During the afternoon service we heard many cannon shots following each other and thought this meant the arrival of Mr. Oglethorpe. But we were told that today, St. Thomas' Day, is not only Mr. Causton's Name Day but also Mr. Oglethorpe's birthday and that it is usually celebrated in Savannah with such expressions of joy.

In Salzburg the people had become very much accustomed to the division of time by the days of the Apostles and we are asked occasionally when this or that Apostle's day will come. The Salzburgers like and derive edification from the Gospels assigned to these days (for they are edifying and worthy of study). For this reason we have announced at the beginning of the church year that this year we will remember the days of the Apostles and use the respective Gospels for edification. But we will go over such texts only briefly during evening prayer and not order a special celebration for the days of the Apostles so that no one will be hindered in his work. If an Apostle's day falls on a Sunday as it does this time, we will take up the Gospel at evening prayers the next day.

The 22nd, Dec. Early yesterday, immediately after the rain, the wind shifted again to northwest and made the air so cold that we cannot compare it with any we have had this winter and almost none last winter. God be praised for having arranged it so that this winter we are better prepared to keep warm than we were last year. Not only is this better for our health but it also makes it possible to use our time more efficiently. We do not hold school when it is this cold because we must first make better preparations, which we will do when we know whether or not we will be moved from Ebenezer. [All the people at our place had to go to the landing today and carry the syrup in little kegs and buckets.]

The 23rd, Dec. The shoemaker from Purysburg returned to us today to serve the people here with his skill. Three people came with him who brought him here in their boat.

The 24th, Dec. Last night Mrs. Burgsteiner was delivered of a young son. As he is healthy, and if it is God's pleasure, he will be christened tomorrow before the entire congregation. At other times we would have preferred to give Holy Baptism to the newborn children on Sundays or holidays, in the presence of the entire congregation, but we were worried because of their weakness.

The 25th, Dec. The men who went to get provisions from Purysburg a few days ago made every effort to return to us by yesterday evening; but they did not arrive until the time of our morning service because the water has once again become higher and faster. There is still some corn and rice to be fetched from Savannah: but because there is nothing in the storehouse there at this time and we want to go to Holy Communion a week from next Sunday, we shall remain together until that time for the sake of our preparation. After our Christmas celebration the people will have enough to do in transporting those provisions that are at our landing.

The 26th, Dec. Although these two holidays have been very cold, no one in the congregation has let himself be kept from regular attendance at the services. We do not doubt that our merciful God will once again place His blessing on the preaching of His word and draw the hungry souls closer into the sweet and blessed company of His Son: for in the evening the dear people come frequently to our dwelling for prayer, and now and then we find people engaged in earnest prayer.

The 27th, Dec. The people are complaining again that two calves have been eaten by wolves. The calves have been put into a nice cane-covered place near our landing. If they were to be herded with the cows they would lose weight and their growth would be retarded because all the good grass around our place has been eaten up. Some have put their cows and calves together in a good pasture, which is better than the others; and so far the animals have not suffered any ill effects. The inconvenience of this is that such cattle become wild; and, in the spring or after they get calves it is very difficult to bring them back to our place. But they should not be hard to find again because a number of cows have had bells tied to their necks and because they always stay together in the same spot. Because of the lack of feed, people have also driven many of the pigs to a region where they can find acorns. They grow wild very quickly and even now they and their young run away like a deer whenever they see a human being. Other wild pigs are not to be found in this country.

The 28th, Dec. So far Mrs. Schweighofer has had to stay in bed and thus has not been able to attend public services; but, for the benefit of her grace-hungry soul she has celebrated Christmas on her sickbed as well as other and healthy people have done. The Word of God was read to her often, by her husband or by other people; and whenever we see her we find her eager for the good and pure milk of the Gospel. She also gives much beautiful testimony about the good which our loving Saviour has done unto her soul. Her affliction has improved a great deal, although she still can make very little use of the foot and hand that were at first almost completely without feeling. And her head and eyes still lack the strength to permit her to read a book by herself. Mr. Zwifler does what he can and we are praying for her with diligence. The rest we entrust to the LORD with whose disposition she is completely satisfied.

The 29th, Dec. The carpenter[105] is making good use of the Means of Salvation; and in doing so he sets a fine example for everybody in his house and in public and also distinctly feels the effect of the Holy Ghost on his heart. O how sincerely he thanks God for bringing him to this state and at the same time to the living knowledge of His Son, to which he had formerly been blind in spite of his church-going and Bible-reading. He cannot marvel enough about the miraculous government of God that he has experienced particularly during the last period of his life, and he cannot give enough praise to the kindness of the Almighty who pulled him out of great temptation, bad examples, self-justification and imagined faith and salvation by giving him to understand that the way to eternal bliss is other than the one He has gone with thousands of others, etc. He still has a sister in Silesia whom he would like very much to have here because he is worried about the salvation of her soul.

The 30th, Dec. Through the preaching of His Gospel our ever faithful and gracious God has shown His kindness to most of our dearly beloved listeners, and this becomes very evident now that they are reporting for Holy Communion. Some of them tearfully praise God for the grace which He has given their hearts at this time and they announce with joy that they are now learning to know and to adore their beloved God as their Abba in Christ. How pleased God and His angels must be when such simple souls are so humbly happy with the good which He has bestowed upon the human race with His Son, and when they thank Him so many times that He has driven them out of their fatherland and into the knowledge of His Son and the enjoyment of the benefits of His grace, at the same time calling them away from manifold temptations.

God has put as much blessing on the simple prayer hour that is being held at our house as He has on the public preaching of His word, for in them we occasionally present matters that are concerned with the main issues of Christianity, while at other times we briefly read and explain some edifying matter, which is then followed by prayer. During this prayer hour we have also begun to sing the old Salzburger hymns so that they will not forget them but remember them for their continuous edification. Psalm 46:5-6. The spirit of God shows itself to be very active also among some of the unmarried people whose Christian spirit has not been growing too well, and this gives us many good reasons to praise God. Those who have put their Christianity on a good foundation are constantly improving this foundation through the grace of their sweet Saviour. They are improving their living knowledge of Christ and his magnificent grace. They consider themselves to be nothing and Christ to be everything, and they express this frequently in the strongest of terms.

The 31st, Dec. In the evening I had those married people with me who intend to go to Holy Communion, in order to prepare myself with them for this important act and to pray with them. Next Friday I will do the same with the unmarried men. They come to me joyfully as often as we ask them.

Now praise and thanks be to our eternally merciful God, for all the mercy and kindness which He has shown us in the year just ended. This year too He has given us, His unworthy servants, more strength of spirit and body, so that His Gospel could be preached to the young and old amongst us, and the Holy Sacraments could be administered. If something was accomplished, through our feeble service, for His glory and for the salvation of the congregation entrusted to us, it must be attributed solely to the extraordinary loyalty and mercy which He let rule over us. May He forgive us, for the sake of the blood of JESUS, the impurity and unfaithfulness which crept into the conduct of our office, and may He make us better and wiser from now on, through the grace and power of His spirit, so that, besides working earnestly for our own salvation, we may lead many, yes, all the souls of our dear congregation to the Arch-Shepherd, that they may stay with him and through Him be saved. Amen.

The following verse is very dear and comforting to me at the end of this and the beginning of the new year: Ye are come to Jesus, the Mediator of the new Covenant, and to the blood of sprinkling, that speaketh better things than that of Abel. Hebrews 12:24. Happy he who learns this coming well!

 SECOND PART

A Few Letters

Of the Two Pastors in Ebenezer

I.

Letter from Mr. Gronau to Professor Francke in Halle, 28th of March, 1735, from Ebenezer.

"In the Lord Jesus, Who has loved us till death, and therewith gained for us a true, steadfast, and eternal consolation."
Very Beloved and Esteemed Professor,

I cannot do otherwise than to render especially heartfelt thanks to you for the transmitted edifying demise of the dear departed Pastor Mischke. Through the grace of our dear Lord this report has been also so edifying to my soul, that I have been awakened through it to look at the departure of this brave fighter in Jesus Christ and true servant of God, and to follow him in his faith. Especially may the Lord Jesus, Who has been so great with His grace in the blessed man, also be my One and All. For I, in my small part, have come to know well that nothing can give more repose and certain consolation to the soul than the knowledge of the superabundant grace in Christ. Yes, nothing else can awaken a man more properly than this, to say good night to the world and sin and to offer up himself entirely to his dear Lord.

When I was in Purysburg eight days ago, and our dear Lord gave me grace to speak something about the sweetness of the love of Jesus and His grace, I have observed how it has not remained unblest. A certain person there, with whom I privately have had especially much inspiration, told me how there were also various servants of God at the place where he was who befittingly hold together to diminish the Devil's realm and to extend the realm of our Jesus. To be sure, the Devil opposed them, but he could accomplish nothing but was confounded. He wished nothing more than that the Germans in Purysburg also might have someone who would help them as a good shepherd. There is, to be

225

sure, already a pastor there in Purysburg, but he preaches only in French: hence the Germans are in a bad way. The harvest is great in America, and in Carolina, too, but the labourers are few. Therefore, all who wish the realm of our Crucified Saviour extended in the whole world will most earnestly implore the Lord of the harvest that He will also send true labourers here.

When it was necessary for me to travel to Charleston a few weeks ago and to stay there a few days, what misery I saw there in matters of Christianity. Oh, how long the time was for me there! Oh, I thought, if only I were in Ebenezer again with the dear Salzburgers! I would rather put up with salt and bread and be in community with the dear Salzburgers than to live permanently in such a place where everything is abundant, unless it were the explicit will of our dear Father. I cite this only as an illustration, for it appears thus at several places. Shall not therefore labourers be needful? Shall not therefore our dear fathers and brothers at other places be the more encouraged to pray right ardently for us poor ones and for this whole country? The Lord Jesus, the eternal God of Mercy, Who has led me up to now and has thus done what the blessed Pastor Mischke wished for me and my dear colleague on the way, (with the words: YOUR MERCIFUL GOD WILL LEAD THEM), will further assist me and not only grant me more diligence in my Christian guidance, but also grant me increased wisdom and fidelity in my conduct of this important office.

Will you, dear Professor, pray diligently for me, so that I may contribute to the glory of my Saviour and not be as an entirely unfruitful tree in the world. You have already bestowed much good upon me physically and spiritually, and may the Lord reward you richly for it and show Himself greater and more magnificent to others both in you and through you. May He also bestow on those dear benefactors who have sent us some linen superabundant richness of His grace and solace for the earnest creation of their bliss. May He lead you according to His counsel and finally receive you with glory. Herewith I commend myself to your fatherly affection, etc.

Israel Christian Gronau

II.

Another Letter to the Same (Gotthilf August Francke), 6th of February, old style, 1735, from Ebenezer.
from Pastors Boltzius and Gronau
jointly signed

Contrary to expectations our dear God has given us the pleasure of seeing a new transport of Salzburgers arrive in Savannah on December 30th of last year. On the 13th they came to our place, with much praise of God on both sides. It also brought along a few letters from Your Grace of August 30th, September 22nd, and October 8th in one cover. Once again we were powerfully convinced of Your Grace's ever continuing fatherly affection to us through your communication and through the books you have sent us; and we thank our dear God sincerely for that. May He Himself be a rich remunerator and again awaken by word and deed good hearts who will aid you and the dear Orphanage with help and counsel, just as He, according to His eternally enduring grace, has never failed to supply you with His spiritual and physical blessing, as we have learned from your letters. May He humbly be praised for that, and may the good report of the increase of His realm at your and other places serve to awaken all of us here to continue working on ourselves and on our dear members with prayer, struggle, and tears. It will not be in vain. For the Lord observes it and hears it, and a memorandum has been written before Him for those who fear the Lord and think on His name.

Up to now we have worked in our little congregation with heartfelt pleasure and, it is to be hoped, also not without all blessing. And we believe with certainty, that our God, in Whom we hope, will strengthen us poor tools further according to the abundance of His grace to contribute to the praise of His Name among the presently growing congregation, for which purpose we, like Your Grace, have been fortified by the ardent inter- cession of many other upright servants and children of God. A sincere and lasting prayer is the best means to stand firm in all trials and to come nearer His goal in the performance of one's office, and also to stand up in armour against all the power of darkness and sundry temptations of the Tempter.

The love and affection of your praiseworthy Society towards us is most extraordinary, as has been freshly proved to us upon the arrival of the Salzburgers. In addition to our salary and also a handsome gift, our apothecary has received many salves and herbs belonging to his profession; and the dear people who have just arrived have been likewise overwhelmed with benefactions, partly in London and partly on the sea journey. May God be praised for everything, and may He crown you for that with grace as with a shield in time and eternity. Even though our worthy benefactors in London make it their business to serve the best interests of the Salzburgers, it still pleases the allwise Ruler of all things to lead these dear people from one trial and tribulation into another. To be sure, He means it in a fatherly way; and we will learn, I hope, to realize better and better His holy and salutary guidance the longer we let ourselves practice the Ways of the Cross.

A goodly number of our first little congregation, namely eleven persons, have already been saved from all misery by a timely and, it is to be hoped, a blessed death. We have yet to see what the Lord has resolved concerning the life and death of the remainder. From time to time there is no lack of bodily weaknesses; and it can not be otherwise because of the unfamiliar country, the unaccustomed food, and the extraordinary hardships. That we both are still fresh and sound in body is a singular blessing of God, etc.

Johann Martin Boltzius
Israel Christian Gronau

III.

Extract from the Letter of Pastor Boltzius to the Same (Gotthilf August Francke), in his and Pastor Gronau's name, the 28th of March, old style, 1735.

We shall remain steadfast in faith to the One Who has said: I SHALL NOT FORSAKE YOU, etc. We are well satisfied with our Father and His saving guidance. Even if our physical circumstances are not always just as the constitution of our body would like, He still sends us and our dear congregation all the more delight and refreshment from His Word, as Your Grace will find traces thereof in our DIARY. Most of the members of our congregation are truly dear souls who love the Lord Jesus with all their hearts and honor Him with godly conduct. Also outwardly everything is proceeding in an entirely orderly and Christian way. And even though Satan sometimes wishes to sow his tares of discord, they resist him and follow the counsel we impart to them from God's Word. They regularly attend the public divine service on Sundays and the daily evening prayer meetings and pay close attention during the preaching of God's Word, that we have become not a little encouraged by that and consider ourselves unworthy of the grace which God has shown us in our calling.

Up to now we have concerned ourselves, among other things, with guarding our congregation from the *opere operato* and always leading them from those external ceremonies and exercises (which, in so far as they are edifying, we use carefully) into the cardinal substance in Christianity. Therefore, we prepare for the public divine service, Holy Communion, and its preparatory training as simply and edifyingly as God's grace grants us to. Also, we accomplish much good with the hymn book of beloved Pastor Freylinghausen.[106] We endeavor from time to time to read an edifying hymn aloud from it, according to the nature of the expounded material, or to give it to them for individual perusal on the way home, which is very profitable for them, as they themselves acknowledge. Now and then we sing unknown melodies in school so that we can easily impart them to the whole congregation later, as a result of which, I hope, the hymns in this book can be gradually utilized to greater edification. A few people are not yet supplied with such hymn books; but we have given them hope, because we hope that our congregation will in the future be presented with some copies of the first part. Likewise, we would welcome the continuation of the *Building of the Kingdom of God*,[107] which I already mentioned in previous letters, and also the *Halle News*.[108]

Up to now we have both been well, God be praised. Even though we have been occasionally taken ill, it still has not hindered us in our official duties or in the school. At this time we can report nothing remarkable or strange. Because of the Spaniards, whose nearest neighbors we are, some people in this colony are a bit concerned and in some fear. In this case we can rely on almost no human aid, because we are stuck in the middle of the country and communication with Savannah and Purysburg is distant and inconvenient. May the Lord further hold His hand over us. We lack the time to write because of the nearing Easter celebration, but we shall seize the first opportunity to do so in the hope our very worthy fathers in Christ will not tire of encouraging us by their replies to more and more earnestness in our ministry and to advise us in this and that. This we especially expect of Your Grace. We entrust you to the grace of our Lord Jesus, etc.

Johann Martin Boltzius
Israel Christian Gronau

Postscript, dated April 1st, old style, 1735.

Contrary to expectations we have been very overjoyed by a letter from Your Grace, written on December 13th of last year. The report, however, of the unexpected death of the beloved servant of God, the late Pastor Mischke, humbles us very much, especially when we recall the divine blessing which God placed on our relations with him and on the very edifying example he set for us. May our eternally gracious God let His blessing be upon the demise of this righteous man in Halle and other places for many years; and, may He place his spirit, his uncommon love for Christ and for the Saviour of souls, his ardor in prayer, etc. in rich measure upon others of His servants, especially upon all those dear labourers in the work of the Lord in Halle.

People often learn only after the departure of upright teachers to recognize and highly treasure that which has been taken away from them. Oh, may our Father in heaven therefore grant that all students of theology and praeceptors at the Orphanage, likewise others, learn to recognize what God has done in His Divine plan. My heart aches when I recall that I have been acquainted with some who not only failed to recognize the remarkable gift of this blessed man and therefore did not want to make use of his catechising instruction and good counsel, but also judged him disdainfully as the world's reward for the service and faithfulness of sincere teachers. The methods which the blessed man had, not only in his public instruction of the divine Word but also in his private relations with both old and young, were of such a nature that it is quite possible something real can be accomplished through them to the honor of Jesus Christ and for the salvation of sinners. This we are learning to recognize now more than before.

Should anyone bring his school-methods and human skills, be they ever so brilliant, before the congregation and to the children in the school or in catechism, he might well find some applause but little blessing. It is to be deplored exceedingly, and it does no little harm to the Kingdom of our Lord Jesus, that so few *Studiosi* wish to turn back and become like children. Many desist from their impudent conduct and become more moderate. Some also reveal in themselves much good that is not hypocrisy. But, since they do not let themselves be brought to the childlike and simple being in Christ, to the correct zeal of love for His glory and for the souls of mankind, etc., no real blessing follows, even though they sometimes carry forward, to be sure, the best truths, even at times with edification to the congregation. It is quite a great advantage in the ministry if a teacher in the school of Christ has learned from this good Saviour to be meek and humble of heart, to follow after Him by renouncing his emotional states and everything earthly. The living impression which we have received anew from the late Pastor Mischke shall stimulate us more into prayer to beg God for those gifts which we perceived in him, and which we still lack in our ministry. May the Lord have mercy upon us and let the prayer of His servants for us poor ones be yea and amen. May He also hear our feeble prayer for you and for the dear Francke Foundation, so that there will never be a lack of such men there who are prepared to help others in a right apostolic and God-pleasing manner for the great harvest in all parts of the world, etc.

Johann Martin Boltzius
Israel Christian Gronau

A Letter from Pastor Gronau to Professor Francke,
from Savannah, on the 6th of July, 1735.

The captain was delayed here with his ship longer than we had expected; therefore we have relayed various parts of the DIARY and letters by him. Because I have to travel to Savannah for the sake of necessary business matters and will meet him there, I have written a few more lines in haste to Your Grace and want to forward the last part of the DIARY, which I brought along in any case. Again, there are noted all kinds of things in it which have occurred among us, so that benefactors and friends may gain some conception of the nature of our circumstances and be able to help us with their intercession and good counsel. In it there are many footprints of divine blessing, aid, and deliverance, because of which the name of the Lord will also be praised where you are.

For a considerable time both of us have experienced various bodily weaknesses; however, our faithful God has let us recover so well that we have had no special hindrance in our ministry. Only my dear colleague seems to suffer certain conditions and attacks again that he had to bear for a good long while a few years ago, as is known to professor Juncker, who demonstrated at that time more than fatherly-faithfulness to him, as his expression frequently goes. He takes care of his health as best he can and commends the remainder to the will of our heavenly Father, Who will cause it to turn out well. I must confess that if our dear God takes him from us or only lets him remain in sickly circumstances, it would not be a good sign. For what he means to me and our congregation is best known to the Lord, and we experience it more and more from time to time.

We have made much use of the last received medicines: and because we again used them to assist a few members of the congregation at their request, some of our medicines are almost completely exhausted. What kind of a blessing the dear God has placed on the use of these, is partly written down in the DIARY. Meanwhile, we wish once more humbly to entreat Your Grace to let us experience such a great benefaction again. God will be very much praised for that; and we believe He, according to His great kindness will also let his love redound as a thousandfold blessing to the dear Orphanage and to its directors.

Israel Christian Gronau

V.

*A Letter from Pastor Boltzius to Professor Francke, from
Ebenezer, on the 1st of September, old style, 1735.*

Once again it has been a thoroughly great pleasure for us to receive some written encouragements and inspirations from Your Grace, as occurred this time abundantly through your letters of February 24th, March 9th, 11th, and 14th and, God be praised!, with much profit. May our heavenly Father be praised, Who has filled the heart of our beloved professor with such uncommon love for us and ours, which we recognized to our mutual joy and praise of God in almost all the lines of the letters we have received and also have indeed experienced the effect of them now as previously. So far we have suffered no want; and, even if it has not been just what the Old Adam would like to have or what would have been beneficial to our weak nature, we recognize, nevertheless, *a posteriori,* that it has harmed neither soul nor body. On the contrary, the remembrance of the trials we have undergone often gives us so much joy now that we sincerely praise God for it.

The God Who has blest Elijah's roasted bread and water and given the scantiest fare to His other children of the Old and New Testaments, so that they therewith could advance further than others with elegant treatments, Daniel 1:12 following, has also so blest our bread that we can carry out our ministry unhindered to the astonishment of ourselves and our dear congregation. We hope, therefore, that our dear fathers, brothers, and friends will apply the reports of our circumstances, which have sometimes been miserable, especially in the first period, only to the purpose for which they have been written down. We have begged forgiveness from our dear Father for whatever there was of disbelief or of little faith therein, and we wish to let it serve for the good through His bestowal of grace.

We believe that, even if there is some external suffering, all hardships will become much lightened if one becomes convinced of the gracious presence of God and of His fatherly goodwill through the experience of the spiritual blessing which God places upon the congregation through ministerial guidance. Yes, a teacher who suffers or has formerly suffered poverty, contempt, and all kinds of discomforts along with his congregation according to divine will can comfort the members much more emphatically and with far better effect and direct their hearts, despite all their external misery, to joy in the grace dearly won for us by Christ as the only consolation of Christians. This he will do better if he live a good life with rich subsistence and comfort and without trials and tribulation, which, to be sure, true servants of God never lack. There is always a reproach in weak souls: Yes, you can well talk, you are experiencing no hardships, if you were in our place, etc. Oh, may God grant that we may rightly struggle in the spirit of Moses and Paul, Hebrews 11:24-27, Philippians 3:7, 8 so that we may be useful in all ways to our members and other souls.

Our dear members now also know how to put up with everything better than at the beginning: and even if their sandy and not entirely productive land shall not be changed, and they must remain here according to divine will, they will not fret, since through the continuous use of the means of salvation they will remain in the Christian frame of mind in which, God be praised! they, for the most part, are. The previous presentations which have been made in our letters to our benefactors in London have had such an effect that those various things which were previously burdensome for the Salzburgers have been alleviated. Mr. Caus-

ton in Savannah, upon order of the Trustees and of the praiseworthy Society, does so much good for them that we could hardly
desire more without sinning, as each of us recognizes clearly
and thanks God.

The affairs of our congregation require me to be present almost
all the time. And our hearts are so bound together that it is
really a painful separation whenever we do not see and hear each
other for one or two days. I am by no means worthy of the grace
which God has bestowed upon me in so powerfully attracting the
hearts of all the Salzburgers to me as well as to my dear colleague, and our hearts to them, that one cannot exist without
the other. Whoever knows details of this considers this no exag-
geration but praises, with us, the Father of all mercy for such
unspeakable grace which contributes very much to external good
order, yes, to the sweetening of our toilsome life. The Lord does
it, why shall I be silent.

From time to time it has occurred to me that my health,
which was quite frail in Germany, would not endure long in this
hot and unaccustomed land and with the previously unfamiliar
diet. After many trials of divine pleasure, this could perhaps
have caused me to return to Germany, as I had promised my
widowed old mother in a letter before my departure. However,
I am now fully assured that the Lord brought me to Ebenezer
to this congregation; and the most unusual love which I, wretched
worm and dead dog, enjoy from old and young is seal and testimony enough that the Lord decided to place a blessing on my
ministry. Consequently I, with my very worthy colleague (as I
must acknowledge to the praise of the Supreme Shepherd), have
so far not worked entirely in vain.

And I have also fully resolved in my heart to await in America
whatever God's loving counsel might perchance have in store
for us. And so that I might have some aid, relief, and advance-
ment in some bodily and official matters in this miserable life,
I decided, in the name of God, to marry the sister of my dear
colleague's wife, a pious Salzburger adorned by God with all
kinds of good endowments. This occurred on the 5th of August,
old style, of this year.[109] This event brought forth much joy and
praise of God in the entire congregation and especially in those
who recognized in it the counsel of God. Therefore I do not
doubt that Christian friends in Germany who wish me well will
also rejoice and thank God that He has done befittingly therein.

I know how foreign wives who are not Salzburgers have caused trouble in the congregation and how slightingly they have treated these simple and God-fearing little people. If such a person in whom the people could have no trust should now come into my own house and into close union with me, without doubt the trust of the good people towards me would diminish and various troubles would arise. Also, it befits a teacher not to look down on his congregation in such circumstances. Since he must often present the Gospel truth, that God is no respecter of persons and that for Him a beggar is dearer and more worthy than a godless man with all his magnificence, I think it behooves a teacher to demonstrate this precious truth by his own example and show that, even with a change in his status, he still has God in mind.

I dare not be ashamed of my helpmate; for in choosing her I have well tested and recognized the will of God. She loves the Lord Jesus with all her heart and seeks nothing else but what I seek; she also has as much natural endowment from God as is necessary to help me in my external circumstances. I shall mention nothing more now but will merely ask God to endow Your Grace further with bodily health and all gifts of grace to promote the glory of our magnificent and beloved Redeemer Jesus Christ in your and in other places. Then may He not let such effective and loyal tools be lacking for promoting the work of the Lord either at the University (Halle) or in the dear Francke Foundation, to which I particularly owe thanks for so much physical and spiritual good, etc.

Johann Martin Boltzius

A Letter from Pastor Gronau to Professor Francke, from Ebenezer, the 1st of September, 1735.

To Your Worthy Grace I am highly indebted that you deemed my petty writing of December 10th of last year worthy of a special answer. Our dear Father in heaven has already blessed it according to His mercy and through it encouraged me to be greatly comforted and not lose courage. He will continue to do so. His ways, which He had previously let me traverse, are, to be sure, often strange, but have been at all times blest; whenever I have been in greatest need His help has been nearest, and that oftentimes so unexpected that I could not imagine it. My disposition is, to be sure, more on the sad than cheerful side; but I frequently see how my dear Saviour has thus lead me according to His great wisdom with the blessed aim above all of lowering me more and more as a little worm in His grace and to draw me into His blessed communion where alone I am happy. Therefore, I am comforted and wish to be led blindly by Him as the wise Saviour. He, as the God of Mercy, will lead me well. The hymn: COME UNTO ME, ALL YE WHO ARE WEARY AND HEAVY LADEN, I SHALL SO SWEETLY REFRESH YOU, etc., has restored me very much. When I read it aloud recently to a certain Salzburger whom the dear God especially leads, it made such an impression on him that he took note of it.

In our relations with the dear Salzburgers, with whom one can associate right simply, our dear God grants much edification. I consider it a great benefaction of God that He has brought me here to the dear Salzburgers. My change[110] has not disturbed me in the least in my brotherly union with the most esteemed Pastor Boltzius, and now that our dear Father has bound us in a wonderful manner so closely in an outward way, He will also bind our hearts closer and closer for the praise of His name and to the benefit of our dear congregation. For me the most comforting thing about the change of my dear brother, Pastor Boltzius, is that no human being contributed anything, but God has done all. I was just at that time in Savannah, and before I departed he had not thought about it in the least, but our dear God directed his spirit to it in my absence.

Concerning my external circumstances, our Father has helped me so far and will also do so henceworth: because that is the easiest for Him. Since He has given me the greater, why shall He not also give me the lesser? If I only have Him and His grace, I am satisfied. He will strengthen me in such understanding and not let me lack divine comfort and help in circumstances which I dare say to no one but to Him alone; and I shall, through His grace, especially make note of the words as they are written in Habakkuk: 2:3, 4: We have a Redeemer, Hallelujah! May the Holy Spirit testify more and more to this in the heart of Your Grace so that you may likewise be able to bear witness of Him, etc.

Israel Christian Gronau

VII.

A Letter from the Same Writer (Pastor Gronau) to a Good Friend in Halle, from Ebenezer, the 1st of September, 1735.

Your esteemed letter of March 9th pleased me thoroughly, and our dear God will let it serve me, as He already has done, for much good and especially for my restoration, strengthening, and consolation. God be praised! we have a Saviour Who can help where no one is able to help, Who says there in Isaiah 51:12. I, EVEN I AM HE THAT COMFORTETH YOU: WHO ART THOU, THAT THOU SHOULDEST BE AFRAID OF A MAN THAT SHALL DIE, AND OF THE SON OF MAN WHICH SHALL BE MADE AS GRASS? Yes, He not only says this, but He truly proves Himself as such to all who give themselves up to Him completely. He will also prove His identity still further in the dear Orphanage so that it shall vex all their enemies. And even if at times He appears to withdraw His comfort and help, He only does it so that He can reveal the same more majestically afterwards so that one may praise Him all the more. He will also single out again such a man who can replace the deceased Pastor Mischke, whose edifying departure brought great benefit and blessing to me and to others to whom I read aloud about it.

If I should report something about how it looks among us in Ebenezer, then I must write: the Lord is with us and is fulfilling His promise, which He has given to His dear disciples and to all believers: LO, I AM WITH YOU ALWAYS, EVEN UNTO THE END OF THE WORLD. As long as He is, and remains, among us, it shall go well: righteousness, peace, and joy will flourish in the Holy Spirit, and all those who are powerless will have strength enough to overcome the devil and all enemies and be comforted in all peril. Therefore we can, and must, confess the praise of our strong Immanuel, that up to now He has revealed Himself as such among us.

Among other things in your esteemed letter I was also glad to hear that you would like to come to us and impart economical advice in our circumstances and, since this cannot be, that you would pray for us all the more sincerely. I thank you affectionately for the assurance of such love, which you further wish to bear towards me, a poor soul, and my dear colleague. The Lord will not scorn such a prayer but rather it will penetrate the clouds and the Almighty will look down upon it. This I can write to the praise of the Lord, that, even though I have had to take up an entirely different way of living in this land than I had in Germany, it has not injured my health so far. Even though this and that has befallen me, it has not lasted long. For now I shall abandon myself to Him further, He shall make it good, I believe that, Hallelujah, etc.

Israel Christian Gronau

VIII.

A Letter Written Jointly from Pastors Boltzius and Gronau to Professor Francke, from Ebenezer, the 8th of January, old style, 1736.

Since the 1st of September, old style, of last year, when a considerable bundle of letters from us and the Salzburgers, together with our DIARY, was sent to England and Germany, we have likewise addressed our DIARY to Court-Pastor Ziegenhagen approximately at the end of October, all of which, I hope, will come into the proper hands through the direction of our heavenly Father, to Whom we most safely entrust the delivery of our letters in prayer and faith. Moreover, Your Grace has formerly written down many edifying and salutary thoughts, which have occurred to you while perusing our letters and DIARIES. We beg you to continue this in the future, because it is certainly necessary and useful and shall be received by us with gratitude. Also, we shall heed fatherly reprimands for our mistakes, which, despite good intentions and design, occur for lack of enough experience, and we shall praise God for them as for a great benefit.

The reports and observations given us by teachers who are upright and experienced in the ways of the Lord have made a deep and lasting impression upon our souls and give us no little help in the conduct of our ministry. In this wilderness we often get into situations where good counsel is dear and we hardly know where we shall set our foot most securely. Therefore, we have learned more and more to appreciate what a cherished benefit it is to be able to avail ourselves of instruction and good advice from experienced teachers, both publicly and privately. Generally, however, one does not use this benefit in the right way when the opportunity is there. One is betrayed by one's own reason and imagined self-cleverness at the time; and then, when it is missing and no longer to be had, one sighs over the loss and over his own stupidity and must humble himself before

God as an unfaithful steward. What our compassionate Father in heaven has done for us and our congregation and how we are faring spiritually and physically, you will see rather clearly from the DIARIES we have sent you. The Lord hears prayers favorably and abandons no one in need, that we can say from experience to the praise of our merciful God. He has already helped us out of many spiritual and physical troubles and has strengthened us in faith and trust in His further help.

With regard to the heathens in the country we do nothing better now than to pray for them sincerely, to set them a good example, and to show them true love as best we can when they come to our place, which, however, seldom happens. Should one of us, according to the will of God and our benefactors, learn the Indian language, he would probably have to be relieved of his ordinary ministerial duties in Ebenezer so that he could not only devote himself seriously to the language, but later also be able to travel further up among those heathens who live together in cities. Although the Indian men there also go hunting for many weeks, even for months, their wives and children are said to stay at home, so schools and other institutes aimed at their salvation could be set up for them. Men, women, and children wander around in the woods here and, to be sure, in as miserable circumstances as the Gypsies in Germany. At the same time, there is no end to the swilling of whiskey and to the dissolute life for which the Christians here in the land give them the opportunity. But if someone had a personal calling further up there among the heathens and had a devout schoolmaster as helper, then perhaps something could be accomplished little by little with divine help.

Now may our faithful and loving God and Father spread His blessings like a cloud of dew over Your Grace, over the dear Foundation and the entire work of the Lord in Halle, and may His faithful servants never lack courage and joy to accomplish their duty uprightly and to prepare, through divine blessing, the many youths studying under them as labourers in the great harvest. May He bless you for all the love and care you bear towards us and grant us soon the pleasure of learning something of your well-being and of the progress of the work of the Lord, etc.

Johann Martin Boltzius
Israel Christian Gronau

IX.

A Letter from Pastor Boltzius to One of his Cousins, Written from Ebenezer, on the 2nd of April, 1735.

I was much gratified by the news of your bodily and spiritual well-being, and that of your family, in your pleasant letter of the 30th of November, new style, of last year. May our dear Lord further reveal to you the proofs of His unspeakable love which He bears in Christ the Beloved for all people, and especially for His dear children, so that you may glorify His miracle in your place and I in mine. I, for my part, must acknowledge to the praise of God, that, up to now, He has done much for me in this strange land. The constant bodily health which I have had up to now is a very great blessing of the heavenly Father: but the grace, which He grants me in my own Christianity and to my dear congregation, is so super-abundant that I lack words to describe it adequately. The knowledge of this divine goodness holding sway over me has so shackled my heart that I want very much to offer up all the strength of my body and soul, yes, all moments of my life, to the honor of my Creator, Saviour, and merciful God.

Our dear Lord let me come to a congregation in which I have the opportunity not to expend my energies in vain, but to apply them according to God's will. In return I enjoy from each and every member a love of which I consider myself unworthy and for which I praise God fervently. Now just as I have never regretted having gone to America with the Salzburgers who were scorned by the world, so I hope that I shall never have the longing to turn back again to Germany. If I wanted to consider things which are pleasing to the flesh, then other preachers might well have an advantage over me and my worthy colleague, Pastor Gronau. However, we both praise our merciful God, Who has taught us in His school to see through everything visible and transitory, and to see the eternal, and Who lets us experience daily for our own good the advantage we have over many in the conduct of our ministry.

I have misgivings in reporting details from here, because not everyone can comprehend everything; also the most necessary items concerning the condition of our congregation and our conduct of the ministry have been made known through the press, as we have seen from a few letters received. May God let it suffice only to the glorification of His great name and to the edification of many people. Such being the case, I shall comply with your request to report a few such things from which, I hope, you and those with whom you choose to communicate your letters will receive some edification. Otherwise, I hope that you have already learned the rest. What is most extraordinary is the love that the English nation, and especially the Society for Promoting Christian Knowledge, shows not only to the Salzburgers but also to us. One must marvel at the details of all the expenses they have applied to us. And this little fountain still flows uninterruptedly. They have advisedly appointed two pastors for these dear Salzburgers so that if one departs in death the congregation will not be as sheep without shepherds.

Because the way is so far and because one can not anticipate the many difficulties and hazardous circumstances to which new colonists are subjected in a previously uninhabited land; things have, to be sure, often turned out differently than the good intentions of our dear benefactors. Meanwhile, each of us is convinced that their single concern is to help those dear Salzburgers to a more comfortable life after the sufferings they have endured, and especially to the free and unhindered exercise of religion. And just as you succeeded through divine blessing in many respects, I surely believe that God will further enable you to help the dear people to the best of your ability in their present circumstances, since difficulties still abide here and there.

As far as my dear colleague and myself are concerned, the affection of the aforementioned Society and the other distinguished benefactors towards us is so great that they have provided, and still provide, as much as possible for our physical subsistence and give us the liberty to report frankly about all the hardships that befall us. Therefore, we must not be in the least bit burdensome to our members, but have so far been well able to give a helping hand in their circumstances with what God has bestowed upon us. We hope, too, that divine Providence will often grant us the pleasure of serving our sincerely loved members not only spiritually but also physically, which is splendidly beneficial to both old and young.

After an esteemed teacher in London learned a short time ago about our Institute, namely, that we were starting to collect some money in a box for the aid of a few needy members in the congregation, he not only approved this project but also sent over for this purpose on the most recent ship, to the great joy of our members, ten pounds sterling, which is over fifty Reichstaler in German money. To be sure, here in Ebenezer God does not let us want for many kinds of trials, but His consolation from the sweet Gospel is also exceedingly great, and the eager desire of the dear people for it is so uncommon that one can testify to them that they have had no other goal in leaving their fatherland than to share in the pure Word of God. Not only do we find edification together three times on Sundays, but they also assemble every evening after their work in my house for singing, praying, and brief edification from God's Word, during which we are not disturbed by anyone.

On our frequent visits to these upright souls in their homes, we have often received more edification from them than they have from us. The Lord Jesus and His so dearly won grace is the All in All for most of them, and they can speak about this in such an artless manner that one can recognize undeniable proofs and signs of the good basis and condition of their hearts and experience by several examples, of which Saint Paul says: THE KINGDOM OF GOD CONSISTS NOT IN WORDS BUT IN POWER. To be sure, a few people have tried to frighten us, as if we in Ebenezer would be exposed first and worst to the attacks of the Indians who are allied with the Spaniards: but we have so fortified ourselves in our Almighty, Merciful God that they will probably have to leave us go untouched or unharmed, unless our commander-in-chief, Jesus Christ, wishes to grant such an enemy an external advantage over us and to let the kingdom of darkness be besieged and overcome through suffering and to draw us all the more sincerely with our souls into His wounds as into our sanctuary and firm fortress. Hebrews 13.6.

The local Indians live with the English in very good friendship and enjoy very many bodily benefits from them. Yes, one aim of the Trustees and of the Society in settling this colony is to provide this miserable people little by little with an ever increasing opportunity to know of our Saviour. In what measure our dear God will bless all those well conceived plans for this purpose may be cleared up little by little and better and better. Now there are still many obstacles and difficulties in the way, therefore all honor will be due God alone if something can be accomplished with these poor people and wretched heathens, etc.

Johann Martin Boltzius

X.

Extract from a Letter of the Same (Boltzius) to His Mother,
from Ebenezer, on the 1st of September, 1735.

In The Lord Jesus Dearly Beloved Mother,

Whatever you hear from me, dear mother, let it serve you to thank our dear God sincerely for all the grace shown unto me up to now and to pray all the more zealously for me, that my ministry as an Evangelical pastor may be accomplished justly and faithfully. For eternity is drawing nigh, where each shall receive according to the way he has acted in the life of the body, be it good or bad. How little, how absolutely little do human beings consider that they are created for eternity, and that either a blessed or an unblest and horrible eternity waits for them according to the state of their hearts. Oh, remind your family often that eternity is coming and that all of us then, whoever we are, must give an exact accounting for thoughts, words, and deeds. The all-knowing Judge, the Lord Jesus, will see in particular whether a person has let himself be brought in the time of grace to true conversion and change of heart and to the loving belief in Him, the Saviour of the world.

Oh, my best loved mother, I have experienced well how much it costs to tear the heart asunder from the sin and substance of this world and to wander in the footsteps of Christ, denying everything earthly to the very end. But let it cost what it will, this is still the only way to heaven and no other leads us to eternal rest in the heavenly Jerusalem, to the multitude of many thousands of angels and chosen ones to God, to the Judge over all, and to the Mediator of the New Testament, Jesus, in a word, to eternal blessedness. I wanted so very much to have all my loved ones with me in heaven, in the blessed place of joy. And the sincere desire for their salvation urges me to write this, especially since I know how easy it is to go to hell and how many people, who should not have erred, are already in it. Our heart is very insidious, it takes a lot of false comfort from Christ and His merits and also from the external acts of the divine service, and wants no part in true conversion and the withdrawing from sin and the world. May God guide you all more and more through His spirit into the only narrow path which will certainly bring us together one day in the house of the heavenly Father, even if we do not meet again in this life.

If you wish to know something of my physical circumstances,

then I must confess, to the praise of God, that I am now entirely well and am working with true heavenly joy in my dear, yes, most beloved congregation. Never in my life have I had such pleasure and refreshment as the heavenly Father is sending me in my present circumstances. The people, young and old, love me so very much that I realize I am entirely unworthy of such love, yet I praise God sincerely for it. For good and fundamental reasons, and especially out of love for my congregation, I was married on the 5th of August, 1735. If you had seen and heard all the emotions, tears, and wishes of all my members, including the children, on the day when I and my helpmate published banns and likewise on our wedding day, your motherly heart would have been happy and praised the dear heavenly Father for the grace of God which I have experienced again.

My dear marriage partner is, to be sure, poor and, like me, born of humble people scorned by the world; but she fears God and is a spiritual bride of the Lord Jesus and, therefore, is dearer to me than a person dressed in gold and silver or adorned with all the transitory splendor of this life. Her name is Gertrude, née Kroher. God has given her so much natural aptitude and such physical and spiritual gifts that she, along with her devout mother, whom I also have with me, will be very useful to me in my affairs and edifying to the whole congregation. You can understand to some extent, if you picture a married couple who seeks nothing in this life than the Lord Jesus, and are entirely of one mind about this, what God has bestowed upon us up to now in the way of spiritual joy, as long as we are together through His direction, and how He has joined our hearts through the bond of divine love. My transformation has certainly occurred through the Lord, and He will also let us participate in His divine blessing as He did in the beginning. May God be your solace and aid in your widowed state, etc.

Johann Martin Boltzius

Notes

1. The autograph diaries of Boltzius and Gronau were copied by a professional scribe into notebooks as an official record for the mission. Pertinent to this volume are the entries from 1 Jan. to 8 Feb. and from 6 July to 31 Dec. 1735. These are found under the signature Missionsarchiv 5 D 1 of the Archiv der Franckeschen Stiftungen of the Universitäts—und Landesbibliothek Sachsen-Anhalt.

2. Published at the Orphanage (*Waisenhaus*) in Halle, 1735. See title page reproduced in Vol. I of these reports.

3. See Geo. F. Jones, ed., *Henry Newman's Salzburger Letterbooks* (Athens, 1966), 293-96.

4. Appleton's sermon, which was printed by Kneeland Green at Boston in 1735, is now available in the *Early American Imprints* microprints of the American Antiquarian Society of Worcester, Mass. (Evans No. 3867). The Conference held at Deerfield on 27 Aug. 1735 between Gov. Jonathan Belcher and the Cagnawaga Tribe was printed at Boston in 1735. (Evans No. 3916).

5. See note above.

6. In this case, Commissioner von Reck. Later the word usually refers to Mr. Vat.

7. As long as the Salzburgers were at Old Ebenezer, the word "river" usually referred to Ebenezer Creek.

8. By open boat through the inland waterways from Charleston.

9. Pallachocolas on the Savannah River. Boltzius consistently called it Pellichokelis.

10. A party of the main emigration to East Prussia. This was the town in which Boltzius and Gronau were ordained en route to Georgia.

11. Von Reck.

12. Jonathan Belcher, governor of Massachusetts.

13. Apparently these never reached Ebenezer.

14. The Huber children.

15. This may have been the case, but it is more probable that they were merely showing a symptom of their high fever.

16. As British subjects, the Georgia Salzburgers had adopted the old or Julian calendar used by the British in place of the new or Gregorian one used in Germany.

17. About five English miles.

18. Gronau married Catherine Kroher (Kraher, Kräer). This is the first mention of the marriage.

19. Gotthilf August Francke.

20. Charleston is, of course, further north than Ebenezer; but, being on the coast, it has a milder climate.

21. *Sammlung Auserlesener Materien zum Bau des Reiches Gottes. Der I. Beitrag* (Leipzig; Samuel Benjamin Walther, 1711).

22. Either Boltzius or Urlsperger seems to have concealed Boltzius' real feelings, for he had complained that Capt. Fry had denied him the use of the great cabin. See Jones, ed., *Henry Newman's Salzburger Letterbooks,* 74, 83, 117, 394, 410, 481.

23. See note 16 above.

24. August Hermann Francke.

25. Some of these Slavs still live near Boltzius' birthplace in Lusatia.

26. Abbreviation for "In the Name of Jesus" (*in nomine Jesu,* also *im Namen Jesu*). Here and henceforth the brackets [ ] indicate matter deleted by Urlsperger.

27. He had threatened to kill Boltzius.

28. This was the second transport, under the leadership of Mr. Vat. See letter no. II of 6 Feb. 1735 in Part Two.

29. *eigene Gerechtigkeit.* By this Boltzius means that they are trying to achieve salvation on their own merits, instead of admitting their sinfulness and throwing themselves on the mercy of God. As a good Pietist, Boltzius was skeptical of all *bürgerliche Ehrlichkeit* (civil respectability), which he considered a proof of pride.

30. In the King James Bible this is v. 22. This is only one of many cases where the German Bible differs slightly in verse numbering from the English one.

31. This word is clearly written in the Halle copy. Perhaps the scribe there misread Boltzius' script.

32. Boltzius wrote the name as Vollerton, which shows that he had heard but not seen it. He corrected the spelling later upon receiving a letter reporting Fullerton's death.

33. Pirogue, dugout.

34. Noble Jones.

35. This last line was added by Urlsperger from the deleted entry for Feb. 6.

36. He answered and said, I will not: but afterward he repented, and went.

37. This time Boltzius, or the type-setter, spelled it Perichockelis, whereas it usually appears as Pellichokelis.

38. Oglethorpe had told them much about the Noble Savage, as we can see from von Reck's reports from Georgia.

39. This sentence is more meaningful with the German word *Passions-Zeit* for Lent.

40. Schauer lodged the first transport at his summer house outside of Augsburg.

41. Christian Friedrich Richter, *Die höchst-nöthige Erkenntniss des Menschen, sonderlich nach dem Leibe und natürlichem Leben,* etc. (Leipzig 1710).

42. Johann Anastasius Freylinghausen's *Geistreiches Gesangbuch* was printed many times at the Orphanage in Halle.

43. Martin Moller, *Soliloquia de Passione Jesu Christi,* etc. (Görlitz, n.d.).

44. Written phonetically as Ogizschy, which shows that he heard but did not see the name.

45. Johann Spangenberg, *Postilla/Das ist Ausslegung der Episteln und Evangelien,* etc. (Nürnberg, 1582.)

46. Joseph Schaitberger, *Neu-vermehrter Evangelischer Send-Brief,* etc. (Nürnberg, 1733.)

47. See note 41 above.

48. The scurvy contracted on shipboard resulted from vitamin deficiency, which continued on land as long as they subsisted mainly on salted meat and cornmeal.

49. Here the "we" refers to the two pastors. Little did they realize that the (anopheles!) mosquitoes were more than just annoying.

50. About five English miles.

51. Cat fish. Being stagnant most of the time, Ebenezer Creek was not suitable for scale fish.

52. According to the record kept by the Earl of Egmont, he died on March 15. Boltzius seems to have welcomed this divine punishment. At least he immediately mentioned pious Madereiter as a perfect contrast.

53. Anton Wilhelm Böhme, *Des Sünders Elend und Trost,* etc. (Wernigerode, n. d.)

54. Paul Anton, *Evangelisches Hauss-Gespräch von der Erlösung* (Halle, 1730.)

55. Johann Goebel, Prussian representative in Salzburg, was trying to collect monies due to the emigrants who went to East Prussia. He promised also to do

the same for those who went to Georgia, but nothing seems to have come of his efforts.

56. Boltzius soon had to report calves killed by wolves. (See entries for Dec. 16 & 27, 1735). The tiger in question was the puma or mountain lion, called "painter" by the settlers (from panther).

57. This most informative letter appears in Jones, ed., *Henry Newman's Salzburger Letterbooks*, 578-83.

58. He eventually did, but most reluctantly. (See entry for Aug. 9, 1735).

59. *Societas de promovendi Christi Cognitione*, Latin for Society for Promoting Christian Knowledge.

60. This must have been one of the books by Callenberg that Boltzius requested from Urlsperger in his letter of March 23, 1734. (See *Detailed Reports*, I, 166).

61. August Hermann Francke, *Kurtze Sonn- und Fest-Tags-Predigten*, etc. (Halle: Waisenhaus, 1718.)

62. Boltzius germanized the name Musgrove into Mossgraf, or "Count of the Moor".

63. See note 46 above.

64. See note 42 above.

65. Daniel Gottlieb Maederjan, *Unterweisung zur Seligkeit* (Sorau 17??.)

66. The remainder of this entry was added by Urlsperger.

67. The last sentence was added by Urlsperger.

68. The last sentence was added by Urlsperger.

69. The last sentence was added by Urlsperger.

70. In Boltzius' original diary the remainder of this entry appears under the date Aug. 4.

71. It is not clear why Urlsperger changed, by one day, this and the following twenty-two dates.

72. This clause was added by Urlsperger.

73. In the original, this paragraph makes the second half of Boltzius' entry for Aug. 6.

74. This seems to have been a French-Swiss woman, apparently the wife of Rauner.

75. Oglethorpe had demonstrated this by giving Kiefer a gift while he was still in London.

76. This last sentence was added by Urlsperger.

77. Carl Heinrich von Bogatzky, *Güldenes Schatz-Kästlein der Kinder Gottes* (Halle, 17??.)

78. This theological term has fallen out of use. It seems to have meant a "method of correction" or a means of putting people on the straight and narrow path.

79. Vv. 11 & 12 in the King James Bible.

80. This last sentence was added by Urlsperger.

81. Johann Anastasius Freylinghausen, *Compendium, oder Kurtzer Begriff der gantzen Christlichen Lehre*, etc. (Halle, 1726.)

82. In the King James version this is Sirach 18:1.

83. In reading these letters as they appear in Part Two, it is clear that they were worded by the pastors themselves.

84. This is an allusion to the violent medicines concocted by Zwifler. See note 89 below.

85. See note 46 above.

86. *Wer nur den lieben Gott lässt walten*. This popular hymn was written by Georg Neumarck.

87. This is the chinkapin or chinquapin.

88. Valentin Wudrian, *Schola crucis & Thessera Christianisimi*, etc. (Hamburg, 1634.)

89. Martialia are ferruginous drugs, named for Mars, the god of iron. The

treibende starcke Artzneyen seem to be the strong purgatives and emetics, of which the Salzburgers complained.

90. Of the Society for Promoting Christian Knowledge and also of the Georgia Company.

91. He was Swiss Reformed.

92. August Hermann Francke, *Schriftmässige Lebens-Regeln,* etc. (Leipzig, 1717.)

93. The Halle copy has Schüländer. This is obviously Rheinländer, for the capital *R* in German script was sometimes confused with *Sc.*

94. *bürgerliche Ehrlichkeit.* See note 29 above.

95. This is a veiled allusion to the Zwiflers, possibly also to the Ortmanns.

96. A medication manufactured by John Caspar Schauer, a benefactor of the Salzburgers in Augsburg. (See note 40 above.)

97. Causton represented the Trustees but not the S.P.C.K.

98. Here, as in several other cases, Boltzius left a space with the intention (not fulfilled) of filling it in later.

99. See note above.

100. Chiefly wood duck (locally called summer duck), which also eat acorns.

101. At this time the word "servant" designated an indentured person of any profession, but most often a field hand.

102. As we shall see, this was Mrs. Rohrmoser, mother-in-law of the two pastors.

103. *Die Stillen im Lande* was a term used of the Pietists.

104. Christian Friedrich Richter, *Erbauliche Betrachtungen vom Ursprung und Adel der Seelen,* etc. (Halle, 17??.)

105. Sanftleben.

106. See note 42 above.

107. See note 21 above.

108. *Hallesche Zeitungen.*

109. Boltzius must have thought that such a personal matter was not worthy of note in his diary, or else he was embarrassed at marrying a girl half his age. She was Gertrude Kroher, the daughter of Mrs. Rohrmoser.

110. "Change" was a common expression for marriage.

Index

Abercorn, Savannah River landing for Ebenezer, 3 *et passim*

Alligators, 89

Anton (Antonius) Paul, pietist theologian, 4, 94, 137, 246 (n. 54)

Appleton, Nathan, New England minister, xv

Arms, Salzburgers trained in use of, 81

Arnd, Johann, pietist author, 55; *Garden of Paradise*, xxiii, 3, *True Christianity*, 3 *et passim*

Augsburg, city in Swabia, xviii, 16

Bach, Gabriel, Salzburger, 154

Bacher, Thomas, Salzburger, 67, 72, 82, 86, 135

Bacher, Mrs. Thomas, 67, 127, 135, 145, 146, 149

Balsamus cephalicus, a medicine, 8

Beans, 44, 86, 198. See Indian beans

Belcher, Jonathan, Governor of Massachusetts, xx, 14

Beyer, pastor in Zezeno, 46

Bibles (Luther trans.), xiii, 13, 40, 45, 58, 78, 83, 85

Bichler, see Pichler

Births, children born to Burgsteiner, 221; Eischberger, 51; Geschwandel, 48; Kalcher, 202; Pichler, 106; Rottenberger (twins), 187; Schweiger, 56; Ruprecht Steiner, 101

Bishop, Henry, English boy apprenticed to Boltzius, 194

Board cutters (English), 45, 69, 77, 100, 103, 111, 129, 152

Boehme, Anton Wilhelm, pietist theologian, 94, 246 (n. 53)

Bogatzky, Carl Heinrich von, pietist theologian, 247 (n. 77)

Boltzius, Martin, pastor to Salzburgers at Ebenezer, xi *et passim*

Boltzius, Mrs., mother of Martin, 243

Books, from Urlsperger, 41

Boston, Massachusetts, 13

Brand, Mrs., 133. Probably error for Brandner

Brandner, Mrs. Matthias, Salzburger, 149

Braumberger, Matthias, Bavarian convert with Salzburgers, 3, 4, 16

Bremen, German seaport, 198

Bridges, 83, 161

Bryan, Mr. (Hugh?), wealthy planter in South Carolina, 97, 100, 101, 157, 188

Burgsteiner, Mrs. Matthias, Salzburger, 221

Burials in Ebenezer, nature of, 52. See Indian burials

Callenberg, Johannes Heinrich, writer of Yiddish books for converting Jews, 247 (n. 60)

Carpenter, Nicholas, English boy at Ebenezer, 194

Carpenters at Ebenezer (English), 8, 12, 13, 45

Cattle, 83, 219; cows, 7, 13, 92, 100, 102, 218, 222; calves, 7, 222; oxen, 7, 13, 135, 188

Causton, Thomas, mayor of Savannah, 2 *et passim*

Celery, wild, 78

Changes made by Urlsperger in reports, xiii

Charleston, seaport in South Carolina, xv, 14, 17, 20, 84, 186, 193

Chinkapin, type of nut, 148, 247 (n. 87)

Christian man from Purysburg (probably Theobald Kiefer), 89

Churching ceremony, 198

Clay for chimneys, 126

Coleman, Rev. Kenneth, minister in Boston, xx

Peaches, 47, 111
Pennsylvania, 186
Philadelphia, 186
Pichler, Thomas, Salzburger, 171
Pietistic vocabulary, xv
Pietists, xiii
Pigs, 2, 3, 24, 119, 219, 222
Pirogue, periagua, 39
Pitch, 197, 199
Postal service to Charleston and Savannah, 10, 20, 29, 56, 76, 151, 204
Poles, speak like Indians, 30
Poultry, 192, 196, 199, 211
Prayer hour, 87
Provisions from Savannah, 27, 28, 33, 35, 36, 40, 71, 81, 86, 102
Prussia, Salzburgers in, 19
Pury, Jean, Swiss founder of Purysburg, 18, 23, 26, 99, 181, 202
Purysburg, Swiss settlement on Savannah in South Carolina, xv *et passim*

Quincy, Rev. Samuel, English pastor in Savannah, 44, 54, 92

Rattlesnake, 5
Rauner, Leonard, Swabian with Salzburgers, xiv, 22, 31, 48, 51, 143
Rauner, Mrs., his wife, 22, 31, 48, 51, 118, 143
Rauner's child, 143
Rauschgott, Simon, Salzburger, 144, 145
Reck, Baron Philipp Georg Friedrich von, commissioner of first Salzburgers, 7, 13, 45, 127, 158, 214
Reck (Röck), shoemaker from Purysburg, 172
Red Bluff, spot on Savannah, site of New Ebenezer, xxii, 191, 196, 219
Regensburg (Ratisbon), city in Bavaria, seat of Diet, xviii
Resch, Andreas, Salzburger, 37, 114, 115, 117
Resch, Mrs. Andreas. See Schwab, Sibylle
Reuter (Reiter), Simon, Salzburger, 78
Rheinländer, German carpenter, xiii, 4, 8, 32, 34, 166, 193, 198
Rheinländer, Mrs., his wife, 4, 9, 10, 32, 34, 198, 204
Rice, 94, 210
Richter, Dr. Christian Friedrich, physician in Halle, 60, 75, 212, 246 (n. 41), 248 (n. 105)
Riedelsperger, Adam, Salzburger, 56, 70, 73, 76, 86
Riedelsperger, Mrs., his wife, 56

Riedelsperger, Nicolaus, 89, 92
Riesch, Rev. Bonaventura, pastor at Lindau, 57
Rieser, Bartholomeus, Salzburger, 191, 200
Rieser, Mrs. Maria (nee Zugseisen), his wife, 191, 200
Rieser's boy, 111, 191
Rohrmoser, Barbara, Salzburger, mother-in-law of Boltzius and Gronau, 205, 209
Roth, Georg Bartholomeus, Bavarian distiller, xii, 32, 90
Roth, Mrs. Mary Barbara, his wife, 31, 32, 39
Rottenberger (Rothenberger), Stephan, Salzburger, 89, 92
Rottenberger, Mrs., his wife, 82, 187, 192
Rottenberger twins, 187, 194, 197
Rotterdam, Netherlands, 40

Salzburg, archbishopric now in Austria, xviii, 95
Salzburger resident of Switzerland, 20
Sanftleben, Georg, Silesian carpenter, 212, 223
Savannah, Georgia, 6 *et passim*
Savy, Mr., (Swiss?), planter in South Carolina, 85, 195
Sawmill, 103
Schaitberger, Joseph, exile from Salzburg, 74, 103, 146, 213, 246 (n. 46)
Schauer, Johann Caspar, Augsburg distiller, 56
Schauer's balsam, medication made by above, 56, 179, 248 n. 96
School in Ebenezer, 3, 45, 47, 54, 69
Schoppacher, Ruprecht, Salzburger, 39, 63, 64, 66, 68, 70, 73, 74
Schoppacher, Mrs. Maria, his wife, 107, 113, 114
Schoppacher child, 39
Schwab, Sibylle, Salzburger, 37, 117, 121, 162
Schweiger, Jerg, Salzburger, 117, 143, 160, 164, 173, 176, 181, 184
Schweiger, Mrs. Anna, first wife of above, 56, 63
Schweiger, Mrs., second wife of above, 143, 144, 164, 173, 175, 183, 184
Schweighofer, Paul, Salzburger, 80, 135, 147, 215
Schweighofer, Mrs. Margaretha, his wife, 70 *et passim*
Schweikert, Christian, servant to Baron von Reck, xiv, 45, 127, 142, 168, 172, 177, 191, 202, 204, 209

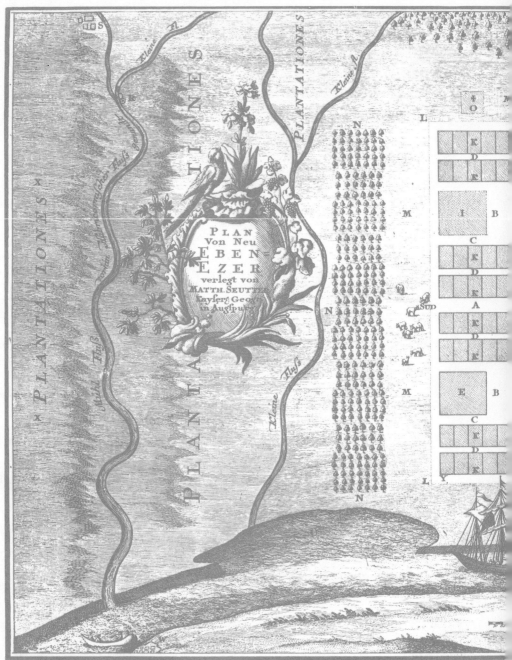

A. Haupt-Straßen. B. Marckt-Plätz. C. Mittle Gaßen. D. kleine Gäßlin. E. Store Hauß. F. Pfarr-Wohnungen. G. die Kirchen u. rer ein jeglicher Zehen Wohnungen faßt; So in einem Hauß Hof u. Garten bestehet. L. ein Schindel Zaun Sechs Fuß hoch we welcher ebenfals eingezaint. P. Holtz. Q. Eigenthumlichs Land einer kleinen Nation Indianer. R. die Mühl. S. Habricorn e Land wo die Saltzburger ihre Vieh Ställe haben. Y. Sind 20 Hauß Plätze zwischen drey Straßen. so Hr. General Oglethς.

This Plan of Ebenezer first appeared in Urlsperger's *Ausführliche Nachrichten, 13te Continuation, Erst*